The Development of Standard English, 1300–1800

Studies in English Language

The aim of this series is to provide a framework for original work on the English language. All are based securely on empirical research, and represent theoretical and descriptive contributions to our knowledge of national varieties of English, both written and spoken. The series will cover a broad range of topics in English grammar, vocabulary, discourse, and pragmatics, and is aimed at an international readership.

Already published

Christian Mair   *Infinitival complement clauses in English: a study of syntax in discourse*
Charles F. Meyer   *Apposition in contemporary English*
Jan Firbas   *Functional sentence perspective in written and spoken communication*
Izchak M. Schlesinger   *Cognitive space and linguistic case*
Katie Wales   *Personal pronouns in present-day English*

The Development of Standard English 1300–1800

Theories, Descriptions, Conflicts

Edited by

LAURA WRIGHT

University of Cambridge

CAMBRIDGE
UNIVERSITY PRESS

CAMBRIDGE UNIVERSITY PRESS
Cambridge, New York, Melbourne, Madrid, Cape Town, Singapore, São Paulo

Cambridge University Press
The Edinburgh Building, Cambridge CB2 2RU, UK

Published in the United States of America by Cambridge University Press, New York

www.cambridge.org
Information on this title: www.cambridge.org/9780521771146

© Cambridge University Press 2000

First published 2000
This digitally printed first paperback version 2006

A catalogue record for this publication is available from the British Library

Library of Congress Cataloguing in Publication data

The development of standard English, 1300–1800: theories, descriptions,
conflicts/ edited by Laura Wright.
    p. cm. – (Studies in English language)
Includes index.
ISBN 0 521 77114 5 (hardback)
1. English language – Standardisation. 2. English language – Middle English,
1100–1500 – History. 3. English language – Early modern, 1500–1700 – History. 4.
English language – 18th century – History. 5. English language – Grammar,
Historical. I. Wright, Laura. II. Series.
PE1074 7 .D48 2000
420′.9 – dc21   99-087473

ISBN-13 978-0-521-77114-6 hardback
ISBN-10 0-521-77114-5 hardback

ISBN-13 978-0-521-02969-8 paperback
ISBN-10 0-521-02969-4 paperback

Contents

Contributors

SUSAN M. FITZMAURICE (formerly Wright) is Assistant Chair, English Department at Northern Arizona University. She is editor with Dieter Stein of *Subjectivity and Subjectivisation: Linguistic Perspectives*, Cambridge University Press, 1995.

RAYMOND HICKEY is Professor of Linguistics at Essen University. He is author of *A Source Book for Irish English*, Benjamins, 2000.

JONATHAN HOPE is Senior Lecturer at the School of Humanities and Cultural Studies, Middlesex University. He is author of 'Shakespeare's "Natiue English"' in D. S. Kastan (ed.), *A Companion to Shakespeare*, Blackwell, 1999.

DEREK KEENE is the Director of the Centre for Metropolitan History, Institute of Historical Research, University of London. He is co-author with B. M. S. Campbell, J. A. Galloway and M. Murphy of *A Medieval Capital and its Grain Supply: Agrarian Production and Distribution in the London Region c. 1300*, Historical Geography Research Series, 30, 1993.

MERJA KYTÖ is Professor of English Language at Uppsala University. She is editor, with Mats Ryden and Ingrid Tieken-Boon van Ostade, of *A Reader in Early Modern English*, University of Bamberg Studies in English Linguistics 43, Peter Lang, 1998.

ROGER LASS is Distinguished Professor of Historical and Comparative Linguistics at the University of Cape Town. He is editor and contributor to the *Cambridge History of the English Language*, vol. III: *1476–1776*, Cambridge University Press, 2000.

GABRIELLA MAZZON is Lecturer in English Language at the University of Palermo. She is author of *Le Lingue Inglesi*, Nuova Italia Scientifica, 1994.

ANNELI MEURMAN-SOLIN is Lecturer in English Language at the University of Helsinki. She is author of *Variation and Change in Early Scottish Prose. Studies Based on the Helsinki Corpus of Older Scots*, Annales Academiae Scientiarum Fennicae, 1993.

JIM MILROY is Professor Emeritus of Linguistics, University of Sheffield, and currently doing research at the Program in Linguistics, University of Michigan. He is author of *Linguistic Variation and Change*, Blackwell, 1992.

MATTI RISSANEN is Professor of English Philology at the University of Helsinki. He is author of the chapter 'Syntax' in the *Cambridge History of the English Language*, vol. III: *1476–1776*, Cambridge University Press, 2000.

SUZANNE ROMAINE is Merton Professor of English Language at the University of Oxford. She is the editor of the *Cambridge History of the English Language*, vol. IV: *1776 to the Present Day*, Cambridge University Press, 1997.

RICHARD J. WATTS is Professor of English Linguistics at the University of Berne. He is editor with Tony Bex of *Standard English: The Widening Debate*, Routledge, 1999.

LAURA WRIGHT is University Lecturer in English Language at the University of Cambridge. She is author of *Sources of London English: Medieval Thames Vocabulary*, Clarendon, 1996.

Acknowledgements

In 1997 the International Conference on the Standardisation of English was held at Lucy Cavendish College, University of Cambridge, with the purpose of re-examining the topic of the history of Standard English. In 1999 several of the themes first aired at Lucy Cavendish College were further developed at the Workshop on Social History and Sociolinguistics: Space and Process held under the auspices of the Centre for Metropolitan History, at the Insitute for Historical Research, Senate House, University of London. The editor would like to thank Lucy Cavendish College and the Centre for Metropolitan History for providing the venues, and the participants at the conference and workshop for their contributions to the events. I would particularly like to thank Reiko Takeda for her invaluable help in running the conference, and Derek Keene for facilitating the workshop. I am also grateful to Cambridge University Press, to the editor, Dr Katharina Brett, and to three anonymous readers for their criticisms.

Introduction

LAURA WRIGHT

Anyone wishing to find out about the rise of Standard English who turned to student textbooks on the history of the English language for enlightenment, would be forgiven for thinking that the topic is now understood. But the story found there is actually rather contradictory. The reader would discover that Standard English is not a development from London English, but is a descendant from some form of Midlands dialect; either East or Central Midlands, depending on which book you read. The selection of the particular Midlands dialect is triggered either by massive migration from the Central Midlands to London in the fourteenth century – or by the migration of a small number of important East Anglians. Why Midlanders coming to London should have caused Londoners to change their dialect is not made clear, nor is it ever spelled out in detail in what ways the Londoners changed their dialect from Southern English to Midland English. Alternatively, you will read that Standard English came from, or was shaped by, the practices of the Chancery – a medieval writing office for the king. Other explanations put forward for why English became standardised at the place and time it did are the prestige of educated speakers from the Oxford, Cambridge and London triangle (although Oxford English, Cambridge English and London English were very different from Standard English then and now); and the naturalness model, whereby Standard English simply came 'naturally' into existence (which seems to invoke an implicit assumption about natural selection; for the dangers of this, see Jonathan Hope's contribution to this volume).[1]

The purpose of the present volume is to reopen the topic of the standardisation of English, and to reconsider some of the work that has been done on its development. I include at the end of this introduction a brief bibliography so that the reader can see specifically what the papers in the present volume are responding to (and reacting against). The predominant names in this field to date are Morsbach (1888), Doelle (1913), Heuser (1914), Reaney (1925, 1926), Mackenzie (1928), Ekwall (1956), Samuels (1963) and Fisher (1977). The claim that Standard English came from the Central Midland dialect as propagated by clerks in Chancery was first developed by Samuels (1963) (based on his analysis

1

of the spelling of numerous Southern and Midland manuscripts, and a selective reading of Ekwall (1956)) and furthered by Fisher (1977). It is this version that dominates the textbooks, and it is sometimes made explicit, but sometimes not, that it has to do with the history of *written* Standard English. In the past, the term 'standard' has been applied rather loosely to cover what could more precisely be termed 'standardisation of spelling'. But questions relevant to the processes of standardisation should also involve lexis, morphology, syntax and pragmatics – for example:

> Over what period of time, and in which text types, have morphological features and lexicalised phrases entered Standard English? This is the area that has received most attention in the last few decades, and it is broached by several contributors to the present volume.

> Was there really a change in the London dialect in the fourteenth century from Southern to Midland, or could the process better be characterised as the diffusion of features from one dialect to another, due to a long peroid of contact between Old Norse and Old English in more Northern parts of the country? What effects have language contact, and dialect contact, subsequently had on Standard English, and how can we tell?

> How did levelled varieties (in the sense of that term as used by Jim and Lesley Milroy; that is, contact varieties that result in the loss of the more marked features of the parent varieties) input into Standard English? Do we find interdialect features (in the sense of that term as used by Peter Trudgill; that is, forms that are the result of dialect contact but that are not found in any of the input systems) in Standard English? Can 'Chancery Standard' (Samuels' term), which is a kind of spelling system, with quite a lot of variation, as used by Chancery clerks in the fifteenth century, be regarded as a levelled spelling variety, or does levelling only apply to spoken forms?

> How did the word-stock of Standard English get selected? How do we know which words are standard and which regional, or which can be written in Standard English, and which do not form part of the written register? Why is it that we are currently rather deaf to one of our most productive word-formation techniques, that of phrasal-verb derivatives (e.g. soaker-upper, turn-onable), and try to exclude them from Standard English writing (and search for them in vain in dictionaries) because we feel that they are 'slangy'?[2] In what sense can they be 'non-standard' – have we over-internalised the prescriptive grammarians' interdict on dangling particles?

There are many questions yet to be answered about the development of Standard English, and there is also the separate topic of the rise of language ideology and language policy, which has fixed the predominant position of Standard English in the Anglophone areas of the world today.

This book is divided into two sections: Part I explores the history of the ideology of Standard English, and Part II presents investigations into ways of describing the spread of standardisation. Derek Keene's paper was specially invited to discuss the supposed migration (tentatively suggested by Ekwall and more firmly stated by Samuels) of East and/or Central Midland speakers into London in the fourteenth century. He demonstrates how historians reconstruct patterns of mobility back and forth between London and the provinces, using as examples transport costs to London, fields of migration, debtors to Londoners, and the origins of butchers' apprentices. He emphasises the importance in language evolution of face-to-face exchange between individuals – particularly when that exchange is reinforced by physical negotiation and contractual obliga- tion, and finds this kind of exchange more important than migration. Jim Milroy is concerned with how the myth about the development of Standard English has had a unilinear effect on the study of the subject. Middle English texts have traditionally been 'edited' (or 'corrected according to the best witness') accord- ing to the editors' notions of what the language ought to have looked like. In a circular way, these edited forms have then been adduced to support the su- periority of Standard English by giving it a historical depth and legitimacy, so that the traditional histories of English are themselves contributing to the standard ideology. He questions the sociolinguist's common appeal to 'prestige' as a motivation for change, and suggests instead the notion of stigma, as does Raymond Hickey. Milroy makes a point that recurs throughout several papers, that changes 'take place in some usages before standard written practice accep- ted them'. Richard Watts examines how the myth of the 'perfection' of Standard English came into existence. He notes that any language ideology can only come about as the result of beliefs and attitudes towards language which already have a long history, prior to overt implementation. He examines prescriptive attitudes before the eighteenth century, and considers the role of teaching books and popular public lectures on the spread of prescription. Both Watts and Milroy consider why the standardisation ideology came about, as well as how it was propagated. The eighteenth-century language commentators tended to prohibit things (like multiple negation) that had long been absent from the emergent standard anyway. Prescriptivism tends to follow, rather than precede, standar- disation, so that by the time a grammarian tells us what we should be doing, we have already been doing it (in certain contexts) for centuries: prescriptivism cannot be a cause of standardisation. To this end, Matti Rissanen pioneers an analysis of legal documents, demonstrating that some of the very things (like single negation) that end up in the standard, can be found centuries earlier in such texts. He directs our attention to the vast repository of data contained in the *Statutes of the Realm*, and investigates *shall/will*, multiple negation, *provided that* and compound adverbs. He finds that the form that ends up as Standard English is found in these governmental texts first. Susan Fitzmaurice examines the myth that late eighteenth-century grammar writers were instrumental in the perpetration of Standard English's rules of grammar. She focuses on the social and political factors that lead to the prescriptivist movement, and tries to reconstruct by means of social network theory how one particular group of people came to have such an influence on what came to be considered 'good' English. She demonstrates how eighteenth-century commentators actually perpetrated the very 'errors' they were busy prohibiting, and touches on the tremendous wealth of self-help literature available for speakers and writers from then up to the present day. In the twentieth century, Gabriella Mazzon considers the implications of the 'correctness' myth for speakers of English as a second language around the world. In a detailed study of linguists' comments on the state of spoken and written English worldwide, she finds that, unsurprisingly, the history of the new varieties was influenced by the ideology of Standard English. In the institutionalisation of present-day New Standard Englishes, schools, media, government and academics all play their part in establishing the variety. Mazzon concludes that the spoken and unspoken consensus of expert and inexpert opinion is that new varieties, whether regarded as localised standards or not, are, in practice, considered to be inferior variants.

Jonathan Hope tackles the Chancery Standard model by pointing out that its very creation is dependent on an earlier type of theoretical thinking, where variation was not fully taken into account. He argues that one should stop looking for a single ancestor to the standard dialect, because such a search is a result of a biological metaphor: the notion of a 'parent' dialect transmitting directly over time into a 'daughter' dialect. He offers an alternative view of standardisation as a multiple, rather than a unitary, process, observing that Standard English ends up as being a typologically rare, or unlikely, dialect. Raymond Hickey also considers the typological unlikelihood of the Standard dialect, and relates it to the notion of stigma. He takes Irish English as his data and notes that Standard Irish English does things that neighbouring dialects do not do, thus providing speakers with 'us' and 'them' choices. He questions by what mechanism speakers come to stigmatise some differences, whilst not noticing others. Irma Taavitsainen looks for Chancery Standard spellings in several fifteenth-century medical manuscripts, and again, does not find the clear-cut move towards Standard English that the Chancery Standard model would lead one to expect. She notes that the importance of scientific writing has been greatly downplayed in accounts of the development of Standard English hitherto, and suggests that its role was not so marginal. Anneli Meurman-Solin takes two corpora of Scottish English as data, the Helsinki Corpus of Older Scots, and the Corpus of Scottish Correspondence, 1450–1800. She investigates the classic Labovian dichotomy of 'change from above' versus 'change from below'; that is, does language change from above the level of consciousness and from the élite social classes, or does it change below the level of speakers' consciousness and percolate from the working classes upwards? To answer this, she divides her corpora according to social spaces as well as the more familiar categories of text-type, gender, etc. Variants lie along clines such as peripheral–central, formal–informal, speech–writing, and her study is further enriched by the fact that Scottish texts exhibit two competing centres of standardisation: Standard English and Standard Scottish English. Texts show varying amounts of deanglicisation (a movement towards Scottish English) and descotticisation (a movement towards Standard English). She concludes that the social function of a text and its audience are paramount in conditioning change in Scottish English, with the drift being from administrative, legal, political and cultural institutions to the private domain. Merja Kytö and Suzanne Romaine compare inflectional adjective comparatives (e.g. *easier*) with the newer periphrastic forms (e.g. *more easy, more easier*) in British and American English. Their work is also corpus-based, using the Corpus of Early American English (1620–1720) and A Representative Corpus of Historical English Registers. As with so many of the investigations reported here, they find that change proceeded along divergent tracks, depending on environment. The use of the newer form peaked during the Late Middle English period, and the older inflectional type has been reasserting itself ever since, to the extent that it seems to be the predominant form in present-day English. British English was slightly ahead of American English at each subperiod they sample in implementing the change towards the inflectional type of adjective comparison. Essentially, they observe the Standard's 'uneven diffusion', and draw a picture of 'regularisation of a confused situation'.

This volume largely concentrates on syntax and morphology, but how speakers expressed their oral version of Standard English has its own history, in the development of Received Pronunciation. Roger Lass plots the spread of RP, and in particular, the spread of /a:/ in *path*. He finds that modern /a:/ largely represents lengthened and quality-shifted seventeenth-century /æ/; with lowering to [a:] during the course of the eighteenth century, and gradual retraction during the later nineteenth century. Lengthening occurred before /r/, voiceless fricatives except /ʃ/, and to some extent before nasal groups /nt, ns/. He calls it Lengthening I, as opposed to later lengthening of /æ/ before voiced stops and nasals, which is Lengthening II. So Lengthening I gives us /a:/ in *path*, and Lengthening II gives us /æ/ in *bag*. Lengthening I is first commented on by Cooper in 1687, and has a complicated history in the following century, as commentators disagreed about which words had the new vowel, although they did agree as to its quality. However, in the 1780s and 90s a reversal occured, and /æ/ seemed to be reinstated, before turning again into the present-day pattern. Simultaneously, the pronunciation of *moss* as *mawse* became stigmatised as vulgar. By 1874, Ellis reported considerable variation – indeed, he saw no conflict between variability and standardisation. It is only in the 1920s that the situation seems to settle down to its present-day pattern.

If, as the papers here suggest, the claim that Standard English came from the Central Midland dialect as propagated by clerks in Chancery is to be revised, where, then, did Standard English come from? The conclusion to be drawn from the present volume is that there is no single ancestor for Standard English, be it a single dialect, a single text type, a single place, or a single point in time. Standard English has gradually emerged over the centuries, and the rise of the ideology of the Standard arose only when many of its linguistic features were already in place (and others have yet to be standardised: consider the variants *I don't have any* v. *I have none*, or *the book which I lent you* v. *the book that I lent you*). Standardisation is a continuing and changing process. It draws its features from many authoritative texts – texts that readers turn to when they wish to ascertain something as serious or true. In the present volume, legal texts, scientific treatises and journalism are investigated; at the workshop and conference we also heard about religious writing and literature. No doubt there are many other written text types which influenced its development – notably, mercantile and business usage. The approach undertaken here has effectively become possible through the creation of the Helsinki Corpus, which takes text type as a fundament from which to look at language change over time. It seems likely that we will increasingly come to see standardisation as arising from acrolectal writings (that is, writings held in high esteem by society, which is not the same thing as texts written by people of high social status) from various places on various subjects growing more and more like each other. My personal view of where to continue the search lies with a thorough examination of *all* text types, not just Chancery texts, written not only in English, but in the languages that Londoners and others used as they went about their daily business, including the commonly written languages Anglo-Norman and Medieval Latin. Such writing is non-regional, as it was produced in each and every region; London is only one of the places where authoritative writing was produced. Merchants, reporters, engineers, accountants, bureaucrats, clerics, scholars, lawyers, doctors and so on wrote everywhere they went. We can define their work as serious in content, educated, and non-ephemeral – that is, written for a public, and often for posterity. Treatises on medicine, copies of the Bible, records of law suits, and records of financial transactions were written not only for the immediate user but for readers in generations yet to come. Standard English is to some extent a consensus dialect, a consensus of features from authoritative texts, meaning that no single late Middle English or early Early Modern authority will show all the features that end up in Standard English. Sixteenth-century witnesses who show standardisation of a given feature do not necessarily show standardisation in any other feature: it did not progress as a bundle of features, but in piecemeal fashion. Subsequently, the rise of prescriptivism in education ensured that 'standards' be enforced; such that I had to write *consensus* and not *concensus* in the above sentence. Some of the papers presented here report data which displays not the familiar S-curve of change, but a more unwieldy W-curve (that is, changes which begin, progress, then recede, then progress again – see for example Kytö and Romaine, and Lass). Standardisation is shown not to be a linear, unidirectional or 'natural' development, but a set of processes which occur in a set of social spaces, developing at different rates in different registers in different idiolects. And the ideology surrounding its later development is also shown to be contradictory. Far from answering the questions 'what is Standard English and where did it come from?', this volume demonstrates that Standard English is a complex issue however one looks at it, and it is to be hoped that future linguists will enjoy its exploration.

Notes

1 For a detailed discussion about these various explanations see Wright (1996), which sets out these contradictions and explains how they came about.
2 See Rolando Bacchielli, 'An Annotated Bibliography on Phrasal Verbs. Part 2', *SLIN Newsletter* 21 (1999), 20 (*SLIN* is the national organisation of Italian scholars working on the history of English).

Selected bibliography of works on the history of Standard English

Benskin, Michael 1992. 'Some new perspectives on the origins of standard written English', in J. A. van Leuvensteijn and J. B. Berns (eds.), *Dialect and Standard Language in the English, Dutch, German and Norwegian Language Areas*, Amsterdam: North Holland, pp. 71–105.

Burnley, J. David 1989. 'Sources of standardisation in Later Middle English', in Joseph B. Trahern (ed.), *Standardizing English: Essays in the History of Language Change in Honour of John Hurt Fisher*, Knoxville: University of Tennessee Press, pp. 23–41.

Cable, Thomas 1984. 'The rise of written Standard English', *Scaglione*, 75–94.

Chambers, R. W. and Daunt, Marjorie (eds.) 1931. *A Book of London English 1384–1425*, Oxford: Clarendon.

Christianson, C. Paul 1989. 'Chancery Standard and the records of Old London Bridge', in Joseph B. Trahern (ed.), *Standardizing English: Essays in the History of Language Change in Honour of John Hurt Fisher*, Knoxville: University of Tennessee Press, pp. 82–112.

Davis, Norman 1959. 'Scribal variation in fifteenth-century English', in *Mélanges de Linguistique et de Philologie Fernand Mossé in Memoriam*. Paris.

1981. 'Language in letters from Sir John Fastolf's Household', in P. L. Heyworth (ed.), *Medieval Studies for J. A. W. Bennett*, Oxford: Clarendon, pp. 329–46.

1983. 'The language of two brothers in the fifteenth century', in Eric Gerald Stanley and Douglas Gray (eds.), *Five Hundred Years of Words and Sounds*, Cambridge: D. S. Brewer, pp. 23–8.

Dobson, E. J. 1955 [1956]. 'Early Modern Standard English', *Transactions of the Philological Society*, 25–54.

Doelle, Ernst 1913. *Zur Sprache Londons vor Chaucer*, Niemeyer.

Ekwall, Bror Eilert 1951. *Two Early London Subsidy Rolls*, Lund: Gleerup.

1956. *Studies on the Population of Medieval London*, Stockholm: Almqvist and Wiksell.

Fisher, John Hurt 1977. 'Chancery and the emergence of standard written English in the fifteenth century', *Speculum* 52, 870–99.

1979. 'Chancery Standard and modern written English', *Journal of the Society of Archivists* 6, 136–44.

1984. 'Caxton and Chancery English', in Robert F. Yeager (ed.), *Fifteenth Century Studies*, Hamden, Conn.: Archon.

1988. 'Piers Plowman and the Chancery tradition', in Edward Donald Kennedy, Ronald Waldron and Joseph S. Wittig (eds.), *Medieval English Studies Presented to George Kane*, Cambridge: D. S. Brewer, pp. 267–78.

Fisher, John Hurt, Fisher, Jane and Richardson, Malcolm (eds.) 1984. *An Anthology of Chancery English*, Knoxville: University of Tennessee Press.

8   Laura Wright

Heuser, Wilhelm 1914. *AltLondon mit besonderer Berücksichtigung des Dialekts*, Osnabrück.

Jacobson, Rodolfo 1970. *The London Dialect of the Late Fourteenth Century: A Transformational Analysis in Historical Linguistics*, Janua Linguarum, series practica, Berlin: Mouton.

Jacobsson, Ulf 1962. *Phonological Dialect Constituents in the Vocabulary of London English*, Lund Studies in English 31, Lund: Gleerup.

Mackenzie, Barbara Alida 1928. *The Early London Dialect*, Oxford: Clarendon.

Morsbach, Lorenz 1888. *Über den Ursprung der neuenglischen Schriftsprache*, Heilbronn: Henninger.

Poussa, Patricia 1982. 'The evolution of early Standard English: The Creolization hypothesis', *Studia Anglica Posnaniensia* 14, 69–85.

Raumolin-Brunberg, Helena and Nevalainen, Terttu 1990. 'Dialectal features in a corpus of Early Modern Standard English', in Graham Caie, Kirsten Haastrup, Arnt Lykke Jakobsen, Joergen Erik Nielsen, Joergen Sevaldsen, Henrik Specht, Arne Zettersten (eds.), *Proceedings from the Fourth Nordic Conference for English Studies*, Department of English, University of Copenhagen, vol. I, pp. 119–31.

Reaney, Percy H. 1925. 'On certain phonological features of the dialect of London in the twelfth century', *Englische Studien* 59, 321–45.

    1926. 'The dialect of London in the thirteenth century', *Englische Studien* 61, 9–23.

Richardson, Malcolm 1980. 'Henry V, the English Chancery, and Chancery English', *Speculum* 55, 726–50.

Rusch, Willard James 1992. *The Language of the East Midlands and the Development of Standard English: A Study in Diachronic Phonology*, Berkeley Insights in Linguistics and Semiotics 8, New York: Peter Lang.

Samuels, Michael Louis 1963. 'Some applications of Middle English dialectology', *English Studies* 44, 81–94; revised in Margaret Laing (ed.) *Middle English Dialectology. Essays on some Principles and Problems*, Aberdeen University Press, pp. 64–80.

Sandved, Arthur O. 1981. 'Prolegomena to a renewed study of the rise of Standard English', in Michael Benskin and Michael Louis Samuels (eds.), *So meny people longages and tonges: philological essays in Scots and mediaeval English presented to Angus McIntosh*, Edinburgh: Middle English Dialect Project, pp. 31–42.

    1981. 'The rise of Standard English', in Stig Johansson and B. Tysdahl (eds.), *Papers from the First Nordic Conference for English Studies, Oslo, 17–19 September, 1980*, Oslo Institute of English Studies, pp. 398–404.

Shaklee, Margaret 1980. 'The rise of Standard English', in Timothy Shopen and J. Williams (eds.), *Standards and Dialects in English*, Cambridge, Mass.: Winthrop.

Stein, Dieter and Tieken-Boon van Ostade, Ingrid (eds.), 1994. *Towards a Standard English 1600–1800*, Topics in English Linguistics 12, Berlin: Mouton de Gruyter.

Wright, Laura 1994. 'On the writing of the history of Standard English', in Francisco Fernandez, Miguel Fuster, Juan José Calvo (eds.), *English Historical Linguistics 1992*, Current Issues in Linguistic Theory 113, Amsterdam: John Benjamins, pp. 105–15.

    1996. 'About the evolution of standard English', in Elizabeth M. Tyler and M. Jane Toswell (eds.), *Studies in English Language and Literature: 'Doubt Wisely', Papers in Honour of E.G. Stanley*, London: Routledge, pp. 99–115.

Part one

Theory and methodology: approaches to studying the standardisation of English

1 Historical description and the ideology of the standard language

JIM MILROY

1 Introduction

It has been observed (Coulmas 1992: 175) that 'traditionally most languages have been studied and described as if they were standard languages'. This is largely true of historical descriptions of English, and I am concerned in this paper with the effects of the ideology of standardisation (Milroy and Milroy 1991: 22–3) on scholars who have worked on the history of English. It seems to me that these effects have been so powerful in the past that the picture of language history that has been handed down to us is a partly false picture – one in which the history of the language as a whole is very largely the story of the development of modern Standard English and not of its manifold varieties. This tendency has been so strong that traditional histories of English can themselves be seen as constituting part of the standard ideology – that part of the ideology that confers legitimacy and historical depth on a language, or – more precisely – on what is held at some particular time to be the most important variety of a language.

In the present account, the standard language will not be treated as a definable variety of a language on a par with other varieties. The standard is not seen as part of the speech community in precisely the same sense that vernaculars can be said to exist in communities. Following Haugen (1966), standardisation is viewed as a *process* that is in some sense always in progress. From this perspective, standard 'varieties' appear as idealisations that exist at a high level of abstraction. Further, these idealisations are finite-state and internally almost invariant, and they do not conform exactly to the usage of any particular speaker. Indeed the most palpable manifestation of the standard is not in the speech community at all, but in the writing system. It seems that if we take this process-based view of standardisation, we can gain some insights that are not accessible if we view the standard language as merely a variety. The overarching paradox that we need to bear in mind throughout the discussion is that, despite the effects of the principle of invariance on language description, languages in reality incorporate extensive variability and are in a constant state of change.

11

It is of course frequently assumed that it is the general public, and not expert linguistic scholars, who are most affected by the ideology of the standard, and, further, that awareness of the standard 'variety' is inculcated through a doctrine of correctness in language. In recent years some linguistic scholars have protested at the narrowness of the doctrine of correctness in so far as it affects the educational system and the welfare of children within it. However, I shall argue in this paper that this ideology has also had its effects on descriptive linguists and historians of English – sometimes quite subtle effects – and it seems that these have their origins in the treatment of language states as uniform and self-contained, rather than variable and open-ended. If the ideology of standardisation is involved in these effects, we need to inquire more closely into this in order to determine more precisely what its role has been. In sections 2 and 3, I shall first consider briefly some of the more obvious effects of the standard ideology on recent linguistic theorising before turning to a brief summary of the characteristics of language standardisation.

2   Standardisation and the database of theoretical linguistics

In the development of linguistic theory over the past thirty years, the database has been profoundly affected by the fact that modern English (unlike some other languages in the world) is a language that can be said to exist in a standard form. The sentences cited in early transformational grammar were virtually always sentences of a kind acceptable in more careful styles (and hence conforming to the norms of the standard), and the sequences cited as 'ungrammatical' in these studies were frequently perfectly acceptable in vernacular varieties and casual styles. Sometimes the norms of the standard as constituting 'English' were appealed to quite directly. One example of a direct appeal is that of Chomsky and Halle (1968) who state that the grammar of English that they are assuming is a 'Kenyon-Knott' grammar (this being a pedagogical account of standard English used in American high schools). This grammar is claimed to be perfectly adequate. Generally, however, the appeal has been less direct and couched in terms of the native speaker's intuition. Radford (1981) points out that in practice the intuition appealed to has to be that of the linguistic scholar who is carrying out the analysis. Yet few such scholars seem to have had any expertise in varying forms of English, and it is obvious to the variationist that they are in practice affected by their own personal experience of using educated and formal styles. I have called attention elsewhere (Milroy 1992) to examples of alleged ungrammatical sentences cited by such scholars where there seems to be no basis for calling them ungrammatical other than a constraint invented by a linguist, and no way of proving that they are indeed ungrammatical.

A fairly recent example in which the influence of the standard ideology may be suspected is Creider (1986), who discusses double embedded relatives with resumptive pronouns of the type: 'It went down over by that river that we don't know where it goes.' An example from our Belfast data is: 'These are the houses that we didn't know what they were like inside.' The embedded *wh*-clause contains a 'shadow' or resumptive pronoun, and what is clear is that it would certainly be ungrammatical if it did not (consider '*These are the houses that we didn't know what were like inside'). Shadow pronoun sequences are commonly found in quite formal styles and can be heard, for example, in high-level discussions of politics and social affairs in the media (one of Creider's examples is an utterance of a US presidential candidate on television). He describes them, however, as 'hopelessly and irretrievably ungrammatical' in English. He then comments (1986: 415) that 'such sentences may be found in serious literature in Spanish and Norwegian where there can be no question of their grammaticality'. This gives us the clue to their grammaticality: it seems that the important criterion is the occurrence of these sentences in serious literature, rather than the intuitions of the native speaker, and it is pointed out further that they exist as named classes ('knot sentences') in Danish and Norwegian grammar books. Thus, they are legitimised by grammarians in Danish and Norwegian, but not – as yet – in English. However, we do not actually know whether the native speaker regards them as ungrammatical in English, and if he does, it may well be because they do not occur in formal written styles. In general, however, the formal literary – even erudite – air of the example sentences used in early textbooks on generative grammar is well known (consider: 'The fact that Hannibal crossed the Alps was surprising to John'), and it can perhaps be fairly readily accepted that the assumption of a standard language has often influenced the notion of grammaticality. In the remainder of this paper I shall attempt to show that historians of English long before Chomsky have been influenced in their judgements by a number of issues that arise from the fact of language standardisation. Before proceeding to this, I will now briefly summarise some of the main characteristics of standardisation.

3   The characteristics of language standardisation

We can observe three interrelated characteristics of standardisation. First, *the chief linguistic consequence of successful standardisation is a high degree of uniformity of structure*. This is achieved by suppression of 'optional' (generally socially functional) variation. For example, when two equivalent structures have a salient existence in the speech community, such as *you were* and *you was* or *I saw* and *I seen*, one is accepted and the other rejected – on grounds that are linguistically arbitrary, but socially non-arbitrary. Thus, standard languages are high-level idealisations, in which uniformity or invariance is valued above all things. One consequence of this is that no one actually speaks a standard language. People speak vernaculars which in some cases may approximate quite closely to the idealised standard; in other cases the vernacular may be quite distant. A further implication of this, of course, is that to the extent that non-standard varieties are maintained, there must be norms in society that differ from the norms of the standard (for example when the dialect of some British city is an [h]-dropping dialect). These must be in some way enforced in social groupings, and in standard language cultures they are effectively in opposition to the norms of the standard. This vernacular maintenance also implies competing ideologies that are in opposition to the standard (or more generally, institutionalised) ideology.

Second, *standardisation is implemented and promoted primarily through written forms of language*. It is in this channel that uniformity of structure is most obviously functional. In spoken language, uniformity is in certain respects dysfunctional, mainly in the sense that it inhibits the functional use of stylistic variation. Until quite recently, linguistic theorists have not in the main used data from spoken interaction as their database. A well-known history of English, for example (Strang 1970), uses dialogue from published novels and plays to exemplify the norms of spoken conversational English. I presume I need not point out in detail how unsatisfactory this is. Thus, the grammars of languages that have been written define formal, literary or written-language sequences as 'grammatical' or well-formed and have few reliable criteria for determining the grammaticality or otherwise of spoken sequences (the discipline of 'conversational analysis' has much to say about this: see for example Schegloff, 1979). Similarly, despite the prominent insistence of Henry Cecil Wyld that our aim must be to write histories of spoken English, the canonical account of the history of English is – arguably – still not as far removed as it ought to be from a history of written English.

Third, *standardisation inhibits linguistic change and variability*. Changes in progress tend to be resisted until they have spread so widely that the written and public media have to accept them. Even in the highly standardised areas of English spelling and punctuation, some changes have been slowly accepted in the last thirty years. For example, in textbooks used in English composition classes around 1960, the spelling *all right* was required, and *alright* (on the analogy of *already*) was an 'error'. It was also required that a colon should be followed by a lower-case letter: the 'erroneous' use of a capital letter after a colon is, however, now accepted and sometimes required. These changes had taken place in some usages before standard written practice accepted them. Standardisation inhibits linguistic change, but it does not prevent it totally: there is a constant tension between the forces of language maintenance and the acceptance of change. Thus, to borrow a term from Edward Sapir, standardisation 'leaks'. In historical interpretation it is necessary to bear in mind this slow acceptance of change into the written language in particular, because even when the written forms are not fully standardised, they are still less variable than speech is. Changes arising in speech communities may thus have been current for long periods before they appeared in written texts. As for standardisation, however, there should be no illusion as to what its aim actually is: it is to fix and 'embalm' (Samuel Johnson's term) the structural properties of the language in a uniform state and *prevent* all structural change. No one who is informed about the history of the standard ideology can seriously doubt this. The intention is to prevent change: the effect is to inhibit it.

In what follows we shall chiefly bear in mind the points about uniformity of structure and the transmission of standardisation through written forms of language – these being the most uniform. We shall first turn to the the the work of the scholars who have built up the tradition of descriptive historical accounts of English. I have elsewhere (Milroy 1996) pointed out the continuing intellectual importance of this tradition and its ideological underpinnings (see further Crowley 1989). What is clearest in the tradition is the equation of the standard language with the *prestige* language.

4   The standard ideology and the descriptive tradition

The groundwork of comparative (and to a great extent, structural) linguistics was laid down in the nineteenth century, and English philology was effectively a sub-branch of this, applying its principles to the description of the history of English. The ideological underpinnings of much of this are quite apparent in retrospect, and one important ideological stance arose from the development of strong nationalism in certain northern European states and the promotion of the national language as a symbol of national unity and national pride. One side-effect of this ideology was a strong Germanic purist movement in England and other northern European countries and an insistence on the lineage of English as a Germanic language with a continuous history as a single entity (for relevant discussions see Leith 1996, Milroy 1977, 1996). This in itself can be seen as a late stage in establishing the *legitimacy* of a national standard language and is conveniently described as *historicisation*. One consequence of this is that, despite the massive structural differences between Anglo–Saxon and Present-day English, historical accounts generally extend the language backward to 500 AD in a continuous line. Indeed, some older histories devote more than half the account to Old English and Germanic. Toller (1900), for example, in a history of English extending to 284 pages, does not arrive at the Norman Conquest until page 203. This ancient pedigree is repeatedly emphasised, and I give here two examples with over a century between them:

> Taking a particular language to mean what has always borne the same name, or been spoken by the same nation or race . . . English may claim to be older than the majority of the tongues in use throughout Europe. (G. L. Craik in 1861, cited by Crowley 1989)

> The story of the life and times of English, from perhaps eight thousand years ago to the present, is both a long and fascinating one. (Claiborne 1983)

Craik was a distinguished scholar in his time, but one has to wonder whether Claiborne believes that Proto-Indo-European was actually English. It should be noted also that another effect of the historicisation of English is the tendency to describe structural changes in English as internally induced rather than externally triggered. In this ideology it is extremely important that the history of the language should be unilinear and, as far as possible, pure. For many scholars, it was a matter of regret that English has sometimes been (embarrassingly but considerably) influenced by other languages.

Apart from the nationalism common to all nation states, there was an additional powerful ideological influence on English studies, and this was of course the movement to establish and legitimise standard English (the Queen's English) as the language of a great empire – a world language. To cite Dean Alford:

> It [the Queen's English] is, so to speak, this land's great highway of thought and speech and seeing that the Sovereign in this realm is the person round whom all our common interests gather, the source of our civil duties and centre of our civil rights, the Queen's English is not a meaningless phrase, but one which may serve to teach us profitable lessons with regard to our language, its use and abuse. (Alford 1889: 2)

It would be wrong to suppose that these Victorian sentiments have been entirely superseded, and the distinction between 'use' and 'abuse' has powerful reverberations not only in Alford's work (his accounts of [h]-dropping – 'this unfortunate habit', 'the worst of all faults' – and intrusive [r] – 'a worse fault even than dropping the aspirate' – leave us in little doubt: Alford 1889: 30–6), but also in many of his successors until very recently. These are 'abuses' – and this means that they are *morally* reprehensible. Those who speak in this way are committing offences against the integrity of the language.

Victorian scholarship actually broke into two streams that on the face of it appear to be divergent. On the one hand there was a tremendous interest in rural dialects of English largely because these were thought to preserve forms and structures that could be used to help in reconstucting the history of the language (a Germanic language) on broadly neogrammarian principles (i.e., emphasising the regularity and gradual nature of internal changes) and extend its pedigree backwards in time. On the other there was a continuing drive to codify and legitimise the standard form of the language, and this is especially apparent in the dictionaries, handbooks and language histories of the period. Among the eminent scholars of the time there were many who advocated both Anglo-Saxon purism and dialect study, and the advocates of the superiority of Standard English could also subscribe to this purism (for a partial account of this see Milroy 1977: 70–98). An important example is T. Kington Oliphant, whose account of the sources of Standard English (Oliphant 1873) includes many lamentations at the damage done to English by the influence of French. In a chapter entitled 'Inroad of French into England', he speaks of the thirteenth century as a 'baleful' century, during which the 'good old masonry' of Anglo-Saxon was thrown down and replaced by 'meaner ware borrowed from France . . . We may put up with the building as it now stands, but we cannot help sighing when we think what we have lost.' But he is also highly critical of

Victorian 'corruptions', which threaten the integrity of the modern language. Henry Sweet, writing in 1899, advocated that schoolchildren should not be taught Latin and Greek until late in their schooling if at all and that they should be taught Anglo-Saxon early. 'The only dead languages that children ought to have anything to do with are the earlier stages of their own language. . . . I think children ought to begin with Old English' (1964: 244–5). In such a context it now seems slightly surprising that Sweet was also a strong defender of Standard English and an opponent of dialect study. For him the dialects of English were degenerate forms.

> Most of the present English dialects are so isolated in their development and so given over to disintegrating influences as to be, on the whole, less conservative than and generally inferior to the standard dialect. They throw little light on the development of English, which is profitably dealt with by a combined study of the literary documents and the educated colloquial speech of each period in so far as it is accessible to us. (Sweet 1971:12)

I do not have space here to tease out the manifold implications of this important passage, which is echoed by Wyld a generation later (1927: 16), and I need hardly comment that to the variationist it seems extraordinarily wrong-headed. The ideological stance is, however, clear, and the resulting history of English has been a history of 'educated speech'. It is as if the millions of people who spoke non-standard dialects over the centuries have no part in the history of English. The diachronic distinction (implicit in Sweet's views) between 'legitimate' linguistic change and 'corruption' or 'decay' is often very clearly stated in the nineteenth century and later, as, for example, by the distinguished American scholar, George Perkins Marsh:

> In studying the history of successive changes in a language, it is by no means easy to discriminate . . . between positive corruptions, which tend to the deterioration of a tongue . . . and changes which belong to the character of speech, as a living semi-organism connatural with man or constitutive of him, and so participating in his mutations . . . Mere corruptions . . . which arise from extraneous or accidental causes, may be detected . . . and prevented from spreading beyond their source and affecting a whole nation. To pillory such offences . . . to detect the moral obliquity which too often lurks beneath them, is the sacred duty of every scholar. (Marsh 1865:458)

Similar views had been expressed by Dr Johnson a century before, but without the moralism, and some of the Victorian 'corruptions' (including 'American-isms') complained of by Marsh and others have long since become linguistic changes. Most of the authoritative histories of English since Sweet's time until quite recently have in effect been retrospective histories of one élite variety spoken by a minority of the population. From about 1550, the story is very largely a historicisation of the development of what is called Standard English (often ambiguously conceived of as a socially élite variety as well as a standard language), and dialectal developments are neglected, confined to footnotes or dismissed as 'vulgar' and 'provincial'. To describe the development of the standard language is of course an entirely legitimate undertaking – and much excellent work has been carried out on the origins of the standard – but it is not a full history of English. The rejection of some varieties as illegitimate and of some changes as corruptions is part of the standard ideology and an intellectual impoverishment of the historiography of the language as a whole.

A very influential scholar in this tradition was Henry Cecil Wyld, whose work has recently come under scrutiny by Crowley (1989, 1991). Wyld's (1927) comments on the irrelevance of the language of 'illiterate peasants' and the importance of the language of 'the Oxford Common Room and the Officers' Mess' are now notorious. Wyld's concept of 'Received Standard' included not only the grammar and vocabulary, but pronunciation (now known as 'Received Pronunciation' or RP), and the effect of this was to restrict the standard language to a very small élite class of speakers, probably never numbering more than 5 per cent of the population. Otherwise it was 'dialect' or the 'Modified Standard' of 'city vulgarians' (these must have been the majority of the population by 1920). Wyld was a very great historian of English and a leader in the field of Middle English dialect study. It now seems paradoxical that he could set such a high value on variation in Middle English and make such an original contribution to the study of variation in Early Modern English (he was a pioneer in the social history of language), while at the same time despising the modern dialects of English. It is interesting to note that a competing tradition of rural dialectology had been represented at Oxford by Joseph Wright, who rose from the status of an illiterate woollen mill worker to become the Professor of Anglo-Saxon, and that Wright was appointed to that Chair in preference to Henry Sweet. However, the ideological bias is clear, and the close association of the standard language with the idea of grades of social prestige appears in Wyld's work, as it also does in American scholarship of the same period (e.g., Sturtevant 1917: 26). The concept of the speech community that underlies this is one in which an élite class sets the standard (the word 'standard' here being used in the sense of a desirable level of usage that all should aspire to achieve), and in which the lower middle classes constantly strive to imitate the speech of their 'betters'. Original as Labov's (1966) approaches have been, his famous graph of the 'hypercorrection' pattern of the Lower Middle Class and his focus on the class system as the scenario in which change is enacted, had certainly been anticipated.

What these earlier scholars did was to equate a standard language with a prestige language used by a minority of speakers and thereby introduce an unanalysed social category – prestige – as part of the definition of what in theory should be an abstract linguistic object characterised especially by uniformity of internal structure. As Crowley (1989, 1991) has recently shown, Wyld was especially important in the legitimisation of the Received Standard as the prestige language in that he gave 'scientific' status (Crowley 1991: 207–9) to what he thought was the *intrinsic* superiority of that variety (Wyld 1934). He did this by citing phonetic reasons. According to him RP has 'maximum sonority or resonance' and the 'clearest possible differentiation between sounds'.

> If it were possible to compare systematically every vowel sound in R[eceived] S[tandard] with the corresponding sounds in a number of provincial and other dialects, I believe no unbiased listener would hesitate in preferring RS as the most pleasing and sonorous form, and the best suited to the medium of poetry and oratory. (Wyld 1934)

What Wyld is describing here is an idealisation and not a reality. It is extremely unlikely that his views could be confirmed by quantitative analysis of the output of large numbers of speakers, and these would have to be pre-defined as speakers of the variety in question: a partly social judgement as to whether they were RP speakers would already have been made. However, it is the question of stylistic levels that is crucial here. In empirical studies it has generally been found that in casual conversational styles there is close approximation and overlap between realisations of different phonemes (see for example Milroy 1981, 1992), and there is no reason to suppose that the *casual* styles of RP would be much different in this respect. People do not pay attention to pronunciation in their casual styles. Thus, we have a third strand in the definition of the standard. The standard language is uniform, it has prestige, and it is also 'careful'. Wyld's idealisation is not merely a uniform state idealisation: it is social and communicative also, and it depends on ideologies of social status and what is desired in public and formal non-conversational language – carefulness and clarity of enunciation. Wyld's 1934 essay was one of the tracts issued by the Society for Pure English, which included in its membership such luminaries as Robert Bridges and George Bernard Shaw, and which was influential in the early development of sound broadcasting. The broadcasters' preference for careful enunciation of RP is clearly relevant. In order to speak this variety you must have a good microphone manner and wear a dinner suit even when you cannot be seen. Although a non-standard variety can be spoken in careful style as well as a casual style, it is much more doubtful whether Wyld's idealised Received Standard can be spoken in anything other than a careful style, preferably in non-conversational modes – poetry, oratory and broadcasting. Yet, if there is such a thing as a spoken standard variety that can function in varying social situations, it cannot be monostylistic.

What is, I think, clear from the tradition is that the focus on uniformity (although implicit in the whole undertaking) was less salient in these scholars' minds than the idea of social prestige and social exclusiveness. References to 'good English' are in fact quite routine in mid-twentieth-century histories of English even if they are sometimes more liberal in tone than Wyld's comments had been. Wyld's focus was on the spoken 'standard' as an élite variety. Its alleged superiority was attributed partly to its supposed clarity of enunciation and widespread comprehensibility, but much more to its use by the higher social classes who had been educated at the English public (i.e. private boarding) schools and/or the Universities of Oxford and Cambridge. The variety described as spoken standard English was in reality a supra-regional class dialect that was not used by the vast majority of the population and aspired to only by a few. It was overtly used in gate-keeping functions in order to exclude the majority of the population from upward social and professional mobility – so much so that Abercrombie (1963), in an excellent and prescient essay first published in 1951, could speak of an 'accent bar' as parallel to the 'colour bar'. Ironically, in its conservative form it is now recessive and avoided by younger speakers, and the strong defence by Wyld could well be an indication that it was already felt to have passed its heyday. It is very doubtful whether this élite supra-regional variety now retains the sociopolitical niche that it once occupied, and it can be plausibly claimed that for this reason it no longer exists. We shall return below to the question of prestige and stigma and their relation to standardisation. First we shall consider the importance of the principle of uniformity and internal invariance in the study of historical states of English.

5   The principle of uniformity in the study of early English

It is well known that Middle English (ME) texts are highly variable in language. Some texts, although geographically divergent, are reasonably consistent within themselves, but many others show considerable internal variation. This can be a result of their textual history – they may have been copied from exemplars in different dialects, and scribes may have varied in the extent to which they 'translated' into their own dialect (see the introductory discussion in Benskin, McIntosh and Samuels 1986). However, there are many early texts that appear to be largely in the 'same' dialect, but which show considerable internal variation in spelling and (less commonly) in grammatical conventions. These include, for example, *Genesis and Exodus*, *King Horn* and *Havelok the Dane* (thirteenth to early fourteenth centuries). This 'inconsistency' has greatly troubled modern editors (who, of course, have been brought up in a society in which uniform spelling conventions are the norm), and they have tended to normalise spelling in their editions and/or explain away the variation in a number of ways. Such variation has been thought to be of no historical linguistic value. Of the *Peterborough Chronicle* continuations, for example, Bennett and Smithers remark (1966: 374) that 'their philological value is reduced . . . by a disordered system of spelling'. Otherwise, editors comment rather routinely that the scribe of a variable text did not know English very well. According to Hall (1920: 637), for example, the scribe of *Genesis and Exodus* 'was probably faithful to his exemplar, for he was imperfectly acquainted with the language'. Yet, as this is a thirteenth-century text composed two centuries after the Norman Conquest, it is very unlikely that the scribe was not a native English speaker. The idea that variation might itself be systematic had not occurred to these scholars. It was merely a nuisance, and the texts that were most highly valued were those that showed relatively little internal variation. These of course were the ones that conformed most closely to the retrospective ideology of the standard.

One important justification for this undervaluing of variable texts was provided by Walter Skeat in an article on *The Proverbs of Alfred* (Skeat 1897). Skeat explains some strange spellings in the manuscript by pointing out that the scribe had used an Old English exemplar and did not recognise some of the OE letter shapes, which were in insular script (and it is in general true that ME spelling conventions were influenced by French and Latin usage), but went on to conclude (unjustifiably) that he was an Anglo-Norman who did not *speak* English natively and that the same was true of many ME scribes. Unfamiliarity with an older writing system does not necessarily mean that the scribe could not speak English. The myth of the Anglo-Norman scribe is set out very fully in Sisam's revision of Skeat's edition of *Havelok the Dane* (Sisam and Skeat 1915: xxxvii–xxxix, and see appendix), and as Cecily Clark (1992) has pointed out, it is still being appealed to a century after its first appearance. It seems appropriate to agree with her that it is indeed a myth – there is no hard evidence for it – but that it is a very powerful myth which leaves its traces everywhere – in onomastics, ME dialectology, standard histories of language and handbooks of ME, and in important work on early English pronunciation by Jespersen, Wyld, Dobson and others. It is clearly an extension of the argument put forward by Sweet, Marsh and others that some forms (or changes) are legitimate and others illegitimate. The alleged Anglo-Norman spellings are illegitimate and can be ignored. What is relevant here are the reasons why this myth was created and the effects of its adoption.

First, it is clear that it is to a great extent the consequence of an ideology that values uniformity and purity above all things. If the texts are 'dirty' they have to be cleansed. Variation is ignored and dismissed again and again in the tradition because it is viewed as random or accidental, or a result of ignorance and incompetence on the part of the scribes. Yet it is arrogant to believe that a modern editor can know Middle English better than a medieval scribe did – the best recent editors of ME do not normalise – and unwillingness to account satisfactorily for the data that have been handed down to us is, in the last analysis, impossible to justify. It seems to be a clear consequence of the ideology of standardisation and part of the retrospective myth of 'pure' English, and this is so despite the distinction of the scholars I have mentioned – Sweet, Sisam, Skeat, Wyld and others – who numbered amongst them the greatest of textual scholars and brilliant pioneers in the development of English philology.

The main scholarly effect of the myth (or ideological stance) is to blind the investigator to evidence for the early stages of sound changes in English, and this is partly because change has been viewed, not as taking place as the result of speaker-activity in speech communities and then spreading through speaker-activity, but as taking place in an abstract entity known as the 'language' or 'dialect'. The date at which the change is deemed to have taken place is typically the date at which there is evidence for it in the writing system – normally a late stage – and it is then determined that at this stage, and not before, the change has entered the abstract linguistic entity known as 'English'. This entity is frequently Standard English (or what is believed to have been Standard English), and if there is evidence for a different change in some particular dialect, that evidence will tend to be dismissed as 'vulgar' or 'dialectal' (some examples are given in Milroy 1996). The historical literature is littered with these recurrent adjectives, and it is tempting to associate this with Marsh's distinction between legitimate changes and 'mere corruptions' and with Sweet's view that dialects are subject to 'corrupting influences'. However, sound changes and other structural changes do not originate in the writing system or in standard languages, but in spoken vernaculars. Thus, if, for example, the phenomenon of *do*-support is detected in fifteenth-century written English, we can be quite sure that it was implemented in a vernacular some time before that, and that the writing system, which is naturally resistant to structural change, had, in effect, been forced to accept it because it had already gained wide currency. In its vernacular stage, it had no doubt been regarded as 'vulgar' or 'corrupt' by many for some time (this being the normal attitude to robust incipient changes). However, the distinction between legitimate change and corrupting influences, typified in the comments of Marsh and Sweet quoted above, and lurking in the background of the myth of the Anglo-Norman scribe, does not seem to be tenable as a general principle that defines what is, or is not, worthy of scholarly attention.

The idea that variation may be structured and orderly seems to be capable of yielding greater insights into early English sound changes. As I have suggested elsewhere (Milroy 1983, 1992, 1993), the spelling conventions of *Havelok* seem to point to a date before 1300 for the weakening and loss of the palatal fricative in words of the type *riht*, *niht* – not to speak of the prima facie evidence in this text and elsewhere for loss of initial [h], substitution of [w] for [hw], stopping of dental fricatives and possible deletion of final dental stops in words of the type *hand, gold*. If these changes were indeed in progress, what this means is not that they had taken place in 'English' as a language, but that they had been adopted in some speech communities long before they reached what we like to call Early Modern Standard English. Furthermore, as variationist experience tells us, change is normally manifested not in sudden replacement of one form by another, but by a period in which older and newer forms alternate. Thus it can be assumed that vernaculars that had lost the palatal fricative co-existed, possibly for centuries, with vernaculars that still retained it, and that two or more variants could persist for some time even within the same speech community. If there is evidence for retention of the fricative (or an aspirate) at some late date in London English, for example (John Hart, 1569, cited by Lass 1997: 220), this does not demonstrate that the loss of the segment had not already taken place in the vernacular of one or more speech communities. In this case, one possible interpretation is that alternation between the older and newer forms may have been present in the community in question, but that the conservative form was considered more 'correct'.

Clearly, such conclusions depend on the idea that language always incorporates variation, and this implies that some of the reasoning that has been used by historical descriptivists needs to be reconsidered. The *terminus ante quem non* argument, that, for example, [h]-dropping in English could not have occurred before the period of colonisation (as it is not generally found today in post-colonial varieties) is from a variationist perspective not necessarily a valid argument, as [h]-dropping almost certainly goes back to the thirteenth century (Milroy 1983). It may have become categorical in some communities and remained a variant in others. In yet other communities, it did not occur. What is striking about this vigorous vernacular change is that – in contrast to loss of the fricative in *right, night* – it has not gone to completion in mainstream English after eight centuries. The forces of language maintenance, including the consciousness of the standard ideology, have so far succeeded in resisting its spread to all vernaculars. Apart from its importance for the principle of variability in language, the case of [h]-dropping raises the question of the social aspects of standardisation – in particular the traditional association of the standard language with a *prestige* variety – and we now turn to this.

6   Prestige as explanation in sociolinguistics

As we saw above, the tradition in English philology assumed an identity between the standard language and the 'prestige' language. In Britain this identification was particularly strong because of the rigid class or status distinctions inherited from the nineteenth century and before, and it is still much more influential than in many other western countries. There is nothing exactly comparable in the USA, for example. In historical description, therefore, the notion of prestige was widely appealed to as a form of explanation for language change. But the concept was never carefully analysed, and the paradox that changes in the history of English did not seem to emanate from the highest status groups was never resolved. It is by no means clear that the 'standard language' at any given time is a direct product of the language of the highest status groups, and the identification of the standard language with the highest prestige language clearly needs further analysis. To start with, it may be suggested that the standard language originates in the need for widespread communication in written form and that, although the highest prestige forms may affect it, the forms adopted are adopted primarily because they are the most likely to be widely accepted or understood in writing. It is not in the élite literary tradition, but in legal and administrative documents, that the need for uniformity of usage is strongest, because these have to be very precise and not subject to differing interpretations.

If historical linguistics was uncritical about prestige, we might expect sociolinguistics to be more critical, but this has not always been so. The idea of prestige is still used rather routinely, and there are many instances in the literature where it is assumed that a scale of prestige parallel to a scale of social status is the same thing as a scale from non-standard to standard. This tendency probably arises from the fact that most of the early quantitative work explored variation in the dimension of social class (Labov 1966, Trudgill 1974), partly continuing the emphasis on social class so prominent in the work of Wyld (but without its assumptions about the 'best' English, 'vulgar' English and so forth). Furthermore, the division of prestige into 'overt' and 'covert' prestige does not seem to get us much further in explanation, as this binary split does not in itself face the problem of what precisely is meant by 'prestige'. How far does it reside in economic power and wealth and how far in subjective perceptions of individual speakers? Why should speakers in their daily life figure forth an abstract class system in their conversations with friends, neighbours and strangers? How far are they motivated by 'prestige' when they use more geographically widespread linguistic forms to communicate with relative outsiders and how far by communicative needs, negative politeness, identity roles, or a host of other possibilities? What is the role of language standardisation in enabling these geographically widespread forms to be used, and if standardisation has a role, what does this have to do with prestige? These unanswered questions come to mind, and there could be many more.

When sociolinguists use prestige explanations, as they so often do, the assumption often seems to be that if a given change cannot be explained by overt prestige, then the explanation must be 'covert' prestige. Labov's distinction between 'change from above' and 'change from below' takes us somewhat further, as it is based on the idea of social awareness of variants. In practice, however, it is nearly always assumed that 'change from above the level of awareness' is the same as change emanating from the higher social classes, and vice versa. Indeed, Labov (1994: 78) has recently stated that these labels refer 'simultaneously to levels of social awareness and positions in the socioeconomic hierarchy'. This dual definition can lead to the possibility of ambiguous interpretation of patterns in the data, as the two are not conceptually the same. But – to return to the notion of the standard language – the many commentaries and projects that identify prestige forms with standard forms do not derive this directly from Labov. He has never included the idea of standardisation in his conceptualisation of 'speech community' and has almost nothing to say directly about standardisation as a process.

The converse social category to prestige is *stigma*, and I will end this discussion by commenting on this. If we focus on stigma rather than prestige we can gain at least one insight that is not so readily accessible in the notion of prestige alone, and that is that features of high-status dialects can be avoided in the speech community just as low-status dialects are. To that extent, it may be reasonably argued that these linguistic features are 'stigmatised' – or at least, avoided – in much the same way as salient features of low-status speech, even if the speakers themselves are not stigmatised. Yet, for these features, both stigma and prestige are strong terms: from a different perspective the conclusion would be that for some reason people often do not want to *identify* with either the highest-status or the lowest-status usage. If features associated with high-status speakers were not sometimes avoided in this way, the élite dialect of the royal court would have controlled the future of early Standard English rather than the dialects of the business and administrative classes that superseded it (we can speculate that if this had happened British English would still have post-vocalic [r] and that [h]-dropping would have become standard). At the present day, conservative RP is receding rapidly among younger speakers, and formerly low-status features, including glottal stops, are entering their speech (Wells 1982). The vowels of the royal family are parodied with spellings such as *hice*, *abite* for 'house, about', and it seems that even high-status people do not particularly want to sound like the Prince of Wales. Similarly, some of the 'U' (upper-class) forms discussed by Ross (1954), such as *looking glass* for 'mirror' are now viewed merely as quaint archaisms. Thus, salient forms that are generally viewed as standard, or mainstream, are not necessarily those of the highest social classes, and they probably have not in the past originated as innovations by those classes. Thus, it seems: 1) that those with highest social prestige are not necessarily seen as desirable models of language use, and 2) that a prestige language is not identical in every respect with an idealised standard language. Prestige (as it is normally used) and standardisation are concepts of different orders – the one being social and speaker-based, and the other sociopolitical and institutional. In interpreting the findings of variationist studies, it is important to keep them separate, define them more precisely, and investigate the subtle relationship between them. The term 'prestige', as used by social and historical linguists, is particularly in need of clarification.

7   Concluding comments

I have attempted to show that, although linguists do not concur with popular attitudes to correctness, they are themselves in some respects affected by the ideology that conditions these popular views – the ideology of language standardisation with its emphasis on formal and written styles and neglect of the variable structure of spoken language. This ideology has arguably strengthened the tendency to think of languages as wholly separate pre-defined entities, consisting of sequences that can be defined as 'grammatical'. It has also strengthened the desire to describe the history of English as a unilinear uniform-state set of developments – as far as possible – and to reject variation as unstructured. Furthermore, the identification of standardisation with 'prestige' is so strong in the descriptive tradition as represented by Wyld and others that, as I have tried to show, it still influences our thinking and has effects in, for example, the tendency to distinguish legitimate internal linguistic changes from 'careless' corruptions – forms that, in Dr Johnson's words, arise from 'some temporary or local convenience'. Very often such forms are the beginnings of linguistic changes, and there are no criteria for assuming a prior distinction between them and those that are more 'legitimate'. I have tried to show that in sociohistorical research it is important to separate the concept of standardisation from that of prestige. If the conceptual confusions surrounding the terminology can be eliminated, we will not only have a more accountable history of English, but also a more coherent account of the history of standardisation.

Appendix

Sisam on Anglo-Norman scribes

'The manuscript spelling appears . . . to be of a very lawless character, but is easily understood in the light of Professor Skeat's discovery (in 1897) that many of our early MSS . . . abound with spellings which can only be understood rightly when we observe that the scribe was of Norman birth and more accustomed to the spelling of Anglo-French than to that of the native language of the country, which he had acquired with some difficulty and could not always correctly pronounce.' (Sisam and Skeat 1915: xxxvii–xxxviii)

Alleged Anglo-Norman spellings 'corrected' in the text:

1   Omission of initial *h* and inorganic addition of *h*
2   *w* for *wh* (*wat*: 'what')
3   *s* for *sh* (*sal*: 'shall')
4   *th*, *cht*, *cth*, *ct*, *t* for *ht* (*rith*, *ricth*, etc: 'right')
5   *th* for *t* (*with*: 'white')
6   *t* for *th* (*herknet*: 'herkneth')
7   *w* for *u*, *wu* (*wl*: 'wool'; *hw*: 'how' – in other texts *wox*: 'fox')
8   'careless' spelling: omission of final *t*, *d* in homorganic clusters (*lan*: 'land').

One effect of this variation is that the spelling *wit*, for example, can represent three different words: 'wight', 'with', 'white' (for the systematic nature of this variation see Milroy 1983, 1992). There is no evidence that the scribe of *Havelok* was a first-language speaker of French and, as the text postdates the Conquest by over two centuries, no good reason to believe that he was.

References

Abercrombie, D. 1963. 'RP and local accent', in *Studies in Phonetics and Linguistics*. Oxford: Oxford University Press.

Alford, H. 1889. *The Queen's English*, 8th edn, London: George Bell (first published 1864).

Bennett, J. A. W. and Smithers, G. 1966. *Early Middle English Verse and Prose*, London: Oxford University Press.

Benskin, M., McIntosh, A. and Samuels, M. 1986. *Linguistic Atlas of Late Medieval English*, Aberdeen: Aberdeen University Press.

Chomsky, N. and Halle, M. 1968. *The Sound Pattern of English*, New York: Harper Row.

Claiborne, R. 1983. *Our Marvelous Native Tongue: the Life and Times of the English Language*, New York: Times Books.

Clark, C. 1992. 'The myth of the Anglo-Norman scribe', in Rissanen, M., Ihalainen, O., Nevalainen, T. and Taavitsainen, I. (eds.), *History of Englishes*, Berlin: Mouton de Gruyter, pp. 117–29.

Coulmas, F. 1992. *Language and Economy*, Oxford: Blackwell.

Creider, C. 1986. 'Constituent-gap dependencies in Norwegian: an acceptability study', in Sankoff, D. (ed.), *Diversity and Diachrony*. Amsterdam: John Benjamin, 415–24.

Crowley, T. 1989. *Standard English and the Politics of Language*, Urbana and Chicago: University of Illinois Press.

1991. *Proper English? Readings in Language, History and Cultural Identity*, London: Routledge.

Hall, J. 1920. *Early Middle English*, 2 vols. Oxford: Clarendon Press.

Haugen, E. 1966. 'Dialect, language, nation', *American Anthropologist* 68, 922–35.

Labov, W. 1966. *The Social Stratification of English in New York City*, Washington DC: Center for Applied Linguistics.

1994. *Principles of Linguistic Change: Internal Factors*, Oxford: Blackwell.

Lass, R. 1997. *Historical Linguistics and Language Change*, Cambridge: Cambridge University Press.

Leith, D. 1996. 'The origins of English', in Graddol, D., Leith, D, and Swann, J., *English: History, Diversity and Change*, London: Routledge.

Marsh, G. P. 1865. *Lectures on the English Language*, London: John Murray.

Milroy, J. 1977. *The Language of Gerard Manley Hopkins*. London: Deutsch.

1981. *Regional Accents of English: Belfast*. Belfast: Blackstaff.

1983. 'On the sociolinguistic history of /h/-dropping in English', in Davenport, M., Hansen, E. and Nielsen, H.-F., *Current Topics in English Historical Linguistics*, Odense: Odense University Press, pp. 37–53.

1992. *Linguistic Variation and Change*, Oxford: Blackwell.

1993. 'Middle English dialectology', in Blake, N. F. (ed.), *Cambridge History of the English Language*, vol. II, pp. 156–206.

1996. 'Linguistic ideology and the Anglo-Saxon lineage of English', in Klemola, J., Kytö, M. and Rissanen, M. *Speech Past and Present: Studies in English Dialectology in Memory of Ossi Ihalainen*, Frankfurt: Peter Lang, pp. 169–86.

Milroy, J. and Milroy, L. 1991. *Authority in Language*, 2nd edn, London: Routledge.

Oliphant, T. K. 1873. *Sources of Standard English*, London: Macmillan.

Radford, A. 1981. *Transformational Syntax*, Cambridge: Cambridge University Press.

Ross, A. S. C. 1954. 'Linguistic class-indicators in present-day English', *Neuphilologische Mitteilungen* 55.

Schegloff, E. 1979. 'The relevance of repair to syntax for conversation', in Givon, T. (ed.) *Discourse and Syntax*, New York: Academic Press, pp. 261–86.

Sisam, K. and Skeat, W. W. 1915. *The Lay of Havelok the Dane*, Oxford: Clarendon Press.

Skeat, W. W. 1897. 'The proverbs of Alfred', *Transactions of the Philological Society*.

Strang, B. M. H. 1970. *History of English*, London: Methuen.

Sturtevant, E. M. 1917. *Linguistic Change*, Chicago: University of Chicago Press.

Sweet, H. 1964. *The Practical Study of Languages*, Oxford: Oxford University Press.

1971. *The Indispensable Foundation*, ed. Eugenie Henderson. Oxford: Oxford University Press.

Toller, T. N. 1900. *History of the English Language*, Cambridge: Cambridge University Press.

Trudgill, P. 1974. *The Social Differentiation of English in Norwich*, Cambridge: Cambridge University Press.

Wells, J. 1982. *Accents of English*, 3 vols. Cambridge: Cambridge University Press.

Wyld, H. C. 1927. *A Short History of English*, London: John Murray.

1934. 'The best English', *Proceedings of the Society for Pure English* 4 (Tract XXXIX), 603–21.

2   Mythical strands in the ideology of prescriptivism

RICHARD J. WATTS

1   Introduction

Benjamin Disraeli's comment in *Sybil; or, the Two Nations* (1845) that Britain consisted of 'two nations . . . who are formed by a different breeding, are fed by a different food, are ordered by different manners' is frequently cited as expressing a conscious awareness of the dichotomous structure of social class distinctions in Britain that would have been shared by his readers. One of the foundations on which such a dichotomous social structure was built was a language ideology which I shall call 'the ideology of prescriptivism' (cf. Watts 1999).

Mugglestone (1995) locates the beginning of prescriptivism in the latter half of the eighteenth century, but the role played by attitudes towards language in helping to create these social distinctions had already been realised explicitly with the emergence of a generally accepted written standard at the beginning of that century. In this chapter I shall argue that we can trace the ideology of prescriptivism back much further.

Mugglestone's principal argument is that one of the most salient ways of marking social distinctions symbolically was through the production and institutionalised reproduction of standard versus non-standard forms of talk. She locates the rise of 'accent as social symbol' in the latter half of the eighteenth century and deals with the ways in which it is socially reproduced throughout the nineteenth century. The impression gained is that before the latter half of the eighteenth century attitudes towards language, particularly towards English, were not nearly as normative as they afterwards became.

However, what she omits to consider is how language came to be used as one of the most potent means by which social structures of power could be constructed and justified. Unless we consider whether prescriptive attitudes towards language were already present before the middle of the eighteenth century and what set of social processes took place to link those attitudes to hegemonic social practices, we only have part of an extremely complex historical process involving language standardisation.

The link that was forged between social discrimination and attitudes towards language in the first half of the eighteenth century became possible for sociopolitical, extra-linguistic reasons. Evidence for this hypothesis can be found in most of the grammars of English published before the appearance of Bishop Lowth's grammar in 1762 (cf. Watts 1999), although I shall focus in this paper on a little-known grammar by Hugh Jones published in 1724. However, without the prior existence of prescriptive attitudes towards language, the rise of Standard English as a 'social symbol' would hardly have been possible.

The most influential social institution in making the explicit connection possible was undoubtedly that of public education. Indeed the beginnings of prescriptivism can be traced back at least as far as the Latin grammar created in 1548/9 out of John Colet's *Aeditio* (1510) and the revision of William Lily's Latin syntax by Erasmus (c.1513; first appearance in English in 1542). It is also in evidence in the sixteenth century in the work on the orthography of English published by John Hart. The 1548/9 edition of the Lily/Colet 'grammar' was published after a proclamation of Edward VI had made the use of Lily's grammar mandatory in English grammar schools. Hart's work is important in that it relates exclusively to the English language. I shall argue, however, that it is still possible to trace many of the strands of prescriptivism further back than this. In addition, it can be shown that outside the institution of 'public' education interest in teaching English was largely instrumental and non-prescriptive. Clear evidence for this can be found in such texts as *A Very Profitable boke to lerne the maner of redyng, writyng, and speaking english and Spanish/Libro muy prouechoso para saber la manera de leer, y screuir, y hablar Angleis, y Español* and *The boke of Englysshe and Spanysshe*, both published anonymously c.1554, and *Familiar Dialogues/Dialogues Familiers*, published by James Bellot in 1586. Indeed, it is in such texts as these that an alternative language ideology can be discerned.

I shall argue in this chapter that work published on the English language during the eighteenth century reveals the development of a widely accepted 'ideology of prescriptivism', but I shall be concerned to demonstrate that any language ideology can only be formed

1   on the basis of beliefs about language, and attitudes towards language, which already have a long history, and
2   as a driving force behind a centrally significant social institution, the institution in this case being public education.

In the following section I shall consider what we understand by the term 'prescriptive' in relation to the study of language. I will then present two conceptualisations of time in classical Greek, *chronos* and *kairos*, since they are central to my understanding of how any ideology emerges. Within the framework of these two concepts of time I will outline my understanding of the concept of language ideology. In doing so, it will also be necessary to define the fundamental term 'myth' in section 3 for the purposes of the discussion in the following sections and to present the principal types of myths which contributed towards the ideology of prescriptivism.

In the fourth section I shall work backwards from two texts in the eighteenth century, one well known and influential, namely Thomas Sheridan's *A Course of Lectures on Elocution* (1762), and the other little known but very enlightening in the insights it provides into language attitudes in the first half of the eighteenth century, namely Hugh Jones' *An Accidence to the English Tongue* (1724), in order to illustrate those types of 'mythical' beliefs about language which form the basis of the ideology of prescriptivism. Some of these examples go back further than the sixteenth century. However, I make no claim to be presenting an exhaustive list of myths. There are undoubtedly several other mythical strands that remain to be discovered.

The fifth section will suggest how the emergence of the ideology of prescriptivism might be related to other historical factors in the eighteenth century. I will also outline very tentatively the alternative ideology that appears to be in evidence in *A Very Profitable boke, The boke of Englysshe and Spanysshe* and *Familiar Dialogues/Dialogues Familiers*. In the final section I shall argue that one of the most fruitful ways to carry out historical linguistic research is to co-ordinate the research findings from other disciplines and to view the process of standardisation as an object of inter-disciplinary research. Such a research programme might also be used to predict the direction not only of processes of language standardisation but also as a critical assessment of our own presentation of the 'story of English'.

2 Prescriptivism and the concept of language ideology

The cognitive matrix of the lexeme *prescription* contains the following five elements which can be transferred from the domain of medical treatment to that of language:

- a patient who needs/wants to be cured; a speaker/writer or group of speakers/writers who need(s) to be cured of 'malformed', 'infectious', 'debilitating' language use
- an improved state of health; a state of 'perfection' in language structure and use which is the desired goal of the treatment
- a means through which the cure can be effected; a set of methods through which that perfection in language can be reached
- a figure of authority (e.g. a doctor) to diagnose the illness and prescribe the course of treatment; a language expert with the authority to diagnose the problem and make the prescription(s), e.g. grammarian, lexicographer, elocutionist, orthographer
- an institution, e.g. a chemist's, from which the medicine can be procured; an educational institution that can dispense the methods for improvement prescribed

For the notion of 'prescription' to make any sense at all when transferred to the domain of language study, however, we need to ask whether there *is* or could ever be a state of perfection in language competence and/or language use, to which a language 'expert' could refer, i.e. that there is an agreed-upon linguistic norm. Given that this norm, or 'standard', exists or is presupposed to exist, linguistic prescriptivism can be defined as the belief in a set of social processes similar to those outlined above.

On the other hand, an ideology of prescriptivism cannot be attained without the prior existence of prescriptive attitudes towards and prescriptive statements on language. In other words, the development of an ideology is dependent on the working of those social processes through time.

We traditionally conceive of time as consisting of a set of discrete, equidistant points ordered linearly and unidirectionally along an axis, the ever-present central point of which is the 'present'. The past is conceptualised as a set of distinct events prior to that point, one preceding, following or running concurrently with another, and since this is the way in which we generally view history, it has tended to dominate our understanding of the historical development of language.

The Greeks referred to this way of conceptualising time as *chronos*. But they also had a second notion of time, *kairos*, which can be understood roughly as a point, or period, in time, for example an event, which only occurs when conditions are such that it should occur. In other words, time in this sense is still conceived of as being directional, but it contains within it certain pre-ordained, predestined events. It therefore transcends the linearity of *chronos*, since, if events are taken to be pre-ordained, there must be a cyclicity or circularity about time which transcends human experience. *Kairos* is thus an evaluative concept which implies not only that there is a 'right' and a 'wrong' time for doing certain things, but also that it may be possible for human beings to predict when the right time will occur. Generally, it implies that we will only be able to judge whether or not an event or action took place at the 'right' time after it has occurred. *Kairos* is not therefore tied to the cycle of animal life as represented by birth, maturity, decay and death, and it may appear to be either momentary and fleeting or inordinately long.

Let us now turn our attention to the term 'language ideology' and fit it into the framework of the notion of *kairos*. An ideology is a coherent set of beliefs constructed socially through chronological time and shared by a community. The precepts of the ideology are the only true precepts for the members of that community, and they are superior to the precepts of any other alternative set of beliefs. A language ideology is thus a set of communally shared precepts about language which have been constructed and reproduced through *chronos*.

However, the precepts themselves, which, I will argue, are mythical, do not come together to form a coherent ideology until the time is 'right' for them to take a hold in the thinking of a community. Hence the emergence of an ideology, including language ideology, is governed by both *chronos* and *kairos*.

If a language ideology gains dominance over other alternative ideologies, it will exert an influence on language attitudes and the way in which language structure and language use are thought of in the community. A dominant language ideology will also owe its emergence to the confluence of non-linguistic socioeconomic, sociopolitical factors with attitudes towards and beliefs about language.

The length of time during which a language ideology is dominant depends on the continued interplay between linguistic and non-linguistic factors, but the longer it exercises its hegemony, the more likely it will be that the community will accept its precepts as 'normal', 'natural', or even, in the terms of the original Greek understanding of *kairos*, as 'God-given'. Hence, if we want not only to understand the ideology of prescriptivism, but also to deconstruct it in order to reinstate *chronos* in the place of *kairos*, we need to identify and unravel the complex threads of beliefs about language that go to make up the pattern of that ideology.

3   Ideology and myths

In order to trace the development of a language ideology, or any ideology for that matter, we need to locate the complex of myths that form the basis of the set of beliefs constituting that ideology. We need to assess the relative strength of those myths in relation to the social factors that have exerted a formative influence in the social construction of the community for whom the ideology is significant.

I am not using the term 'myth' to mean any belief, or set of beliefs, which can be shown to be empirically false. Myths are, of course, essentially fictive, but they contain elements of reality in them, derived as they are from the mutually shared past experiences of members of the community. If myths are judged solely on the basis of a present-time, commonsense point of view, they will have to be rejected as fantasy. The two fundamental defining features of myths are that they are narrative and communal. They are shared stories which tell part of the overall 'story' of the sociocultural group; they are not the property of any single individual. Telling the stories helps to reproduce and validate the cultural group, and in this sense myths fulfil a vital function in explaining, justifying and ratifying present behaviour by the narrated events of the past. Myths can also be changed, altered, lost, abandoned, inverted, etc., in other words they are continually reproduced and reconstructed socially.

The myths that form the basis of the ideology of prescriptivism are stories or remnants of stories about links between language and the sociocultural group. The principal mythical types that I would identify as forming the basis of the ideology of prescriptivism will be outlined below. In some cases they are contradictory, so in order for the kairotic moment for the ideology to emerge in the second decade of the eighteenth century the contradictions must somehow be resolved.

Language is frequently taken to be one of the most important core values of a sociocultural group (cf. Smolicz 1981, 1997), and it is hardly surprising that it should figure among the creation myths of many cultures. The relationship between territory and ethnic identity usually makes use of a shared language to link the two, thus establishing the central or core function of language in the production of ethnicity. I shall call this type of myth the *language and ethnicity myth*.

Linked to the language and ethnicity myth are two contradictory types of story, about the creativity and variety of the English language, on the one hand, and its central importance in the development of a sense of unity between the nation (the people linked by the bonds of ethnicity) and the state (the political representative of the nation in its dealings with other nations), on the other. The concept of the nation is a social construct created by those in power in the important social institutions of the state. In order to create the unity between nation and state, the former must be represented as culturally homogeneous, and it is precisely this function which a standardised variety of language is pressed into service to fulfil. If all the members of a 'nation' speak the same language, then this is a significant ratification of the social construction of the nation and a justification for the institutions of the state. I shall call this type of myth the *language and nationality myth*.

The creativity and variety stories, on the other hand, work in exactly the opposite direction. One of the virtues that English has been said to possess is the number of dialectal varieties it displays. Whenever this myth, which I shall call the *language variety myth*, is raised as an argument in favour of the English language, it does not seem to motivate against the need to codify Standard English and to raise it to a position of pre-eminence over the other varieties. But it does very clearly contradict the language and nationality myth, as we shall see, and during the first twenty years of the eighteenth century it was superseded by that myth.

Until the beginning of the eighteenth century the language variety myth was frequently connected with other assumed qualities of English which placed it in a position of superiority with respect to other European languages. It was said to be easier to learn, to have more 'significancy', to be 'sweeter' and 'more copious' than other languages, and a number of writers went to great lengths to give examples of these assumed qualities. This *myth of superiority* was undoubtedly linked to the language and nationality myth, and there is evidence of this link before the sixteenth century. But the period in which the standard language, rather than simply 'English', became firmly associated with the myth of superiority coincided precisely with rapid mercantile and imperial expansion by Great Britain and colonial competition with other European powers in the first half of the eighteenth century, particularly competition with France. In other words, the assumed superiority of the standard language was taken as a potent symbol for the assumed economic and political superiority of the state of Great Britain.

In order to give some substance to the myth of superiority, it was necessary to represent Standard English as having already reached a state of perfection, creating the *myth of the perfect language*. This, however, called into being two further mythical stories. If the language had already reached perfection, there must have been a 'golden age' which writers and speakers should aspire to recreate: thus we can speak of the *golden age myth*. Since any change in the 'perfection' of the standard language was bound to be change for the worse if left to the whims of natural development, change should be prevented, if possible by a language academy or some such body of authority. The only change that such a body of 'experts' should allow would be with the express intention of enriching the language still further. I shall call this myth the *myth of the undesirability of change*.

The complex of language myths outlined in this section forms the set of major tenets of the ideology of prescriptivism which arose during the first half of the eighteenth century, and in the following section I shall give a number of examples of these myths.

4   Tracing the myths

If the myths that I outlined in the previous section do indeed contribute towards the emergence of an ideology of prescriptivism, they should be in evidence in texts on language in the eighteenth century, and it should be possible to trace them back through time. In order to test out this hypothesis I shall comment on some extracts from Thomas Sheridan's lectures on elocution and Hugh Jones' grammar.

4.1   *Language myths in Sheridan's* Course of Lectures on Elocution

In 1762 Thomas Sheridan delivered a series of lectures on elocution in London and other large cities in Britain in his efforts to establish a standard form of oral English to complement the written standard variety (cf. Mugglestone 1995). In order to secure himself a greater income than the quite considerable sums of money he had already amassed from entrance fees charged at the public lectures – the majority of which were held in large halls in front of capacity audiences – Sheridan had the text of the lectures published together with certain other tracts on the same subject. At every lecture he opened a subscribers' list which is printed in full at the front of the *Course of Lectures on Elocution* and contains more than 800 names, the vast majority of which clearly indicate the middle-class social provenance of his audiences.

By the eighteenth century the myth of language and ethnicity no longer needs to be retold in Britain, since the relationship between territory and ethnic identity has already been firmly established by emphasising the importance of a standard form of English. The two grammars which appeared in 1711, Greenwood's and Gildon and Brightland's, were among the last to give this myth any real attention. It is interesting to note, however, that the positive version of the language variety myth is still evident in Greenwood's grammar, whereas it is interpreted in a negative way by Sheridan. In 'Lecture II' Sheridan discusses the two types of English to be found in London (cf. Disraeli's 'two nations'), court English, or what Sheridan chooses to call 'polite pronunciation', and 'cockney'. His comment on these two varieties is as follows:

> As amongst these various dialects, one must have the preference, and become fashionable, it will of course fall to the lot of that which prevails at court, the source of fashions of all kinds. All other dialects, are sure marks, either of a provincial, rustic, pedantic, or mechanic education; and therefore have some degree of disgrace attached to them. (Sheridan 1762: 30)

Dialects thus indicate the provinciality, rusticity and manual occupation of the speaker, all of which are negatively evaluated terms to which 'some degree of disgrace' is attached.

This attitude is expressed in a slightly different way in a section of the text which is entitled 'Heads of a Plan for the Improvement of Elocution' (1762: 206):

> it can not be denied that an uniformity of pronunciation throughout Scotland, Wales, and Ireland, as well as through the several counties of England, would be a point much to be wished; as it might in great measure contribute to destroy those odious distinctions between subjects of the same king, and members of the same community, which are ever attended with ill consequences, and which are chiefly kept alive by difference of pronunciation, and dialects; for these in a manner proclaim the place of a man's birth, whenever he speaks, which otherwise could not be known by any other marks in mixed societies.

The variety of dialects and pronunciation is presented by Sheridan as being divisive and as maintaining differences between the citizens of Great Britain. However, it is not social differences that a uniform pronunciation may help to eradicate, but rather the linguistic signs of geographical provenance.

For Sheridan 'vitious articulation' is 'caught perhaps from a nurse, or favourite servant' and it 'often infects a man's discourse thro' life' (1762: 23), which makes the metaphorical comparison of bad speech with an illness or infection quite explicit. The remedy for this illness is to teach elocution in schools so that the learners

> may avoid provincial dialects, accents and phraseology, which prevail more or less thro' all the counties of Great Britain; and which, thro' want of proper care in early years, are necessarily caught, in some degree, by all who are trained in those counties, and generally stick to them during the remainder of their lives. (1762: 204)

The language and nationality myth is invoked throughout the *Course of Lectures on Elocution*, although it is generally kept implicit. Explicit mention of it is made at certain places, however, particularly when in a further section of the overall text entitled 'A Dissertation on the Causes of the Difficulties, which occur in Learning the English Tongue' he advocates the writing of a definitive grammar and dictionary of Standard English and imposing it universally throughout the public school system:

> Upon the whole, if such a Grammar and Dictionary were published, they must soon be adopted into use by all schools professing to teach English. The consequences of teaching children by one method, and one uniform system of rules, would be an uniformity of pronunciation in all so instructed. Thus might the rising generation, born and bred in different countries, and counties, no longer have a variety of dialects, but as subjects of one king, like sons of one father, have one common tongue. All natives of these realms would be restored to their birthright in commonage of language, which has been too long fenced in, and made the property of a few. (1762: 261–2)

The 'one method' and 'one uniform system of rules' used through the education system would create a common language, which Sheridan considers the 'birth-right' of the 'natives of these realms'.

The myth of the perfect language and the myth of the undesirability of change are less obviously in evidence in Sheridan's text, but they do emerge from time to time, as in the following passage from the same section:

> Such a grammar and dictionary will lay the foundation for regulating and refining our speech, till it is brought to the degree of perfection whereof in its nature it is capable; and afterwards fixing it in that state to perpetuity, by a sure and settled standard. For tho' in a living tongue changes are not to be prevented, whilst any plausible colour can be given that such changes are made for the better; yet, after the general rules of analogy shall have been laid open, all alterations hereafter will be made in conformity to those rules, in order to render our language more regular and complete. Nor will novelty or caprice (the sources of fashion); or partial views of the constitution of our tongue, have it in their power to innovate as usual. (1762: 259)

The message here is quite clear. The language may be allowed to change but only in strict conformity with the rules and only if it is thereby enriched. Sheridan suggests, as Swift did earlier in the century, that English has not quite reached a state of perfection, but that it is about to do so. For this reason, any mention of a previous golden age lies outside Sheridan's view of the development of Standard English.

4.2   Language myths in Hugh Jones' An Accidence to the English Tongue

The grammar of English published in 1724 by Hugh Jones is certainly one of the
least known grammars of the eighteenth century, but it is an intriguing mixture
of traditional normative grammar, presented almost too briefly and succinctly to
be of any real use to the learner of English, and a lengthy digression on the 'rules'
of polite conversation in English. Its value as a book to be used in the eighteenth-
century schoolroom is almost zero, but its value to the twentieth-century
researcher into language attitudes is very considerable.

   Although Jones' grammar was printed in London, it was written in Williams-
burg, Virginia, and is often classified as the first 'colonial' grammar of English.
All the language myths that can be identified in Sheridan can be found in Jones'
grammar. As in Sheridan, the language variety myth is presented negatively and
the language and ethnicity myth is not represented at all.

   The title page of the grammar is significant in that it identifies the groups of
people at whom the grammar is aimed. In effect, we have a rank order of
addressees, at the top of which we see 'boys and men' who have never 'learnt
Latin perfectly', women, and finally those non-English-speaking citizens of
Great Britain and other 'foreigners':

> An Accidence to the English Tongue, chiefly for the Use of such Boys and
> Men, as have never learnt Latin perfectly, and for the Benefit of the
> Female sex: Also for the Welch, Scotch, Irish, and Foreigners.

The inclusion of the 'Welch' in this list of addressees is the more surprising
given the thorough 'Welshness' of the author's own name, Hugh Jones.

   Like Sheridan, Jones also adopts a critical, even mocking tone in his criticism
of the variety of dialects in Britain, indicating that 'a polite Londoner' – note,
not a cockney! – would be amused to listen to a conversation between 'downright
Countrymen' from different parts of the country:

> For want of better Knowledge, and more Care, almost every County in
> *England* has gotten a distinct Dialect, or several peculiar Words, and
> odious Tones, perfectly ridiculous to Persons unaccustomed to hear such
> Jargon: thus as the speech of a *Yorkshire* and *Somersetshire* downright
> *Countryman* would be almost unintelligible to each other; so would it be
> good Diversion to a polite *Londoner* to hear a Dialogue between them.
> (Jones 1724: 11–12)

He goes on to classify the variety of dialects as a 'Confusion of English', but in
classifying five principal types of English, he also includes the 'Proper, or
London Language':

> Out of this Confusion of English may we collect 5 principal Dialects and
> Tones.
> 1   The *Northern Dialect*, which we may call *Yorkshire*.
> 2   The *Southern*, or *Sussex Speech*.

3   The *Eastern*, or *Suffolk Speech*.
4   The *Western*, which we may call *Bristol Language*.
5   The *Proper*, or *London Language*.
All these are manifestly distinguishable by their Sound, and some Terms, to any curious Observator. (1724: 13)

The myths of perfection and superiority, and the myth of the undesirability of change are evident in the following passage, in which Jones uses two of the very terms that Richard Carew used in 1586, namely 'copiousness' and 'significancy', to stress the pre-eminence of English with respect to other languages:

> In *this Age our Language* seems to be *arrived* at its *Crisis*, or highest Pitch; being sufficiently copious, significative, and fluent; and it is doubted whether future Alterations may prove real Amendments. (1724: 21)

Since Jones assumes English to have reached perfection in the eighteenth century, there is no need for him, as there was no need for Sheridan, to make use of the myth of language and ethnicity.

The myth of the undesirability of change appears to have been first voiced by Swift in *A Proposal for Correcting, Improving and Ascertaining the English Tongue* (1712):

> But what I have most at Heart, is, that some Method should be thought on for *Ascertaining* and *Fixing* our Language for ever, after such Alterations are made in it as shall be thought requisite. For I am of Opinion, that it is better a Language should not be wholly perfect, than that it should be perpetually changing; and we must give over at one Time or other, or at length infallibly change for the worse. (1964 [1712]: 14)

But it reoccurs in Samuel Johnson's *The Plan of a Dictionary of the English Language* (1747):

> But the chief rule which I propose to follow, is to make no innovation, without a reason sufficient to balance the inconvenience of change; and such reasons I do not expect to find. All change is of itself an evil, which ought not to be hazarded but for evident advantage; and as inconstancy is in every case a mark of weakness, it will add nothing to the reputation of our tongue. (1747: 10)

Although the myth of the golden age does not appear explicitly in Jones or Sheridan, it is certainly present in other writers in the eighteenth century, notably, once again, in Swift and Johnson:

> The Period wherein the *English* Tongue received most Improvement, I take to commence with the Beginning of Queen *Elizabeth*'s Reign, and to conclude with the great Rebellion in Forty-two. (Swift 1964 [1712]: 9)

the accession of Elizabeth, from which we date the golden age of our language. (Johnson 1762: 28)

4.3   Tracing the myths back through time

If we trace these myths back through time by locating attitudes towards the English language expressed by various authors, an interesting pattern emerges, which suggests an obvious relationship in their development. A rough visualisation of this pattern is given in Figure 2.1.

The figure indicates that the stronger the language and nationality, language superiority and language perfection myths became, the weaker became the language and ethnicity and language variety myths. In effect, whereas the language and ethnicity myth gave way to the language superiority, and language and nationality myths, the language perfection myth was in competition with the language variety myth from roughly 1550 to 1700, the latter also being part of the language superiority myth. The myth of the undesirability of change is therefore the inverse of the language variety myth. The myth of the golden age simply added substance to the myth of the undesirability of change and the language perfection myth, these three in turn strengthening the language superiority and language and nationality myths. The period during which the crucial inversion between the language variety myth and the myth of the undesirability of change took place can be located around the end of the reign of Queen Anne.

Before I focus on this period in a little more detail, however, it would be interesting to trace the development of those two mythical strands which disappeared at or immediately prior to this period, the language and ethnicity myth and the language variety myth. The language and ethnicity myth has a long tradition in writing on English. The link between culture and territory associated with language is evident in historical and geographical descriptions which go back at least as far as Bede. In Higden's *Polychronicon* at the beginning of the fourteenth century the myth is developed quite extensively, as we can see from John of Trevisa's translation of Higden's Latin text later in the fourteenth century:

> As hyt ys yknowe houȝ meny maner people buþ in þis ylond? þer buþ also of so meny people longages & tonges // noþeles walsch men & scottes þᵗ buþ noȝt ymelled wiþ oþer nacions? holdeþ wel nyȝ here furste longage & speche // . . . also englysch men þeyȝ hy hadde fram þe bygynnyng þre maner speche souþeron norþeron & myddel speche in þe myddel of þe lond as hy come of þre maner people of germania? noþeles by conmyxstion & mellyng furst wiþ danes & afterward wiþ normans in menye þe contray longage ys apeyred and som vseþ strange wlaffyng chyteryng harryng & garryng grisbittyng // (Higden c. 1327: fo.50v)

In effect, this text simply echoes Bede's belief in the three Germanic tribes that

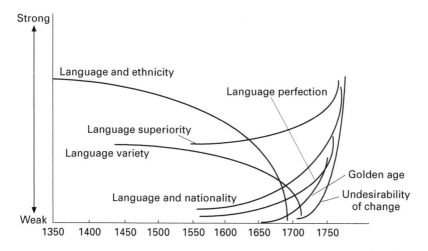

Figure 2.1 Assessment of the relative development of the myths along an axis strong–weak.

migrated to England from roughly the fourth to the fifth centuries. Note, however, that there is already a critical undercurrent here with regard to how English is used in country areas: 'som vseþ strange wlaffyng chyteryng harryng & garryng grisbittyng'.

The critical undercurrent is developed at other points in the text. In the original Latin text Higden appears to be critical of the diversity of accents and dialects in Britain when he compares this diversity with the supposed unity of Anglo-Norman in England:

> Ubi nempe mirandem videtur, quomodo nativa et propria Anglorum lingua, in unica insula coartata, pronunciatione ipsa sit tam diversa; cum tamen Normannica lingua, quæ adventitia est, univoca maneat penes cunctos. (Higden [c.1327] 1964: 160)

Trevisa translates this section in the following way:

> Hyt semeþ a gret wond*er* houӡ englysch þ' ys þe burþ tonge of englysch men & here oune longage & tonge ys so dyuers of soon in þis ylond & þe longage of normandy ys co*m*lyng of a noþ*er* lond & haþ on man*er* soon among al men þ' spekeþ hyt aryӡt in engelond (fo. 51)

But he immediately adds the following comment of his own, countering Higden's belief in the unity of Anglo-Norman French, to the effect that there are just as many dialects and accents in France:

> Noþeles þ*er* ys as meny dyuers man*er* frensch yn þe rem of fraunce as ys dyuers manere englysch in þe rem of engelond

Higden's Latin text goes on to suggest that the 'pure' variety of 'Saxon' – that untainted by the influences of Old French or Old Norse – is now only spoken by 'a few wild rustics' (*in paucis . . . agrestibus*), which is translated by Trevisa as 'wiþ fewe vplondisshe men', and that only the Mercians (*sive Mediterranei Angli*) can understand those to the north, south, east and west of them. Higden follows this with a scathing criticism of the language of Northumbria:

> Tota lingua Northimbrorum, maxime in Eboraco, ita stridet incondita, quod nos australes eam vix intelligere possumus. (p. 163)

Trevisa embellishes his translation of *stridet incondita* as follows:

> ys so scharp slyttyng & frotyng & vnschape (fo. 51)

Jones' negative attitude towards dialectal variety in English is thus prefigured in both Higden's early fourteenth-century text and John of Trevisa's late fourteenth-century translation of it.

In Raphael Holinshed's *Chronicles of England, Scotland, and Ireland*, printed in 1577, the chapter 'Of the Languages Spoken in this Land' was written by William Harrison. Harrison's text was reused and adapted several times in the prefaces to grammars of English right into the eighteenth century, although the last significant adaptation and extension of it was written in Latin by John Wallis in his *Grammatica Linguæ Anglicanæ* in 1653 and again reused and extended in English by James Greenwood in his *Essay Towards a Practical English Grammar* in 1711. In Harrison's text, for example, we read the following:

> Thus we sée how that vnder the dominion of the king of England, and in the south parts of the realme, we haue thrée seuerall toongs, that is to saie, English, British, and Cornish, and euen so manie are in Scotland, if you accompt the English speach for one: notwithstanding that for the bredth and quantitie of the region, I meane onelie of the soile of the maine Iland, it be somewhat lesse to see than the other. ([1577] 1965: 25)

Harrison talks here of three languages spoken in England in the sixteenth century, English, Cornish and British (i.e. Welsh), and suggests that if Scotland were included, there would be even more. He makes an interesting link between the quality of the soil and the number of languages, as if languages grew like plants, and expresses his surprise that the poor quality of the soil in Scotland still gives rise to three languages.

Greenwood's translation of Wallis' preface deals more with the relationship between language and history than that between language and soil quality:

> Now the Saxons, as has been observ'd, having made themselves Masters of the Ancient Seats of the Britains, nam'd that Part of Britain which they had conquer'd, England; and the Tongue which they brought with 'em, English. But the Anglo-Saxon, as likewise the Frank, or French Tongue, the present German, Dutch, Swedish and Prussian Tongues, are Branches of the old Teutonic. The Anglo-Saxon Tongue, remained here,

in a manner, pure and unmix'd, till the Time of the Normans; only it received some Welch Words, as the Welch did likewise some of theirs; for altho' the Danes, in the mean Time came into England, yet the Tongue suffer'd no considerable Change, the Danish Tongue being almost the same, or very near a kin to it. (Greenwood 1711:8)

In both these texts the author's concern is to give the English language an ethnic pedigree by tracing it back through time and relating it to other languages and the nature of the territory in which these languages coexisted. The language variety myth is also implicit in them, as it was in Higden's *Polychronicon*, and at other points in those same texts is explicitly dealt with. The concern with language variety, however, arises explicitly in the fifteenth century. The anonymous translator of Higden in the first half of the fifteenth century, for example, writes the following:

> Where it is to be hade in meruayle that the propur langage of Englische men scholde be made so diuerse in oon lytelle yle in pronunciacion, sythe the langage of Normannes is oon and vniuocate allemoste amonge theyme alle. (Higden [c. 1327] 1964: 159)

The translator expresses his surprise that there should be so many varieties in 'oon lytelle yle'.

At the end of the sixteenth century Richard Carew, in a chapter in William Camden's *Remains Concerning Britain* (1674) entitled 'The Excellency of the English Tongue', explicitly focuses on the myth of language variety as an important part of the language superiority myth:

> Moreover the copiousness of our Language appeareth in the diversity of our Dialects, for we have Court and we have Countrey English, we have Northern and Southern, gross and ordinary, which differ from each other, not only in the terminations, but also in many words, terms, and phrases, and express the same thing in divers sorts, yet all write English alike. ([1674] 1870: 49)

The term 'copiousness' reappears consistently till well into the eighteenth century, although, as we saw in the case of Hugh Jones' use of the word in 1724, its meaning has become inverted.

In Guy Miège's preface to his *The English Grammar* (1688) Carew's text appears almost verbatim, as we can see from his version of the language variety myth:

> Nor does its Abundance ly here [i.e. in the fact that English has borrowed liberally from other languages]. For we have Court and Country *English*, *Northern* and *Southern* Dialects; which differ not only in Pronunciation, but also in Words and Terms. (1688: A4)

Three myths reach back before the watershed of the early eighteenth century to the age of Queen Elizabeth in the latter half of the sixteenth century: the language and nationality myth, the language perfection and language superiority myths. Since the language superiority myth contained the other two and also the myth of language variety, I have assessed it in figure 2.1 as being at medium strength around the year 1550 and rising quite sharply together with the other myths of the ideology of prescriptivism in the eighteenth century. The myth of language perfection and that of language and nationality, on the other hand, are certainly represented in writings on language, but more weakly so. With respect to language perfection, Harrison in Holinshed's *Chronicles* writes the following:

> Afterward also, by diligent trauell of Geffray Chaucer, and Iohn Gower, in the time of Richard the second, and after them Iohn Scogan, and Iohn Lydgate, monke of Berrie, our said toong was brought to an excellent passe, notwithstanding that it neuer came vnto perfection, vntill the time of Quéene Elizabeth. ([1577] 1965: 25)

Harrison thus links the attainment of perfection to the Elizabethan age, in which he himself was writing, and it is precisely that period which later writers refer back to as the golden age.

The idea of perfection is also expressed by Miège in 1688 (A4), although without making any explicit mention of a golden age:

> Thus, when Substance combines with Delight, Plenty with Delicacy, Beauty with Majesty, and Expedition with Gravity, what can want to the Perfection of such a Language? Certainly such is the Mixture of the *English*.

Carew's text, however, is the clearest expression of the myth of the superiority of English over other languages and its implicit link with the development of a sense of nationality:

> I come now to the last and sweetest point of the sweetness of our tongue, which shall appear the more plainly, if like two Turkeyses or the London Drapers we match it with our neighbours. The Italian is pleasant, but without sinews, as a still fleeting water. The French, delicate, but even nice as a woman, scarce daring to open her lips for fear of marring her countenance. The Spanish, majestical, but fulsome, running too much on the O, and terrible like the devil in a play. The Dutch, manlike, but withal very harsh, as one ready at every word to pick a quarrel. Now we, in borrowing from them, give the strength of consonants to the Italian, the full sound of words to the French, the variety of terminations to the Spanish, and the mollifying of more vowels to the Dutch, and so (like Bees) gather the honey of the good properties and leave the dregs to themselves. ([1674] 1870: 50)

To prevent the impression from being formed that it is only Carew's text in which these myths find their expression, here is a more cautious expression, if not of superiority, then at least of equality, by Richard Mulcaster in his *The*

Elementarie (1582):

> Yet notwithstanding all this, it is verie manifest, that the tung it self hath
> matter enough in it self, to furnish out an art, & that the same mean, which
> hath bene vsed in the reducing of other tungs to their right, will serue this
> of ours. ([1852] 1925: 88)

In the following section I shall turn to the period located visually in figure 2.1
as the rise of the ideology of prescriptivism and relate attitudes towards language
during this historical period with extralinguistic, sociohistorical factors which
helped to contribute towards its emergence. I shall also argue in favour of the
need to carry out interdisciplinary historical research in attempting to display
and partially unravel the immense complexity of the process of the standardisation of English. As a final point I shall suggest briefly that there was at least one
alternative language ideology in evidence in the sixteenth century, which also
deserves to be researched in a little more detail, since such research might throw
an interesting light on what we might call the 'mainstream' development of
Standard English.

5   The rise of the ideology of prescriptivism

The beginning of the eighteenth century saw the reigning monarch of England
also firmly established as King (or Queen) of Scotland and Ireland. Although
with the accession to the throne of James VI of Scotland in 1603 the Union of the
Crowns of England, Wales, Scotland and Ireland was achieved, it was not until
1707 that the Act of Union was passed in which the Scottish parliament ceased
to exist and Scottish representatives were elected to a centralised Westminster
parliament along with English and Welsh members. From that point on the
monarch became King (or Queen) of Great Britain and Ireland. British imperial
power had also been extended by the establishment of the American colonies
and the acquisition of most of the West Indian islands in the Caribbean. In
North America Britain was in fierce colonial competition with France, both in
what later came to be Canada and in the United States.

Strong trading links were established in competition with the Dutch in South
and South East Asia, resulting in the establishment of the British East India
Company and the eventual economic and, ultimately, political takeover of the
Indian subcontinent. The financially lucrative slave trade in Africa resulting in
the enslavement and enforced transportation of Africans to the New World was
also in full swing, involving Britain once again in fierce competition with the
French and the Dutch.

All of these developments, and many more which I do not have space to
develop here, had to do with an unprecedented rapid expansion in international
trade and a struggle for colonial power which necessitated the establishment of a
strong national identity as 'British', rather than 'English', 'Scots' or 'Irish'. In
effect, creating such a uniform national identity was a new development which

rested almost entirely on the centralisation and enforcement of the powers of jurisdiction exercised in the monarch's name by the central government in London. Whatever happened in the rapidly expanding British empire was focused on London, in which all the complex threads of administration, trade and finance were concentrated.

If we accept the central role which language plays in the development of a national cultural identity and the significance that a system of public education has in constructing this identity, we can perhaps understand how the form of written standard *English* at the beginning of the eighteenth century, which had already attained a high degree of uniformity, became the vehicle for expressing a *British* identity. This will also enable us to understand why dialect variation and the existence of other languages within the territory of Great Britain and Ireland, Irish, Gaelic, Welsh, Manx and Cornish, motivated against this drive for linguistic uniformity, why it was necessary to assume that Standard English had achieved a state of near perfection which would be seriously threatened by linguistic change, and how and why Standard English had to be exalted above the languages of Great Britain's competitors.

6   Future research

In investigating the development of Standard English, however, what we now need is linguistic research which will link up with historical research into the nature of the economic and colonial competition with France and the Netherlands from the end of the seventeenth and the beginning of the eighteenth centuries, with research into the unprecedented rise of London as an imperial metropolis at the core of a world-wide 'empire', with research into the development of public education in Britain at the end of the seventeenth and beginning of the eighteenth centuries, and so forth. These and many other avenues of investigation will entail micro-level and macro-level study involving a variety of academic disciplines.

From the point of view of cultural myths which become the mainstay of a set of beliefs constituting an ideology, however, we still need to locate other alternative sets of beliefs about and attitudes towards language. In the first section of this chapter I intimated that there were indeed texts in the sixteenth century in which such alternatives might be found and which therefore merit careful study (cf. also Watts in press). In sixteenth-century London there were relatively sizeable communities of foreign immigrants, some of whom had come to England for economic reasons, others as refugees from religious and political persecution on the continent. Those foreign residents took a more everyday, instrumental view of the English language than native English commentators on it, and their need to acquire enough of the language to be able to get by in their day-to-day dealings with Londoners was served in part at least by didactic texts, many of which were written in the form of dialogues (e.g. James Bellot's *Familiar Dialogues / Dialogues Familiers*, 1586). Such texts raise intriguing questions which promise to reveal alternative attitudes towards English:

How were the learners taught English?

What sort of English appears from the texts to have been taught?

What age were the learners and what did they need to use their English for?

Are there similar texts from other periods of English which can be compared with them, e.g. in the seventeenth century?

Above all, what do the texts tell us about the forms of English currently in use in the latter half of the sixteenth century in London and the degree of integration of such communities of non-native English speakers?

In addition to these questions, all of which will provide a rich vein of alternative myths deserving future research, we might also give some thought to the mythologisation contained in our own teaching of the 'story of English'. How much of that story can, and indeed should, be re-examined along similar lines to the approach I have sketched out in this chapter? For example, is it perhaps not a myth to locate the beginnings of Standard English in Chancery English? Can we make such neat distinctions as 'Old English', 'Middle English', 'Early Modern English' and 'Modern English' when confronted, for example, with wills from East Anglia written between c.980 and 1020 which look and feel distinctly like texts from the twelfth or even thirteenth century?

There are countless other questions we could ask ourselves, but perhaps the most important questions of all are the following: What is the nature of the ideology that guides our own teaching, and how is that ideology grounded in the hegemonic practices of academic discourse? If we once dare to unpack those questions and reveal the myths that underlie them, the story of Standard English might look rather different from the *standard* way in which we teach it.

References

Anonymous 1554. *A Very Profitable boke to lerne the maner of redyng, writyng, and speaking english and Spanish / Libro muy prouechoso para saber la manera de leer, y screuir, y hablar Angleis, y Español*, London.

1554. *The boke of Englysshe and Spanysshe*, London.

Bellot, James 1586. *Familiar Dialogues / Dialogues familiers*, London.

Carew, Richard 1674. 'The excellency of the English tongue', in William Camden, *Remains Concerning Britain*, ed. T. Moule, London: John Russell Smith, 1870, pp. 42–51.

Gildon, Charles and John Brightland 1711. *A Grammar of the English Tongue, with Notes, giving the Grounds and Reason of Grammar in General*, London.

Greenwood, James 1711. *An Essay towards a Practical English Grammar*, London.

Harrison, William 1577. 'Of the languages spoken in this land', printed in Raphael Holinshed, *Chronicles of England, Scotland, and Ireland*, ed. Vernon F. Snow, vol. I, New York: AMS Press, 1965, pp. 107–9.

Hart, John 1551. *The Opening of the Unreasonable Writing of Our Inglish Toung*, repr. in Danielsson, Bror (ed.), *John Hart's Works on English Orthography and Pronunciation [1551, 1569, 1570]*, part 1, Stockholm: Almqvist and Wiksell, 1955.

Higden, Ranulf c.1327. 'De incolarum linguis', trans. John of Trevisa, British Library
   MS Cotton Tiberius D. vii, fos 50v, 51; printed in Babington, Churchill (ed.),
   *Polychronicon Ranulphi Higden Monachi Cestrensis: Together with the English Trans-
   lation of John Trevisa and of an Unknown Writer of the Fifteenth Century*, vol. II,
   London: Longmans, Green and Co., 1869; repr. in Wiesbaden: Kraus, 1964,
   156–63.
Johnson, Samuel 1747. *The Plan of a Dictionary of the English Language*, London.
Jones, Hugh 1724. *An Accidence to the English Tongue*, London.
Lily, William and John Colet 1549. *A shorte introduction of grammar, generally to be vsed in
   the Kynges maiesties dominions . . . to atteyne the knowledge of the Latin tongue*,
   London.
Miège, Guy 1688. *The English Grammar*, London.
Mugglestone, Lynda 1995. *Talking Proper: The Rise of Accent as a Social Symbol*, Oxford:
   Clarendon Press.
Mulcaster, Richard 1582. *The Elementarie*, repr. in Campagnac, E. T. (ed.), *Mulcaster's
   Elementarie*, Oxford University Press, 1925.
Sheridan, Thomas 1762. *A Course of Lectures on Elocution: Together with Two Disserta-
   tions on Language; and some Tracts relative to those Subjects*, London.
Smolicz, Jerzy 1981. 'Core values and cultural identity', *Ethnic and Racial Studies* 4.1,
   75–90.
   1997. 'In search of a multicultural nation: The case of Australia from an international
   perspective', in Watts, Richard J. and Jerzy Smolicz (eds.), *Cultural Democracy and
   Ethnic Pluralism: Multicultural and Multilingual Policies in Education*, Frankfurt:
   Peter Lang, pp. 51–76.
Swift, Jonathan 1712. *A Proposal for Correcting, Improving and Ascertaining the English
   Tongue*, ed. Herbert Davis and Louis Landa, Oxford: Blackwell, 1964, 1–21.
Wallis, John 1653. *Grammatica Linguæ Anglicanæ*, London.
Watts, Richard J. 1999. 'The social construction of Standard English: Grammar writers
   as a "discourse community"', in Watts, Richard J. and Anthony Bex (eds.),
   Standard English: The Continuing Debate, London: Routledge.
   in press. '"Refugiate in a strange countrey": Learning English through dialogues in
   the sixteenth century', in Jucker, Andreas (ed.), *Historical Dialogue Analysis*, Amsterdam: Benjamin.

3 Rats, bats, sparrows and dogs: biology, linguistics and the nature of Standard English[1]

JONATHAN HOPE

1   Introduction

Linguistic historians of English like to claim that they have the nature and origin of Standard English nailed. The standard, *as any fule kno*, is a non-regional, multifunctional, written variety, historically based on the educated English used within a triangle drawn with its apexes at London, Cambridge and Oxford. Even more specifically, the propagation of this 'incipient' standard can be linked to a particular branch of the late medieval bureaucracy: the court of Chancery.[2]

At least, that is the standard account of the rise of Standard English in most classrooms and textbooks. In a series of articles on business texts, however, Laura Wright has now challenged the second part of this account, pointing out that the central governmental bureaucracy is not the only place where the necessary conditions for standardisation obtained;[3] and other chapters in this book offer further evidence of a growing unease with the status of 'Chancery Standard' as the simple and sole source of Standard English. In this chapter, I want to question the first part of the standard account – and in particular the general theoretical basis of the hypothesis, which I take to be the evolutionary, family-tree model of language change. I claim that linguists have tended to accept what I will call the 'single ancestor-dialect' hypothesis (the SAD hypothesis), not because the linguistic data supports it (in fact it does the opposite), but because the family-tree metaphor demands it. Following from this rejection of a unitary source for Standard English, the paper offers an alternative characterisation of standardisation itself as a multiple rather than a unitary process; I end by claiming that this reformulation accounts for the hybrid linguistic nature of Standard English.

2   The 'single ancestor-dialect' hypothesis

Under a SAD-based analysis, the rise of Standard English becomes the story of the selection of one Middle English dialect, and its evolution into that standard. The SAD hypothesis places the chosen dialect in a direct genetic relationship to

Standard English: one evolves from the other in the linear way that man evolves from one of the early primates. Strang, for example, discusses 'the evolution of a sequence of competing types, of which one (the direct ancestor of PE [Present-day English] standard) dominated from about 1430' (1970: 161). Pyles and Algeo state: 'Throughout this chapter, the focus of attention is on the London speech that is the ancestor of standard Modern English . . . the term *Middle English* is used here to refer to the language of the East Midland area and specifically to that of London' (1993: 143). The attractiveness of the SAD hypothesis is clear: it provides a neat explanation for the emergence of Standard English from the morass of competing variants in the Middle English period, and it is an economical account, since by operating at the level of dialect rather than linguistic feature, it automatically explains why any and every linguistic variant was selected to become part of the standard. The alternative would be an 'every variant has its own history' account, which would have to treat each variant as a separate entity. Such an account would present us with standardisation as a random, haphazard process with no overall organisation. The SAD hypothesis is also highly teachable, because it leaves no loose ends, and because (in its 'Chancery Standard' realisation) it provides a clear motivation for changes: they happened because an identifiable group of people made identifiable decisions. Finally, the success of this hypothesis is also due in no small part to the parallels it draws between evolutionary biology and linguistic change.

Reasonable as the SAD hypothesis may appear, there are at least two problems with it. The first is that the linguistic data does not support the notion that Standard English evolved from a single dialect: as most historians of the language accept, Standard English features can be traced to an inconveniently wide range of dialects. Thus Pyles and Algeo: 'It is not surprising that a type of speech – that of London – essentially East Midlandish in its characteristics, though showing Northern and to a lesser extent Southern influences, should in time have become a standard for all of England' (1993: 141). It is tempting to ask what dialects are *not* present in this Londonish-East Midlandish-Northernish-Southernish 'single' ancestor. The second problem with the hypothesis is that languages and dialects are not equivalent to biological species: the metaphor of the family tree is inappropriate as a way of representing their development.

A biological species does, of course, evolve from a single ancestor species. This is inevitable, since the definition of different species is that they do not interbreed and exchange genetic material: the branches of the evolutionary tree indicate direct, linear relationships. Genes for a particular feature can only be handed down through related species: insects, birds and bats all have 'wings', but they are unrelated structures which look similar because of their similar functions. Birds evolved wings in a separate process to that of insects, and those of bats are the result of a third, again separate, development. Mammals might have developed wings more quickly if they had been able to borrow bird wing-genes, but until recently this kind of genetic modification, or borrowing, has been impossible. Languages, however, operate very differently. Linguistic structures *can* be mixed and recombined across dialect and language boundaries: it is very easy to mate linguistic sparrows with rats to get bats – with the consequence that a linguistic dialect, unlike a biological species, does not have to have a single immediate evolutionary ancestor. Use of the family-tree model encourages linguists to assume that Standard English must have evolved from a single dialect just as new organisms evolve from single ancestor species. If there is a missing link between man and the primates, the metaphor whispers temptingly in our collective ear, then surely there is also one between Standard English and the mass of competing Middle English dialects.[4]

3   What is 'standardisation'?

With the rejection or modification of the SAD hypothesis of Standard English comes a reconsideration of our notion of what standardisation is. Standardisation is commonly defined as the reduction of variation in language, or (more specifically, and not quite the same thing) as the selection, elaboration and codification of a particular dialect. Implicit in section 1 is the claim that the 'selection' process of standardisation is not the selection of a single dialect, but the selection of single linguistic features from a range of dialects – features which are then recombined into a new dialect which lacks a common ancestor. Standardisation thus becomes, not a unitary process operating on a single dialect at a single time, but a group of processes operating on all dialects over a much longer time. *Selection* becomes *selections*, and this accords much more closely with the observed nature of Standard English (the mixing of northern and southern forms, for example). Standardisation is not simply a set of decisions made by one identifiable group of late medieval bureaucrats: it is a complex of processes, growing out of the decisions made by a much wider range of writers in English (including, for example, the hundreds, perhaps thousands, of people involved in keeping and exchanging business records).

Reconsidering standardisation in this way suggests that it may be much more of a 'natural' linguistic process than has previously been thought. One of the paradoxes of the relationship between standardisation and prescriptivism is that prescriptivism always *follows*, rather than precedes, standardisation. It is therefore wrong to see prescriptivism as the ideological wing of standardisation: standardisation can be initiated, and can run virtually to completion (as in the case of English in the early seventeenth century), in the absence of prescriptivist comment. In fact, it is arguable that prescriptivism is impossible until standardisation has done most of its work – since it is only in a relatively standardised context that some language users become conscious of, and resistant to, variation.

If this is the case, we can characterise prescriptivism, uncontentiously, as language-external: a cultural, ideological phenomenon which plays itself out in language, but which is not in itself a linguistic process. Standardisation, however, looks more like a language-internal phenomenon: something motivated and progressed below the conscious awareness of language users. I would suggest that we think of standardisation as a set of 'natural' linguistic processes (selections, self-censorships) which are started when language users encounter formal written texts, and become unconsciously sensitive to linguistic variation. This awareness triggers natural processes of competition (for example, those suggested by Ehala 1996 and Kroch 1994) which operate independently for each linguistic variable, producing the hybrid features of Standard English.[5]

4   On the linguistic nature of Standard English

Grant the inadequacy of the SAD hypothesis, and accept that standardisation is a natural, but multiple, process, triggered by shifts in the medium and context of linguistic communication: are we then left with nothing but randomness as the factor that selects the variants that make it into the standard? Must we conclude that, for any given variable, the outcome of standardisation is unrelated to any overarching principle? This would be an unsatisfactory conclusion, especially given the repeated findings of studies of linguistic variation and change that apparent randomness in language is frequently an illusion. If the features that make up Standard English do not all share an ancestor dialect, how can they be linked? I am now going to contradict somewhat the characterisation of standardisation I gave above, as a series of events connected only by their triggering context, by hypothesising a principle which shapes the linguistic nature of Standard English.

Human languages share typological features which are unevenly distributed amongst languages: some features are relatively common; others relatively rare. Examination of the variants that make up Standard English shows some interesting shared properties, especially when Standard English is compared to other dialects of English. A number of the variants of Standard English can be characterised as the *least* likely to have been selected (if 'naturalness' or frequency is a criterion) from a pool of variation:

(i)   retention of *-s* inflection in the third-person singular present tense, typologically the least likely slot to be morphologically marked – even highly synthetic languages often have this slot unmarked (e.g. the Finnish language, and see Molesworth (Willans and Searle) *passim*)

(ii) the typologically unusual five-person pronoun system:

singular	*I*	*she/he/it*
singular/plural	*you*	
plural	*we*	*they*

Middle English, Early Modern English, and most present-day dialects have a six-person system retaining or reinventing singular and plural second person reference, e.g. *thou/you, you/youse, you/you-all*[6]

(iii) failure to allow *what* as a relativiser, despite the use of other *wh-* interrogatives as relatives, and the use of *what* as a relativiser by most (perhaps all) non-standard dialects[7]

(iv)   failure to allow double negatives, despite their frequency in speech and dialects

Thus, in each case, Standard English arrives at a typologically unusual structure, while non-standard English dialects follow the path of linguistic naturalness.[8] One explanation for this might be that as speakers make the choices that will result in standardisation, they unconsciously tend towards more complex structures, because of their sense of the prestige and difference of formal written language. Standard English would then become a 'deliberately' difficult language, constructed, albeit unconsciously, from elements that go against linguistic naturalness, and which would not survive in a 'natural' linguistic environment.[9] There are also implications for the learnability of Standard English from this: note how well this type of 'difficult' structure feeds into (or perhaps produces) the ideology of prescriptivism, since learners will typically require formal instruction in order for them to hit linguistically unlikely target utterances, and to remove the linguistically likely, but non-standard, alternative realisations from their idiolects.

5   Summary and conclusion

To summarise: one trend in the history of Standard English can be called the 'single ancestor dialect' (SAD) hypothesis. This claims that Standard English has developed directly from one dialect. However, this hypothesis is not supported by our knowledge of the mixed appearance of Standard English. The SAD hypothesis can be seen as a construct of the evolutionary metaphor, which is inappropriate in its application of linear biological processes of change to languages. Paradoxically, this is also what has made the hypothesis so successful as a theory (it is teachable, and fits in with our expectations from other fields).

The alternative hypothesis presented here is that standardisation came about in English when changes in the medium (writing) and context (distance) of language use created a situation in which multiple instances of grammar competition occurred. Since these are multiple processes rather than one, no single dialect of English provided all of the successful variants. A secondary hypothesis of this paper is that in the processes of competition speakers unconsciously favoured linguistically less likely variants because of their sense of the formality of written language. These two hypotheses explain the mixed dialectal sources of the variants which make it into the standard, and the linguistically unlikely nature of Standard English.

Notes

1 This is a deliberately polemical paper from which I have rigorously excluded almost all linguistic data. Preliminary versions of the paper were given at Lancaster and Middlesex Universities, and further thought was prompted by the papers and discussions at the International Conference on Standard English. I am grateful for comments and

suggestions made on all those occasions by the various participants. I am also grateful to an anonymous reader for Cambridge University Press who hated my tone, and pinpointed numerous lazy weaknesses in an earlier version. The unattributed non-standard quotation in the first paragraph is from the *oeuvre* of schoolboy Nigel Molesworth (Willans and Searle 1958: 8).

2 For examples of this geographical claim, see: Strang 1970: 161–5; Pyles and Algeo 1993: 140–3; Crystal 1995: 54–5; Barber 1997: 10. For work on 'Chancery Standard', see: Fisher 1977, 1979, 1984, 1988 and Fisher, Fisher and Richardson 1984; and see Smith 1996: 68–78 for a sophistication of the theory which none the less retains the essentials.

3 See, for example, Wright 1994 and 1996.

4 This challenge to the family-tree model is not new, of course. Consideration of the effects of using biological models in linguistics can also be found in Ehala 1996, Lass 1997 and Smith 1996. Smith (43) makes a similar point about the exchange of genetic material, and suggests (50–2) that the wave model of change is better able to deal with this aspect of language. In a recent posting on the *Histling* e-mail discussion group (5.8.98), Larry Trask made the point that there is a long tradition of resistance to the family-tree model within linguistics, and a growing current interest in convergence phenomena (as distinct from the divergence phenomena highlighted by the family-tree model).

5 It could be said that the SAD hypothesis is in fact a branch of prescriptivism – even though many of those who support it would certainly reject the description. Its prescriptivism lies in the unitary, motivated account it gives of standardisation: one dialect is privileged, and linguistic change becomes a process dedicated to bringing that dialect to prominence (a similar teleological fallacy dogs biology: in this case, seeing man as the purpose or 'end' of evolution). Its underlying ideological aim is to give coherence to Standard English by establishing a unitary origin, and to give it prestige by associating that origin with political, economic and intellectual power. Prescriptivism, like the SAD hypothesis, has been highly successful as a social ideology, while failing to account for linguistic data.

6 See Lutz 1998.

7 E.g.: 'Are you the little bastards *what* hit my son over the head?' Cheshire 1982: 72 – example quoted from Ball 1996: 240. In an otherwise impressive article, Ball classifies *what* with *who* and *which* as WH relatives, commenting: 'Hughes and Trudgill (1979: 18) noted that "[t]he form with *what* is particularly common" in non-standard BrE dialects. If we classify this form as a WH-pronoun, then we have further evidence that WH has indeed affected spoken (British) English.' (Ball 1996: 240–1). Given the stylistic and dialectal distribution of relative *what*, such a lumping of it with *who* and *which* would seem to be a serious misrepresentation: Tottie and Rey 1997: 227–8, tables 3 and 5, show that relative *what* is the only one of the three found in a corpus of African American Vernacular English; Pat Poussa (1991, 1997) has also worked on the dialectal distribution of relative *what*.

8 This list is not meant to be exhaustive. At ICSE, in response to a paper by Larisa Oldireva (1997) on the use of the preterite and past participle in the seventeenth and eighteenth centuries, Dieter Kastovsky posed a question which seems to illustrate a further example of Standard English being contrary: why, in choosing the form of spelling for the past tense ending, does Standard English select *-ed* from the range of possible choices: *-ed -d -'d -t -'t*? Especially given that *-ed* corresponds to the

phonetically *least* common form. Further speculation that standard languages may be in some sense unnatural can be found in Kiesling 1997: 101–2: see also his reference to Chambers 1995 (final chapter: 'Adaptive significance of language variation', especially pages 230–53).

9 The example of the exclusion of double negatives from Standard English may be a case of this. Although this is one of the great bugbears of prescriptivism, and has been hailed as one of its few successes, it is notable that double negatives had virtually disappeared from written English long before prescriptivism (Iyeiri 1997, and Rissanen, this volume). How else to explain an apparently unnatural change occurring before explicit comment on it?

References

Ball, Catherine N. 1996. 'A diachronic study of relative markers in spoken and written English', *Language Variation and Change* 8, 227–58.

Barber, Charles 1997. *Early Modern English*, 2nd edn, Edinburgh University Press.

Chambers, Jack 1995. *Sociolinguistic Theory*, Oxford: Blackwell.

Cheshire, Jenny 1982. *Variation in an English Dialect*, Cambridge University Press.

Crystal, David 1995. *The Cambridge Encyclopedia of the English Language*, Cambridge University Press.

Ehala, Martin 1996. 'Self-organization and language change', *Diachronica* 13.1, 1–28.

Fisher, John Hurt 1977. 'Chancery and the emergence of Standard written English in the fifteenth century', *Speculum* 52, 870–99.

    1979. 'Chancery Standard and modern written English', *Journal of the Society of Archivists* 6, 136–44.

    1984. 'Caxton and Chancery English', in Robert F. Yeager (ed.), *Fifteenth Century Studies*, Hamden, Conn.: Archon.

    1988. 'Piers Plowman and the Chancery tradition', in Edward Donald Kennedy, Ronald Waldron and Joseph S. Wittig (eds.), *Medieval English Studies Presented to George Kane*, Cambridge: D.S. Brewer, pp. 267–78.

Fisher, John Hurt, Jane Fisher and Malcolm Richardson, 1984. *An Anthology of Chancery English*, Knoxville: University of Tennessee Press.

Hughes, A. and Peter Trudgill 1979. *English Accents and Dialects: An Introduction to Social and Regional Varieties of British English*, London: Arnold.

Iyeiri, Yoko 1997. 'Standardization of English and the decline of multiple negation: a case of Caxton's *Reynard the Fox*', paper presented at the International Conference on the Standardisation of English, Lucy Cavendish College, Cambridge, July 1997.

Kiesling, Scott F. 1997. Review of Chambers 1995, *Australian Journal of Linguistics* 17.1, 99–103.

Kroch, Anthony 1994. 'Morphosyntactic variation', in Katharine Beals et al. (eds.) *Papers from the 30th Regional Meeting of the Chicago Linguistic Society*, vol. II: *The Parasession on Variation in Linguistic Theory*, Chicago: Chicago Linguistic Society. pp. 180–201.

Lass, Roger 1997. *Historical Linguistics and Language Change*, Cambridge University Press.

Lutz, Angelika 1998. 'The interplay of external and internal factors in morphological restructuring: the case of *you*', in Jacek Fisiak and Marcin Krygier (eds.), *Advances in Historical Linguistics (1996)*, Berlin: Mouton, pp. 189–210.

Oldireva, Larisa 1997. 'The use of the preterite and past participle form in 17th and 18th century English', paper presented at the International Conference on the Standardisation of English, Lucy Cavendish College, Cambridge, July 1997.

Poussa, Pat 1991. 'Origins of the nonstandard relativisers WHAT and AS in English', in P. Sture Ureland and George Broderick (eds.), *Language Contact in the British Isles*, Niemeyer.

1997. 'Reanalysing *whose*', paper presented at the International Conference on the Standardisation of English, Lucy Cavendish College, Cambridge, July 1997.

Pyles, Thomas and John Algeo 1993. *The Origins and Development of the English Language*, 4th edn, Harcourt Brace.

Smith, Jeremy 1996. *An Historical Study of English: Function, Form and Change*, Routledge.

Strang, Barbara M.H. 1970. *A History of English*, Methuen.

Tottie, Gunnel and Michel Rey 1997. 'Relativisation strategies in Earlier African American Vernacular English', *Language Variation and Change* 9, 219–47.

Willans, Geoffrey and Ronald Searle 1958. *The Compleet Molesworth*, Max Parrish.

Wright, Laura 1994. 'On the writing of the history of Standard English', in Francisco Fernandez, Miguel Fuster, and Juan Jose Calvo (eds.), *English Historical Linguistics 1992*, John Benjamins, pp. 105–15.

1996. 'About the evolution of Standard English', in Elizabeth Tyler and M. Jane Toswell (eds.), *Studies in English Language and Literature: 'Doubt Wisely'. Papers in Honour of E.G. Stanley*, Routledge, pp. 99–115.

4   Salience, stigma and standard

RAYMOND HICKEY

1   Introduction

The concern of the present contribution is to look at a phenomenon which is generally recognised by linguists but which is notoriously difficult to quantify. This is the notion of *salience*. There are two points which need to be distinguished here. The first is defining what one means by salience and the second is to examine the extent to which it may play a role in language change. The first task appears relatively simple. Salience is a reference to the degree to which speakers are aware of some linguistic feature. It is immediately clear that one is dealing with conscious aspects of language. For instance, if speakers of a non-rhotic variety of English notice that other speakers use an /r/ sound in syllable codas, then this sound is salient for the speakers of the first variety. Note here that salience may apply to one's own speech or that of others. The concern in the present study is with salience in one's own speech, or at least in that of speakers whose speech is closely related.

If one wishes later to consider the role of salience in language change then one must determine if a feature can be said to be salient for more or less the entire community using a variety. This implies a notion of homogeneity, i.e. that all speakers are aware to more or less the same degree of a given feature or features and that, conversely, for certain other features they do not show this awareness. Short of interviewing an entire community, how can one determine this? One means is to look at what features are commented on by non-linguists. A further step would be elicitation, i.e. to ask of speakers to listen to a stretch of speech and comment on this for peculiarities; this method would only provide useful results in a synchronic study. For the present chapter the degree to which linguistic features have been salient in the past is central. One clear indication of this is found if features are regarded as stereotypes and ridiculed, something which is obvious, for example, in the many satirical dramas which purport to represent Irish English.

In this context one should be wary of one false conclusion, namely that if speakers do not comment on a feature they therefore do not show systematic variation with regard to it. Indeed it can be seen from investigations of sociolinguistic changes (Hickey 1998) that intricate and sophisticated variation is found precisely with those features which are below the level of conscious awareness for speakers. This variation which lies below the threshold of perception is especially significant for language change because no prescriptive brake is applied to such variation. Furthermore, it is clear that speakers show well-ordered and largely predictable variation for features of which they are not conscious. This is not a contradiction: as most linguistic activity is not conscious for speakers it is only to be expected that variation, particularly in phonology and syntax, is not something to which speakers devote their explicit attention. This fact is tied up with the nature of the linguistic level affected: closed class areas, the sounds of a language or its set of syntactic structures, typically enjoy only limited awareness by speakers, whereas open classes, first and foremost the lexicon of the language, show a high degree of awareness, probably due to the fact that this is a class whose acquisition is not completed during early childhood and where conscious choices are continually made as to which lexical items to use in the sentences one speaks. The lexicon allows for continuous growth, both for the individual and on a collective scale, so that it must of necessity remain open-ended.

It is probably fair to say that the elements in a variety or language which are most salient for its speakers are those used in linguistic stereotypes. These are prominent features which speakers manipulate consciously, largely to achieve some kind of comic effect. Furthermore, stereotypical features are not usually determined afresh by each generation, still less by each speaker. Rather they are part of the inherited knowledge of features which are putatively typical for a certain variety. For instance, the unraised mid vowel used in words like *Jesus*, *decent* are regarded as stereotypical for colloquial forms of Irish English, particularly of Dublin. The regard for these sounds as stereotypical does not necessarily rest on direct experience of the variety which is being alluded to. This fact explains why stereotypes are so frequently off the mark. An example from syntax would be the use of *after* and a continuous form of the verb (used in a perfective sense), again as a stereotypical feature of Irish English. But it is often used by non-Irish speakers in syntactic frames which do not allow it, e.g. with stative verbs as in **She after knowing Paddy for years*.

1.1   Stereotypes

Stereotypes in varieties of English have a long pedigree. For Irish English their occurrence can be traced back to the late sixteenth century, to Richard Stanyhurst's *Description of Ireland* in Holinshed's *Chronicles* (1586). No less writers than Shakespeare and Ben Jonson attempted to indicate Irish English in their plays. Shakespeare did so in the figure of Captain Macmorris in the 'Three Nations Scene' in *Henry V*, whereas Jonson dedicated a small piece to a (ridiculous) portrayal of Irish English, *The Irish Masque at Court* (1613/16). The basis for his linguistic characterisation are certain features of Irish English which had become established by then and indeed had become obvious to English observers. For example, virtually every instance of /s/ is written as *sh*, i.e. [ʃ], and all cases of initial *wh-* [ʍ] are rendered orthographically as *ph-* or *f-*, deriving from Irish /f/ [ɸ]. Jonson also indicates all ambidental fricatives as *t* which stands for either [t] or [t̪]: going on his orthographic evidence it is not possible to say which.

(1)   *For chreeshes sayk, phair ish te king?*
      ['For Christ's sake, where is the king?']
      Peash, ant take heet, vat tou shaysht, man.
      ['Peace, and take heed, what thou sayest, man.']
                                      The Irish Masque at Court (Jonson 1969: 206)

This type of accent imitation became quite a vogue and is to be found in later literary parodies, particularly those of Restoration comedy in the second half of the seventeenth century (see Bliss 1979), establishing the literary stereotype known as the 'stage Irishman', which has had a long tradition continuing into the twentieth century (see Duggan 1969 [1937] for a comprehensive treatment of this topic). Apart from the character and the situations typical for such a dramatic figure there is also a conception of the speech suitable for his portrayal, and many guides and handbooks for actors include chapters on Irish English and the modifications of an actor's speech necessary to simulate an Irish stage accent.

Jerry Blunt lists in his *Stage Dialects* (1967) five features which also have a foundation in local speech in Ireland, particularly that of Dublin where feature five is prominent:

(1)   central /aː/ for /ɑː/   *grand*   /graːnd/
(2)   unrounding of /ɒ/ to /a/   *top*   /taːp/
(3)   the raising of /ɛ/ to /ɪ/   *bed*   /bɪd/
(4)   the retention of /ʊ/ for /ʌ/   *bun*   /bʊn/
(5)   'the elongation of vowels'   in *mean* /   mijən/[1]

A more thorough discussion is to be found in Bartley and Sims (1949), who attempt to reconstruct stage Irish pronunciation before the nineteenth century and list six essential features:

(1)   /ʃ/ for /s/
(2)   affricate simplification /tʃ/ → /ʃ/
(3)   plosivisation of /θ/
(4)   use of /f/ for /ʍ/
(5)   substitution of voiced stops by voiceless ones
(6)   /eː/ for both ME /eː/ and /ɛː/, e.g. /dʒeːzɪz/ for
      Jesus; *meat* /mɛːt/

All authors used English literary works as their sources and hence one can conclude that for the perception of Irish English by speakers (and writers) of mainland English these stereotypes had a certain significance. But they cannot be said to play a central role in language change. In general the stereotypical features are simply avoided. The use of [ʃ] for /s/, particularly before high vowels and in syllable codas before consonants, is not something which is relevant for present-day forms of Irish English. It may be found – recessively – in some contact varieties in the west of the country. Apart from that it is confined to linguistic caricature of a rather crude type.[2]

One should point out here that what is salient for one group may be non-salient for another. Within varieties of Irish English the alveolar [l] in syllable-final positions – rather than [ɫ] – has never been the subject of comment and has close to zero salience. But for Scottish speakers this is one of the features which is claimed to be typically Irish (Roger Lass, personal communication). There would seem to be a fairly obvious explanation for this: in most forms of Scottish English a velarised variant of syllable-final /l/ is available, so that the Irish realisation contrasts strongly with it. Within Ireland there is no variation in the pronunciation of /l/ (except in the few varieties still in contact with Irish). This highlights an essential aspect of salience: it only arises where there is contrast.

1.2   Indicators and markers

Those linguistic features which are not so obvious are of greater interest to the linguist, as their role in the development of a variety is likely to be more central. Recall that there is a distinction in sociolinguistics between two basic types of variable. Those which are subject to *stylistic variation* as well as class, sex or age variation are referred to as markers. Variables which are not involved in systematic variation in style are called indicators. These do not contribute to the description of class differences as markers do, since speakers appear to be less aware of the social implications of an indicator than of a marker.

With reference to salience there would appear to be grounds for maintaining that markers are more salient for speakers than indicators. Again, take an example from (southern) Irish English. There is a general weakening of alveolar stops in open positions (intervocalically and in an open-syllable coda before a pause). The allophones found here are apical fricatives, rather than stops, and can be transcribed as [ṯ] and [ḏ] for the realisations of /t/ and /d/ respectively.

(2)   fricatives for alveolar stops   *but*   [bʌṯ]
                                            bud   [bʌḏ]

These indicators are found on all stylistic levels of (southern) Irish English and enjoy a low level of awareness among speakers. They are furthermore not singled out for caricature in stereotypical characterisations of Irish English and are not, for instance, indicated in the various guidelines on Irish English for actors; see Blunt (1967), and Bartley and Sims (1949) discussed above.[3]

The situation with markers of Irish English, especially that of the capital Dublin, is quite different. Among the various features found here is one which is salient for speakers who come into contact with socially lower registers of Irish English, namely the use of a high back vowel for /ʌ/.

(3)   unlowered [ʊ] for /ʌ/   *coming* [kʊmŋ]

Indicators and markers show the same lack or high degree of salience, respectively, when the differences are morphological. A clear example of this is afforded by the forms of the second person plural in Irish English (Hickey 1983). In this instance the archaic form which is retained in this variety is non-salient and shows a phonetic gradient in its realisation from [ji] to [jə] where it meets with the reduced form of the standard /ju/.[4]

(4)   *ye* [jiː] [jɪ] [jə]   2nd person plural
            [jə] [juː] *you*   2nd person singular

The form which enjoys a much greater degree of awareness is that with an added plural {S}, phonetically [z]. This can be appended to either the standard or the archaic form of example (3).

(5)   *youse*   [juz]   'you'-plural
        yez   [jiz]

For middle-class speakers of (southern) Irish English this form is quite stigmatised. It is only found among uneducated speakers or in deliberate imitations of the speech of such groups and is thus characteristic of stereotypes. Once this situation arises a realisation also becomes the object of sociolinguistic censure. It is the unwitting use of a stigmatised feature which provokes the disdain of less regionally bound speakers who themselves retain the right to use these features in conscious imitation of an accent they wish to ridicule.

1.3   Language levels

The above examples of putatively salient elements are all phonological in nature. In this connection one should stress that there is an essential difference between phonological and syntactic variables in that the latter do not occur as frequently as phonological ones. Syntactic variation is more likely to be conditioned by linguistic and 'situational-stylistic' factors rather than social ones, since syntactic structures are repeated less often than phonological ones and are thus less available for social assessment. Syntactic structures seem not to have an identification function equal to phonological factors as there may well be stretches of speech in which a given syntactic variable does not occur at all. Within syntax there would appear to be two types of context: 1) high-profile contexts used for variables which have high social significance for speakers and which are typically found in main clauses containing emphatic declaratives or explicit negatives (see the discussion in Cheshire 1996); and 2) low-profile contexts used for variables which are incoming and in the process of being adopted by diffusion into a community. This might be a plausible scenario for the spread of aspectual categories from Irish to English for the section of the community involved in language shift, as will be discussed in 2.5 below.

2   How does salience arise?

The discussion thus far has been fairly general, and for the remainder of the present article I would like to consider how it is that a certain linguistic feature becomes salient in a language and perhaps conjecture about whether there is a degree of predictability involved here. The following can thus be regarded as a preliminary checklist of salience triggers. It should be borne in mind that no one of these can be singled out as decisive and that frequently a combination of triggers is present.

2.1   Acoustic prominence

Acoustic prominence certainly contributes to salience. For instance, features such as the substitution of /ʃ/ for /s/ as with /ʃtɒp/ and /ʃkɪp/ are acoustically obvious given the ease with which the phonetic distinction between the two sounds can be perceived and the fact that these two sounds are phonemes in English (*sue* ≠ *shoe*). This kind of acoustic prominence can be appealed to in the history of English as well, for instance the substitution of /-θ/ by /-s/ in the third person singular[5] or the progressive productivity of /-s/ plurals from Old English onwards and their encroaching on already established plural types – cf. ME nasal plurals, such as *eyen* → *eyes* – can be accounted for on the grounds of the phonetic salience of /s/ and hence its suitability as a grammatical suffix.

2.2   Homophonic merger

This type of situation assumes that at some stage in the development of a variety continual variation became discrete variation, the latter involving two phoneme realisations. Homophonic merger would appear to have occurred in varieties of Irish English with the shift of dental plosives (themselves from dental fricatives in English) to alveolar stops.

(6)   *thank* [t̪æŋk] → [tæŋk]
       tank   [tæŋk]

But this seems to apply only to central phonemes. Peripheral ones such as /w/ versus /ʍ/ can be collapsed with this hardly being noticed.

(7)   *which* [ʍɪtʃ] → [wɪtʃ]
       witch   [wɪtʃ]

Of course there is a phonological issue involved here. If one analyses [ʍ] as a sequence of /h/ + /w/ then there is no phonological merger but deletion of an initial /h/.

The converse of homophonic merger is the acceptance of conditional realisations which appear not to be salient. For instance the alveolar realisation of /t̪/ in *athlete* is not stigmatised but the unconditional [t] in a word like *thick* is. Note that the unconditional merger of dentals and alveolars in Irish English is always to an alveolar articulation. There is no unconditional merger to dentals. A conditional merger to a dental articulation is found in the recessive case of a shift forward in articulation before /r/. This shift has traditionally been indicated orthographically by *dh* or *th* as in *murdher* (found in Shakespeare's *Macbeth* for instance), *shouldher*, *wather*.[6]

2.3   System conformity

Quite apart from the question of merger one can maintain that salience can be determined by the unusualness of features for a given variety, i.e. whether realisations conform to the possible range in the sound system. What is meant by this can be seen in the combination of [+ round] and [+ front] which may occur when the realisations of the /ʊ/, /uː/ or /əʊ/ vowels in English are fronted, as in the areally characteristic [ʉː] in Donegal Irish, Mid Ulster English, Ulster Scots and of course in Scotland. Equally unusual would be the fronting of the onset of the /əʊ/ diphthong as in *boat* [bøʊt] or that of the /ɜː/ vowel as in a pronunciation such as *bird* [bøːd]. The essential point about these realisations is that they flout a principle of English that [+ front] and [+ round] are features which do not combine with positive values.

2.4   Deletion and insertion

Any taxonomy of salience must also take the processes of deletion and insertion into account. Deletion often takes the form of cluster simplification which can be regarded as a fast-speech phenomenon which may become established in a variety. For instance, in fifteenth-century Dublin English (as documented in the *Calendar of Ancient Records* (1447) and the *Records of the Dublin Guild of Merchants*) this reduction of final clusters affected a nasal and a following stop, e.g. /nd/ → /n/ in *beyan* for 'beyond', *fown* for 'found', *grown* for 'ground' (Henry 1958: 74). There are indeed a few cases of unetymological /t/, in *forent* for 'foreign', for example, which shows the extent of the deletion of stops: speakers reinstated them even where they were not there originally.

For later varieties of Irish English this deletion is not attested. It is gone by the seventeenth century, and the texts which Bliss (1979) examines do not show it. Now replacement of deleted segments is a common phenomenon when moving upwards on a register cline (not just in Irish English) and is part of a more careful pronunciation, hence the reinstatement of alveolar stops after homorganic nasals.

Today similar deletion is attested. In Dublin English the kind just described is still found; in Ulster English the deletion of intervocalic /ð/ is common, but does not appear to enjoy high salience, again perhaps because deletion is accepted in allegro speech and is regarded to a certain extent as expected and natural. Conversely, insertion does appear to show salience, e.g. palatal glide insertion as in *car* [kjaːr] and *gap* [gjaːp] – again in certain forms of Ulster English.

In southern Irish English the insertion of a centralised short vowel (epenthesis) is common in most varieties and fulfils the phonological function of breaking up heavy syllable codas by disyllabification.

(8)   *film*   /fɪlm/   → [fɪləm]
      helm   /hɛlm/   → [hɛləm]

What is crucial here with regard to acceptance is the scope of epenthesis. It is tolerated in the supra-regional variety of the Republic of Ireland when it occurs between a /l/ and a nasal but not with other sonorants.

(9)   *burn*   /bərn/   → [bəɹen]
      girl   /gərl/   → [gəɹəl] ~ [gɛɹəl]

2.5   Grammatical restructuring

A more tentative claim is that any feature which involves grammatical restructuring would appear to be salient for native speakers, an obvious example being the use of the productive plural ending on either plural forms *you* or *ye* to yield *youse* or *yez* respectively. It may well be the morphological transparency of the forms which contributes to their salience – it also has acoustic prominence because of [-z] from {S}. Note that this salience does not apply to *ye* for plural of *you*, as noted above in the discussion of indicators and markers.

An example from syntax is the use of non-emphatic *do* for habitual aspect as in the following sentence.

(10)   *He does be in his office on Tuesday.*
       'He is in his office for a certain time every Tuesday.'

This represents a restructuring of English, albeit with models from dialects and earlier English (Harris 1984). The use of *after*, frequently with a continuous form of a verb, is not stigmatised within Irish English (but may be observed by the non-Irish).

(11)   *He is after his (eating) dinner.*
       'He has eaten his dinner.'

Here one could postulate that this use of *after* is not re-structuring on a morphological or syntactical level (as with the second person plural form /juz/

or the habitual with *do*) but a grammaticalisation of the temporal use of the adverb into a perfective sense.

Restructuring of a section of grammar is an operation which does not usually allow any transitional stages in form. But grammaticalisation normally results from a metaphorical extension of a literal use of a category (Hopper and Traugott 1993). In the example just given one has an extension of a locative meaning of *after* into the temporal sphere which yields the distinction in aspect (immediate perfective, Hickey 1997: 1007). The low salience of grammaticalised structures may account for their ready adoption across varieties; again, consider Newfoundland English where the perfective with *after*, while originating in the Irish-based communities of the island, has become a feature of the speech of the English-based section (mainly West Country) as well (Clarke 1997: 280).

2.6   Openness of word-class

As noted above, salience almost certainly has to do with the openness of a word-class. This must be what contributes to the high awareness which native speakers have of lexical items which are archaic or typical of varieties more colloquial than the supra-regional one. If such lexical items have a greater semantic range in the vernacular, then the extension beyond the standard may enjoy increased awareness. Take the instance of *grand* in Irish English. This has broadened in its scope considerably to form a general adjective of approval as in *You did a grand job on the cars*. The adjective has all but renounced its meaning of 'displaying grandeur'. In addition this word has adopted a pronunciation with a low back vowel [grɒːnd] (an attempted imitation of Received Pronunciation) with the specific meaning of 'posh, snobbish' as in *She speaks with a grand* [grɒːnd] *accent*.

2.7   The loss of vernacular features

In the development of a language or variety there is frequently a relatively sudden loss of a vernacular feature, typically in urban varieties, or at least in areas which are geographically well delimited. One view of this could be that when a pronunciation item becomes salient and conscious for the members of a speech community – for instance, when the variant crosses a barrier and becomes identical with an allophone of another phoneme – it is then abandoned or the merger is reversed (if varieties are around which do not have the merger, as with /ai/ and /ɔi/, cf. *bile* (noun) and *boil* (verb), in Early Modern English). This could account for the seeming disappearance of the raising tendency for /æ/ in Dublin English. The realisation as /ɛ/ is remarked on by many authors in the eighteenth century: Sheridan (1781)[7] originally noted this in words like *ketch* for 'catch' and *gether* for 'gather', but then the raised version seems to disappear shortly afterwards and is no longer commented on in the nineteenth century. Nowadays, if anything, there is a tendency to lower the realisation of /æ/ in Irish English.

2.8   Retention of conditional realisations

A subtype of this phenomenon involves phonetically conditioned realisations. If for a given segment a realisation is used, which is the normal allophone of another phoneme in more standard varieties, then this variant may be retained if the environment clearly defines it. The question here is whether the generalisation is valid that the loss of a feature follows a path through conditional realisation. Consider the following examples, the first of which is common on the east coast of Ireland and the second in the south-west of the country.

		previously	now	
(12)	raising of /a/	unconditional	only before /r/	*park* [pɛːɹk]
	raising of /ɛ/	unconditional	only before nasals	*pen* [pɪn]

Up to the last century, to judge by representations in dramas with stage Irish characters, such as those by Dion Boucicault (1820–1890) (see Krause (ed.) 1964), the unconditional raising of /ɛ/ and /ɪ/ was still to be found, for instance in *togithir* for *together* and *nivir* for *never*. The unconditional forms were replaced sometime later by more mainstream pronunciations deriving from British English.

The raising of /a/ before /r/ must be seen in the context of another vowel realisation in the same phonetic environment. This is where an original /ɛ/ is lowered to /a/ before /r/. There are many examples of this which are now established in English, e.g. *barn*, *dark* (from earlier *bern*, *derk*), and the orthography of *clerk* (British English) and various county names such as *Berkshire*, *Hertfordshire* still indicate the former pronunciation. It looks as if there were two movements in opposing directions in early modern Irish English: /ɛ/ → /a/ and /a/ → /ɛ/, both before /r/ but with different lexical sets. There are many written attestations of the /ɛ/ → /a/ shift, as in *sarve* for 'serve', *sarvint* for 'servant'. By a process of re-lexification (see below) these were gradually replaced by mainland British forms so that nowadays there are no unexpected cases of /-ar/ deriving from a former /-ɛr/.

The case of the raising of /a/ to /ɛ/ before /r/ is somewhat different. Whereas the lowering before /r/ was conditioned *from the beginning*, the raising of /a/ was not conditioned, as Sheridan with the examples from his grammar of 1781 shows. What one has now is the retention of the conditional realisations, which might be explained by the fact that these are not salient and so survive longest (recall that the alveolar realisation of /t̪/ in *athlete* is not stigmatised in Irish English but the unconditional shift of /t̪/ to /t/ in a word like *thick* [tɪk] is).

The retreat of salient non-standard forms might be used to explain phonetically unexpected distributions, such as vowel raising before /r/ whereas one normally has retraction of /a/ to /ɒ/ before /r/ as in many other varieties of English. This is a case where the conditional realisation is the only remnant of the former wider distribution, much like a pillar of stone left standing when the surrounding rock has been eroded.

A former widespread distribution can also take another path, as an alternative to conditional realisation or parallel to it. This is where individual lexical items with the former realisation become confined to a specific register, usually a more colloquial one. Hence the general raising of /ɛ/ to /ɪ/ has been retained for many forms of English in the south-west of Ireland, but the non-conditional (i.e. not pre-nasal) realisation is normally excluded from supra-regional varieties and is only found in a few lexicalised items such as *divil* for *devil* in the sense of 'rogue' and in [gɪɫ] for *get* to add local flavouring to one's speech (see section 3.4 below).

3   Reactions to salience

3.1   Possible hypercorrection

The desire to distance oneself from what are considered undesirable pronunciations is a common trait. And in the Ireland of the eighteenth and probably also the nineteenth centuries, when many of the pronunciations discussed above were not confined to specific styles, hypercorrection would appear to have occurred. Both Sheridan (1781) and Walker (1791) remark on the fact that the 'gentlemen of Ireland' frequently say *greet, beer, sweer, occeesion* ignorant of the fact that these words have /eː/ rather than /iː/, the normal post-vowel shift realisation of the vowel in *tea, sea, please*, for example. This is also found in words like *prey* and *convey* which had /iː/ as a hypercorrect pronunciation by the Irish, although the words in question did not have /eː/ when borrowed originally from French.

Sheridan also has /ʌ/ in the words *pudding* and *cushion*. These could be explained as inherited pronunciations from English but also – in their maintenance – as reactions to popular Dublin English which now, and certainly then, had /ʊ/ in these and all words with Early Modern English /ʊ/. Indeed, according to Sheridan, /ʌ/ was found in *bull, bush, push, pull, pulpit*, all but the last of which have /ʊ/ in (southern) Irish English today.

3.2   Phonological replacement

Hypercorrection is a dubious means of ridding one's speech of salient local features. Most people who engage in hypercorrection notice (at some stage in their lives) that their hypercorrect pronunciations are not in fact standard and may well be the object of derision by those who do indeed speak something approaching the standard. And if the relationship of those who hypercorrect to those who do not is one of colony to coloniser then the shame of being detected is so much the greater. For these or similar reasons the hypercorrect forms noted by Sheridan died out by the nineteenth century and are only of historical interest today.

Indeed when viewing Irish English diachronically one can see that several of its marked features have simply been replaced by the corresponding mainland British pronunciations. Where a replacement affects all instances of a sound one can speak of phonological replacement. A simple example of this is the retraction of /a/ after /(k)w/, which was apparently not present in eighteenth-century Irish English (cf. *squadron* [skwadrən] in Sheridan), but which is now universal in Ireland, i.e. /-wa-/ has become /wɒ/. Another instance of this replacement is provided by unshifted Middle English /aː/, which was obviously a prominent feature up to the late eighteenth century. George Farquhar in his play *The Beaux' Stratagem* (1707) uses many of the stereotypes of Irish pronunciation, including this one:

(13)   FOIGARD Ireland! No, joy. Fat sort of plaace [= [plaːs]] is dat saam [= [saːm]] Ireland? Dey say de people are catcht dere when dey are young.

Sheridan also rails against the low vowel in *matron, patron*, etc. But by the nineteenth century there are no more references to this. Boucicault, who does not shy away from indicating the phonetic peculiarities – inasmuch as English orthography allows him to – does not indicate anything like unshifted /aː/ when writing some seventy years later.

Prosodic replacement is the supra-segmental equivalent to the segmental features just discussed. Stressing of the second syllable in many Romance loan words meant that they were long in Irish English but short in mainland English (Sheridan 1781: 145f.):

(14)   *malicious* [məˈliːʃəs]   *endeavour* [ɪnˈdeːvɚ]

In some cases English already had initial stress, but Irish English retained this on the second syllable, which was long: *mischievous* [mɪsˈtʃiːvəs]. Nowadays the only remnant of this late stress is found in verbs with long vowels in the third syllable, e.g. *educate* [ɛdʒuːᵘkeːʈ], *demonstrate* [dɛmənˈstreːʈ]; the other words have been aligned to British pronunciation.

3.3   Lexical replacement

Apart from global changes like the Great Vowel Shift there are a number of archaic pronunciations which are still to be found in early modern documents in Irish English. Two instances can illustrate this well. The word for *gold* still had the pronunciation *goold* /guːld/ (as did *Rome*) in late eighteenth-century Ireland – a pronunciation criticised by Walker. The word *onion* /ʌnjən/ had /ɪnjən/, an archaic pronunciation attested up to the twentieth century with Patrick Weston Joyce (1910: 99). This was recorded by the lexicographer Nathan Bailey in 1726

(*Universal Etymological English Dictionary*) but was not typical of mainstream pronunciations, as Walker notes at the end of the eighteenth century. The quantifiers *many* [mæni] and *any* [æni] did not, and sometimes still do not, show the /e/ vowel which is characteristic of their pronunciation elsewhere.

If sound replacements are sensitive to the lexicon then it makes sense to speak of lexical replacement. Consider archaic pronunciations, found in Ireland in the early modern period (from earlier), e.g. *sarch* for *search* or *sarve* for *serve*. Here the early modern lowering of /e/ before /r/ is seen to have a much wider scope than in southern British English where it is not quite as widespread. These instances were all reversed on a lexeme-by-lexeme basis assuming that British English did not have the lowering. If it did, as with *clerk* /klaːk/, then the low vowel was retained (in rhotacised form in Ireland).

Vowels before /r/ provide further instances where Irish English was out of sync with developments in England. *R*-lowering did not occur in words like *door* /duːr/, *floor* /fluːr/, *source* /suːrs/, *course* /kuːrs/, *court* /kuːrt/ which, according to the Appendix to Sheridan's *Grammar* (pp. 137–55), were typical Irish pronunciations. This means that the southern mainland English lowering of back high vowels before /r/ had not occurred in Ireland by the late eighteenth century but was introduced by lexically replacing those pronunciations which conflicted with mainland British usage.

3.4   Local flavouring

An important point to be made concerning salience is that speakers may deliberately manipulate salient features, on the fly so to speak, for instance for the purpose of caricature or when style-shifting downwards. A simple instance is the replacement of *ye* by *youse*, the use of [lɛp] for *leap* [liːp] or the high vowel in *get* [gɪt] *out of here!*, all typical of colloquial registers of Irish English.

In the course of its development Irish English has evolved a technique of attaining local flavouring. This consists of maintaining two forms of a single lexeme, one the British standard one and another an archaic or regional pronunciation which differs in connotation from the first. This second usage is always found on a more colloquial level and plays an important role in establishing the profile of vernacular Irish English. The following are some typical examples to illustrate this phenomenon.

Eejit for *idiot* has adopted the sense of a bungling individual rather than an imbecile. *Cratur* /kreːtəɹ/ shows a survival of the older pre-vowel shift pronunciation (with /ɛː/) and denotes an object of pity or commiseration. Indeed for the supra-regional variety of the south, unraised /ɛː/ implies a vernacular register. Other words which, colloquially, still show the mid vowel are *Jesus*, *decent*, *tea*, *queer* (found orthographically as *Jaysus*, *daycent*, *tay*, *quare*) or expressions like *leave* [lɛː] *me alone*.[8] This situation is quite understandable: the replacement of an older pronunciation by a more mainstream one has led to the retreat of the former into a marked style, here one of local Irishness.

Bowl /baul/ for *bold* and *owl* /aul/ for *old* illustrate the same phenomenon. The older pronunciations have a simplified final cluster (the post-sonorant deletion is a very archaic feature reaching well back into the first period of settlement in the late Middle Ages) and a diphthong, arising probably due to the velarisation of the syllable-final /l/ – which is now alveolar [l], not [ɫ]. The special connotations of the archaic word forms can be seen in the following examples:

(15)   *The bowl' Paddy*   'The bold Paddy' (with sneaking admiration)
       The owl' bus   'The old bus' (said affectionately)

4   Conclusion

The factors considered in the present paper seem to suggest that salience results in the very first instance from language-internal causes, for example because of the appearance of features with high acoustic prominence, or because of homophonic merger or grammatical restructuring. The features involved are always strongly local and contrast with their lack in varieties which are less regionally bound, more 'standard' in the sense that they are not primarily indicative of a specific geographical area or of a social group. Once features have gained this prominence they experience an additional momentum as they are now part of the colloquial registers, including those for accent imitation, which the more educated sections of a community exhibit. In some cases salient features are deliberately maintained for local flavouring in which case they are transmitted through time and hence become part of the linguistic knowledge of later generations. At some later time such features may no longer be characteristic of the accents they are intended to allude to, but this fact does not necessarily lead to a revision of the features, as the salience of a low-status accent has as much to do with its perception by others as with its actual reality.

Notes

1 See the chapter 'Key sounds of an Irish dialect', pp. 75–90.
2 The traditional term for an obvious Irish English accent (lower-class urban or rural) is 'brogue'. This label has three possible sources (1) Irish *bróg*, 'shoe'; (2) Irish *barróg* 'rip, hold' as in *barróg teangan* (lit.: grip on the tongue), 'lisp'; (3) Northern Irish *bachlóg* also meaning 'lisp'. Irish *bróg* is itself from Old Norse *brók*, cognate with Old English *brōc* (plural *brēc* = Modern English *breeches*).
3 In her sociolinguistic investigation of language use in the capital of Newfoundland, Clarke (1986: 68) found that the apico-alveolar fricative realisation of /t/ – an inherited feature from Ireland – is not stigmatised in St John's and is common in the speech of women in the city, who tend otherwise to gravitate towards more standard usage.
4 Again in Newfoundland the *ye* /ji/ form is common among Irish-based communities and not subject to social stigma; see Kirwin (1993: 72). The restructured form /juz/

with the plural morpheme is not recorded for Newfoundland.

5 Ladefoged and Maddieson (1996: 145–72) suggest a division of fricatives into sibilant and non-sibilant given that with the former (/s, ʃ/ articulations in English for instance) the constriction at the alveolar ridge produces a jet of air that hits the obstacle formed by the teeth. In non-obstacle fricatives, such as /θ, ð/, the turbulence is produced at the constriction itself. Laver (1994: 260–3) discusses the auditory characteristics of fricatives as does Fry (1979: 122), who notes that the noise energy for [s] is prominent between 4000 and 8000 Hz. It is similar in frequency distribution to [θ] but has much greater energy which means it is more clearly audible (see diagrams, Fry 1979: 123).

6 See Hickey (1989) for a fuller treatment of the vacillation between ambi-dental fricatives and dental/alveolar stops in the history of English.

7 This work, *A rhetorical grammar of the English language*, contains an appendix on pp. 140–6 entitled 'Rules to be observed by the natives of Ireland in order to attain a just pronunciation of English' which is revealing in its description of Dublin English in the latter half of the eighteenth century. Sheridan states explicitly that his remarks concern the speech of 'the gentlemen of Ireland', i.e. he is describing the educated Dublin usage of his day.

8 Note here that some of these words had /eː/ in Middle English and some /ɛː/ but with the collapse of the two in Irish English the contrast became simply mid- versus high-front.

References

Bartley, J. O. and D. L. Sims 1949. 'Pre-nineteenth century stage Irish and Welsh pronunciation', *Proceedings of the American Philosophical Society* 93, 439–47.

Bliss, Alan J. 1979. *Spoken English in Ireland 1600–1740. Twenty-seven Representative Texts Assembled and Analysed*, Dublin: Cadenus Press.

Blunt, Jerry 1967. *Stage Dialects*, San Francisco: Chandler.

Cheshire, Jenny 1996. 'Syntactic variation and the concept of prominence', in Klemola, Kytö and Rissanen (eds.), pp. 1–17.

Clarke, Sandra 1986. 'Sociolinguistic patterning in a New World dialect of Hiberno-English: The speech of St.John's, Newfoundland', in Harris et al. (eds.), pp. 67–82.
    1997. 'On establishing historical relationships between New and Old World varieties: Habitual aspect and Newfoundland Vernacular English', in Schneider (ed.), pp. 277–93.

Clarke, Sandra (ed.) 1993. *Focus on Canada*, Varieties of English around the World, 11, Amsterdam: Benjamins.

Duggan, G. C. 1969 [1937]. *The Stage Irishman. A History of the Irish Play and Stage Characters from the Earliest Times*, New York: Benjamin Blom.

Fisiak, Jacek and Marcin Krygier (eds.) 1998. *English Historical Linguistics 1996*, Berlin: Mouton de Gruyter.

Foulkes, Paul and Gerard Docherty (eds.) 1999. *Urban Voices. Accent Studies in the British Isles*, London: Arnold.

Fry, Dennis Butler 1979. *The Physics of Speech*, Cambridge: Cambridge University Press.

Harris, John 1984. 'Syntactic variation and dialect divergence', *Journal of Linguistics* 20, 303–27.

Harris, John, David Little and David Singleton (eds.) 1986. *Perspectives on the English Language in Ireland. Proceedings of the First Symposium on Hiberno-English, Dublin 1985*, Dublin: Centre for Language and Communication Studies, Trinity College.

Henry, Patrick Leo 1958. 'A linguistic survey of Ireland. Preliminary report', *Norsk Tidsskrift for Sprogvidenskap [Lochlann, A Review of Celtic Studies]* supplement 5, 49–208.

Hickey, Raymond 1983. 'Remarks on pronominal usage in Hiberno-English', *Studia Anglica Posnaniensia* 15, 47–53.

   1989. 'The realization of dental obstruents adjacent to /r/ in the history of English', *Neuphilologische Mitteilungen* 90, 167–72.

   1997. 'Arguments for creolisation in Irish English', in Hickey and Puppel (eds.), pp. 969–1038.

   1998. 'The Dublin vowel shift and the progress of sound change', in Fisiak and Krygier (eds.), pp. 79–106.

   1999. 'Dublin English: Current changes and their motivation', in Foulkes and Docherty (eds.), pp. 265–81.

Hickey, Raymond and Stanislaw Puppel (eds.) 1997. *Language History and Linguistic Modelling. A Festschrift for Jacek Fisiak on his 60th Birthday*, Berlin: Mouton de Gruyter.

Hopper, Paul and Elizabeth Traugott 1993. *Grammaticalization*, Cambridge: University Press.

Jonson, Ben 1969. *The Complete Masques*, ed. Stephen Orgel, New Haven and London: Yale University Press.

Joyce, Patrick Weston 1910. *English as We Speak it in Ireland*, London: Longmans and Green.

Kirwin, William J. 1993. 'The planting of Anglo-Irish in Newfoundland', in Clarke (ed.), pp. 65–84.

Klemola, Juhani, Merja Kytö and Matti Rissanen (eds.) 1996. *Speech Past and Present. Studies in English Dialectology in Memory of Ossi Ihalainen*, Frankfurt am Main: Peter Lang.

Krause, David (ed.) 1964. *The Dolmen Boucicault*, Dublin: Dolmen Press.

Ladefoged, Peter and Ian Maddieson 1996. *The Sounds of the World's Languages*, Oxford: Blackwell.

Laver, John 1994. *Principles of Phonetics*, Cambridge University Press.

Schneider, Edgar (ed.) 1997. *Englishes Around the World*, 2 vols, Amsterdam: Benjamins.

Sheridan, Thomas 1781. *A rhetorical grammar of the English language calculated solely for the purpose of teaching propriety of pronunciation and justness of delivery, in that tongue*, Dublin: Price.

Stanyhurst, Richard 1808 [1586]. 'A treatise containing a plaine and perfect description of Ireland . . .', in R. Holinshed, *Chronicles of England, Scotland and Ireland*, 6 vols., vol. VI: *Ireland*, repr. 1965, New York: AMS Press.

Walker, John 1791. *A Critical Pronouncing Dictionary of the English Language*, Menston: The Scolar Press.

5 The ideology of the standard and the development of Extraterritorial Englishes

GABRIELLA MAZZON

The period of the formation of Extraterritorial Englishes coincided with a time in which language prescriptivism was in full swing in Britain. This has necessarily left some traces in the way Extraterritorial Englishes have developed, and it is the aim of this paper to examine some of these influences, as well as the impact of political and socioeconomic matters on linguistic attitudes within the context of the birth of new varieties. The countries where there are first-language Extraterritorial Englishes (Ireland, Scotland, the USA, Canada, Australia, New Zealand, South Africa) and those where English is a second language (India, Nigeria, Singapore etc.) show situations that are not straightforwardly comparable for several aspects, such as different times, mechanisms and forces involved in the shaping of the new forms of English, different social and pragmatic roles of the use of English and different linguistic contexts and backgrounds. The basic common factor in all these situations is the fact that the history of the new varieties was influenced by the idea of Standard English and by the ideology surrounding this notion, though not in the same ways or to the same extent.

1 Roots of the ideology of the standard; the standard as colonial instrument

The rise of the first Extraterritorial Englishes was accompanied by strong criticism,[1] and often these varieties were the object of ridicule, even before the full development of prescriptive attitudes in Britain, i.e. when the 'English English' standard itself was barely established (Pennycook 1994: 113).

A good part of the argument supporting a standard is based on its supposed 'excellence', but a not insignificant part is also made up of criticisms of other varieties. This is not revealed by histories of standardisation alone: in many cultures, the very names for languages refer to the excellence and uniqueness of the particular code, often in the same way as the names for tribes and ethnic groups often mean just 'people'. Of course, these groups are aware of the

73

existence of 'others', but this naming practice is a way of establishing oneself as *'the* people' *par excellence*: the others are just (as highly civilised Greece defined foreigners) οι βάρβαροι, barbarians.

Within the process of imposing colonial domination over a territory whose local traditions and languages have a long-standing existence, the imposition of a standard colonial language is an instrument of imperialism, aiming at suppressing or at least undermining the identity sensibilities of the people colonised and at establishing a whole range of new social divisions totally alien to the local culture. Therefore, it can be said that the role of the standard within the process of the spread of English has been that of creating a sense of inferiority, of establishing a new social scale based on the degree of knowledge of English and to the extent of adherence to its (exo-normative) standard, and in general it has served as an instrument of imperialism as much as political and economic strategies and policies.

2   Local standards and identity sensibilities in first-language Extraterritorial Englishes

In communities using a primary Extraterritorial English, there does not seem to have been, at first, a real preoccupation with enforcing the position of English, let alone the prescription of a standard, since the predominance of English was never questioned, due to the historical circumstances of settlement. But the traits of the local varieties that emerged as most prestigious in the older colonies show that the influence of some norm must have been there, however covert and vague. All main Extraterritorial Englishes are based on British varieties from the Southeast whatever the input, i.e. whatever the predominant geographical provenance of settlers. It is only rarely, and in very peripheral areas such as Newfoundland, that the localised varieties show a more than negligible influence from non-southeastern British English. This phenomenon of dialect levelling (Lass 1990 calls it the 'Law of Swamping [of non-southeastern features]') is in some cases connected to the numerical predominance of settlers of southern provenance (as possibly in Australia, see Eagleson 1982: 415–16; Delbridge 1990: 67ff.). In other cases, however, it must have been due to the prestige attributed to forms of speech brought along by the first settlers, especially in North America, first peopled by groups of pilgrims who were usually fully literate, if not quite educated.

The first Extraterritorial Englishes were not immediately recognised as varieties in their own right, and certainly not as new standards, since the first records of their 'difference' were accompanied by the expression of negative attitudes and judgements. The problem is that ever since these first opinions, the approach to these varieties has invariably been a 'deviationist' approach (Sridhar 1989: 41), i.e. the new varieties have been seen and assessed in terms of their relationship with the mother country's standard, so that the process leading to the recognition of an independent variety has been long and troubled.

This kind of attitude, emerging originally in the mother country but easily transferred, helped to reinforce linguistic insecurity and negative (self-)assessment in the colonies.[2]

Among the strategies adopted to this end there is the non-recognition of the autonomy of the local variety, autonomy being one of the constitutive features of a standard. This has given rise to the argument which often goes under the name of 'colonial lag', i.e. the fact that the older Extraterritorial Englishes, notably US English, look remarkably like older British English. These varieties were formed in Early Modern English times, the argument goes, and have not changed very much since then: they preserve older features and show very little innovation. Among the most frequently quoted examples of 'colonial lag' there are the lack of lengthening of the vowel in words like *glass*, and the retention of post-vocalic /r/. The argument implies that the language is still 'British', that it is still a secondary product: the umbilical cord with the mother country cannot be cut, and autonomous development is impossible besides minor, very marginal changes.

The 'colonial lag' argument has been refuted, e.g. by Görlach (1987) as regards US English, but it is still put forth occasionally (see e.g. Bliss 1984: 135; Barry 1982: 98 on Ireland; see reviews in Knowles 1997: 132–4, Dillard 1992: 35–6 on American English) and, what is more important for the ideology of the standard, it has filtered into the education system and public opinion, and so has the argument to the effect that Extraterritorial Englishes like US English are 'dialects' (in the non-technical, prejudice-laden sense) of British English.

Conversely, claims to the existence of local varieties of English and their validity as autonomous standards have become part of the struggle for political independence. Arguments like 'colonial lag' typically tend to perpetuate language colonialism, and are put forth the more vocally in moments of deeper political strife, e.g. when independentist movements are more vital. Scotland and Ireland are often claimed to have 'high' varieties that are 'very close' to Standard British English (Trudgill and Hannah 1985: 82; Douglas-Cowie 1984: 533–5), and studies on attitudes and on pressures to conformity in school pupils and university students reveal that such pressures towards the use of the 'English English' standard can be strong indeed (Iacuaniello 1991: 157–79). There is however also a strong reaction against these pressures, and the process of standardisation of these varieties often works towards the elimination of RP-like variants (see e.g. Harris 1991: 40 on Irish English).

The connection between language and politics was particularly salient in the emergence of US English. Kahane (1982: 229–31) claims that immediately after independence there was still a typically colonial linguistic situation of the diglossic kind, with British English as the 'high' variety to be preserved (a notion that still underlies language attitudes in first-language Extraterritorial English communities, cf. Bailey 1992: 124). The history of US English is a story of 'linguistic democratisation', with informal expressions and foreign elements becoming more and more widely accepted, to the detriment of the 'gentlemen's language', a process which mirrors the fluidity and mobility of early American society.

The sociopolitical role of language was also relevant in the building of the idea of the USA as a nation (Leith 1983: 196–200; Bailey 1992: 104); in this sense, the most representative figure is certainly that of Noah Webster (1758–1843), who employed language issues as a vehicle for his patriotism (Fodde 1994). Among his best-known statements is the following:

> As an independent nation, our honor requires us to have a system of our own, in language as well as in government. Great Britain, whose children we are, and whose language we speak, should no longer be *our* standard; for the taste of her writers is already corrupted, and her language on the decline. (Quoted in Carver 1992: 138)

More recently, the use of the phrase 'The American Language' as a title of a book by Mencken (1941), and the protests that this choice raised (since it did away with the label 'American *English*'), are illustrative of the fact that the issue of the linguistic independence of this variety is far from established even in the twentieth century (Llamzon 1983: 92–3).

R. Quirk (1983: 11) claims, 'From as early as 1776, it became clear that there could be no single standard of English – not one at any rate based on the English of England.' In most academics' opinion, however, as in that of the public at large, American English was not at first recognised at all, and later mostly despised (Bailey 1992: 130). As mentioned, early comments and opinions on 'new' varieties are usually fiercely negative, abusive of some features of the variety in question and of its speakers, and they reveal the power of the ideology of uniformity. The few positive comments are usually produced locally or by people deeply involved with local matters; furthermore, these positive arguments are products of the same ideology, since among them are:

1) The 'colonial lag', i.e. the preservation of older, and therefore 'purer', features of the mother-country variety, as compared to the 'debasing and corrupting innovation' of the latter. This leaves the 'language-change-is-bad' assumption untouched.
2) The 'uniformity' of the new variety over a large territory, i.e. the alleged lack of local dialects. That uniformity should be valued *per se* is one of the most important tenets of the ideology of the standard.

Two other English-speaking countries, with partly different language histories, also show the power of the ideology of the standard. Canada is an instance of the development of 'hybrid' usage, due to the splitting of allegiance between two different norms: the British and the American. The notion of a local Canadian standard has been resisted for some time; even nowadays, in tests and exams reference is made to an international, not to a local standard (cf. Pringle 1985: 183). The term 'Canadian English' itself was used for the first time in print in 1857 (Chambers 1991: 92). In the period immediately following the American revolution, several groups of loyalists took refuge in Canada and contributed to the spread of positive views of the US and its standard (Avis 1973, Orkin 1971), thanks to the fact that they were generally quite educated, and able to influence the school system. Apart from these groups, however, public opinion trends seemed to be more in favour of the original British connection, to emphasise their difference from their 'neighbours' in the US. Even now, when the uniqueness of Canadian English is accepted, there is a form of purism that takes as its reference British rather than American authority, although there is a fair amount of ambiguity in such attitudes (Bailey 1982; Pringle 1985: 188ff.).

Australia is a somewhat different case: the strife here was not between two competing standards (a real competition from the US standard has only recently begun to be felt) but for the preservation of the British standard as against the non-standard forms prevalent in the use of the majority of the population, especially given the origin of the colony as penal settlement (Gunn 1992: 204, 216; Bailey 1992: 130–3). Much has been made of the 'Cockney flavour' which seems to characterise Australian English, and a whole class of loyalists and bureaucrats fought against this influence and for the maintenance of adherence to the British standard. The speech habits of the convicts, as in-group jargons, were of course likely to spread over the country; among the elements considered revealing of Cockney influence there are greetings and swearwords (McCrum et al. 1987: 282–3), i.e. mainly pragmatically relevant language items. Among pronunciation phenomena that indicate conservativism there is, for example, the preservation of a long vowel in words like *off*. Other features, like the raising and closing of the vowels in *bid, bed, bad*, are seen e.g. by Trudgill (1986: 130ff.) as signs of the influence over Australian English of other groups, for instance of East-Anglian rural provenance. It is clear that, in spite of the documented numerical predominance of Londoners in the colony, one must always be cautious of assigning clear-cut 'parenthood' to any variety. In any case, the high 'visibility' of the Cockney element contributed to the creation of a deep feeling of linguistic insecurity which made the recognition and acceptance of a local norm rather slow and difficult (Eagleson 1982; Delbridge 1990; Leitner 1984: 56ff.).

Other situations in the English-speaking world vary: in South Africa the normative tradition is still strong, and is revealed by the difference in status between Conservative (i.e. RP-like) and Respectable (localised standard) South African English (Lanham 1985; Lass 1987: 302–3). On the other hand, in Hawaii there have been attempts at imposing 'standard' norms in the school system, to the exclusion of the widespread though stigmatised Hawaiian Creole. This has given rise to unprecedented public reaction against the ousting of the non-standard variety, to the extent of creating a tendency to spread an 'anti-norm' which counteracts the process of decreolisation within some groups of speakers (Sato 1991). Such diverse situations are all illustrative of the role that adherence to a specific norm can acquire when it becomes a vehicle for identity sensibilities and political allegiance.

3   'New Englishes', (partly) similar problems

The emergence of new, localised varieties in countries where English is a second language (ESL), like India or Nigeria, is also fraught with political, social, ideological overtones which are only partly similar to those of the older colonies. One significant difference is that the adoption of English in the new colonies was not a natural process, but an imposition representing a precise imperialistic strategy. This involves two main consequences:

1)   The presence of local languages used as first languages implied that the use of English had become a new social marker, a process that often deeply modified the sociolinguistic profile of the country.
2)   The spread of English took place through formalised learning, rather than through spontaneous acquisition (on the role of the school system and of language planning see the next section).

The 'life cycle' of the New Englishes therefore starts with a progressive *indigenisation* (Moag 1982b: 271): one of the fundamental steps in this process is the adoption of the language for intranational (as opposed to international) use (Strevens 1982: 25). The next stage of the cycle is the *expansion* of the new variety, which comes to be used in more and more numerous and diverse contexts. This phase is particularly fast where there is no pidgin or other variety that can act as a *lingua franca*, and it brings about the multiplication of the registers and styles of the 'localised' English, each with its own formal characteristics (Moag 1982b: 273–7).

In the meantime, a change from an *exonormative* model to an *endonormative* one takes place (i.e. the community shifts from *norm-dependent* to *norm-developing*; Kachru 1985: 16–19), which involves fundamental changes in the speakers' attitudes. When the typical features of the variety appear frequently and regularly, they are no longer seen as 'mistakes', i.e. they are de-stigmatised, especially if they are associated with the usage of educated speakers. At the same time, the language becomes detached from the original British cultural apparatus, and undergoes a re-acculturation in the new context: the vocabulary is enlarged to adapt it to local needs, and conversational rules change according to the social norms of the new community (Kachru 1982a).

At this point, detachment from British English is no longer felt as 'deficiency' but as a further, conscious affirmation of newly acquired independence (Kachru 1986: 21–5). The advantages that come from the use of English are thus not given up, but the local variety used by the higher social classes is adopted, and creative writing in English comes to be felt as part of the national literature.

It is usually at this stage that the adjective of nationality that qualifies a particular variety of English ceases to be felt as a depreciative and becomes just descriptive. This shift, which is part of a global change in attitudes, can take place at different paces, according to the degree of political (and hence linguistic) insecurity of the nation in question. For instance, the first mention, in a publication, of the label 'Maltese English' (in 1976) generated strong criticism and some resentment. Still in the late 1980s, several Maltese people, when questioned about language use, claimed that 'Maltese English' did not exist or was just 'broken English'. On the other hand, others (especially in the younger generations) accepted the label, claimed that it referred to a local but acceptable form of English, and admitted that they used this variety (Mazzon 1992: 11–12, 110–11).

This leads us to the next stage in the evolution of a 'new' variety, i.e. its *institutionalisation*, in which schools, media and government all have important roles, as have local intellectuals (Moag 1982b: 278–81). Localised varieties arise as performance varieties, i.e. they are connected to individual and occasional uses. These varieties, however, gradually acquire extension of use, length of time in use, the emotional attachment of users to the variety, functional importance and sociolinguistic status (the terms are used by Kachru 1983b: 152): this makes them into institutionalised varieties, with a wide range of registers and styles, a body of literature, and so on.

The institutionalisation of varieties has important sociolinguistic consequences, since it usually coincides with the stigmatisation of those forms which adhere too closely to the old native model. The new variety becomes part of the speakers' repertoire and is thus associated with identification values; although the exonormative model may continue to predominate within the school system, prestige becomes transferred onto the local variety, and eventually the local governments themselves will insist on its use (Loveday 1982). This is the highest grade of expansion of the new varieties; in some ESL communities there can be a last stage in the 'cycle', involving a *restriction* in the use and functions of English, with a local language gradually taking its place as a prestige and bridge language, a process that can virtually bring about the death of the local 'New English'. Such a dramatic development has never taken place so far, and it is actually highly improbable, due to the role that English continues to fulfil in the life of all these communities (for the beginning of such a restriction in the Philippines see Llamzon 1986).

The question of the possible standardisation of the New Englishes has been debated for a long time. The sheer multiplicity and diversity of situations of ESL communities makes any decision about variety-defining and boundary-placing very difficult, even in merely technical terms, i.e. even abstracting from the problem of prejudice and the sociopolitical loading of the concepts involved. First of all, it must be kept in mind that to speak about only *one* Indian English, Nigerian English etc., is only an abstraction, since in several ESL communities there has been the development of whole ranges or *clines*[3] of sub-varieties (Kachru 1986: 89–90), including sets of registers and styles.

This kind of development has, however, rarely been studied, since most reports so far have been concentrating on 'high' or 'educated' forms of the New Englishes.[4] Moreover, a real cline seems easy to identify only in rather large communities where the local variety is more or less institutionalised. In situations where the community is smaller and uses are less rigidly codified (or more difficult to capture within a given survey format), the only possible generalisations seem to concern the relative frequency of certain items or constructions in the spoken compared with the written language. For one such case see Mazzon (1992: 121–58) on Maltese English.

Thus, the labels assigned to the various New Englishes actually simplify and reduce a highly complex and diversified reality, even without considering the fact that, in ESL communities, some of the functions of different registers and styles are often taken over by 'mixed varieties'. This should lead us to reconsider the whole sociopragmatic setting of the 'New Englishes' and thus to revise the standard/non-standard polarity and other sociolinguistic categories in view of this different set of options. This is not normally done because code-switching and code-mixing have so far been considered non-systematic or dependent on the micro-context of situation, but this is not necessarily the case (Kachru 1978; 1986: 53, 65–6, 71–2). To an extent, switching can be used to signal one's identity, and therefore mixed varieties fall into a speaker's repertoire as tools for interaction. This is proved by the fact that, in some communities, mixed varieties have become institutionalised and follow rules that we are just starting to understand (e.g., switching may take place at some points in the sentence, but not at others; it may concern content words rather than function words, etc. Cf., beside Kachru's works cited above, Crystal 1987; Gumperz 1978; Gibbons 1987).

Before sociolinguistically oriented studies on ESL varieties started, around the mid-1960s, the only sources on the New Englishes were works by missionaries or educators that hinted at nativisation phenomena, and some more or less casual comments by British observers who reported, often in deprecatory tones, the linguistic 'deviations' of the natives (for some examples, see Bailey 1992: 142–3; Kachru 1983c for India; Sey 1973 for Ghana). The 'academic codification' of this field came only with the publication of several handbooks in the first part of the 1980s (Bailey and Görlach 1982; Kachru (ed.) 1982; Pride (ed.) 1982; Noss (ed.) 1983; Platt, Weber and Ho 1984; Quirk and Widdowson 1985; see also Görlach 1988: 2–3). In the meantime, the first dictionaries of local varieties started to be published, although such enterprises were made more difficult by the problems involved in the attempt at codifying situations which were far from being thoroughly institutionalised, and by the fact that written varieties tend to adhere more closely to the exonormative standard (Görlach 1985; 1988: 20).

Today, research on the New Englishes seems to have slowed down, especially since some authors have become doubtful about the possibility of applying current methods of sociolinguistic investigation to ESL situations, because they are based on a model of social structure not necessarily extendable to these communities. Moreover, the range of stylistic levels and the notion of prestige are not necessarily identical to those applied to western societies, so that non-native speakers, for instance, often sound exceedingly formal (Görlach 1988: 7–9; Jibril 1986: 70–2). Furthermore, this field has often suffered from ostracism from some academic milieus (Kachru 1986: 29–30). Aiming to explore almost unknown situations, these studies have often appeared too generic and based on fragmentary and impressionistic, if not anecdotal, evidence. According to K. K. Sridhar (1989: 35–7), several studies on these varieties were the products of a pre-theoretical stage, and this, together with the long-standing prejudice that leads to identifying whatever deviates from the standard with 'broken English', contributed to the creation of this negative attitude. It remains true, however, that the studies of the 1960s and 1970s have paved the way for more rigorous ones, e.g. those in Cheshire (1991), and still constitute important reference points for this kind of research.

The lack of comprehensive descriptions of these varieties is, however, responsible for the difficulties connected to the individuation, within the respective clines, of possible 'standards'. These difficulties are partly due to the fact that differences within a cline often appear to be a matter of degree, or 'rule-governed stylistic variants of the more "standard" varieties in use in the speech communities in question' (Pride 1982: 6). But the problems are also connected to the fact that, for a long time, it has been difficult for observers to try to define these varieties (taking into account speakers' perceptions about their status) mainly because speakers refused to admit that they were speaking anything but 'pure British English', and the very idea of a 'national English' of their own raised indignation, scorn, derision – since whatever deviated from the British norm could only be classified as a 'mistake' (see Moag 1982a: 32; Sey 1973: 6–10 for Ghana; Kachru 1983c: 73, 94–5 for India; Bamgbose 1982: 99; Jibril 1982: 74; Akere 1982: 87 for Nigeria).

Thus, it is often the very presence of the external model that obscures local developments and variation (Das 1982: 142; Fraser Gupta 1986), and this is connected to the myth of the 'native speaker' as a model for language use (Parakrama 1995: 39). After some time there arises a new model based on a local 'educated' norm (Kachru 1983a: 24–6 defines it as a norm developed through the influence of both a literary canon and social sanction, which allows a certain scope for internal variation), which is often only a shift of prestige from one powerful group of speakers to another. Moreover, the concept of 'educated norm' does not apply to all ESL communities, as pointed out by Tay and Fraser Gupta (1983: 174–6).

Another factor that is often considered decisive in establishing a standard for a 'New English' is intelligibility. In countries where English functions as a bridge language with the rest of the world, it is argued, the form of the language cannot be allowed to deviate too much from some internationally recognised, and recognisable, standard (see e.g. the discussion of a paper by Kachru in Greenbaum (ed.) 1985: 31–4). This clashes with the need to have a variety of English that clearly signals national identity (as expressed e.g. by Tay 1982: 55), and often hides prescriptive attitudes masked by utilitarian motives.

It is undeniable that the 'New Standards' have an elusive character, which prevents a categorical inclusion or exclusion of features. Given the existence of clearly recognisable 'localisms' (some variety-oriented and some text-specific) revealed by linguistic analysis, the question is (as for any standard and, indeed, for any language variety): where does one draw the line between what can be considered 'Standard (Indian, etc.) English' and what cannot? These entities, whose existence has for so long been denied, appear to have blurred boundaries, especially since they appear closer to British English in syntax, but further in pronunciation. Should one therefore define a standard differently according to the different linguistic levels (morphology, vocabulary, etc.), as is done with Standard English English and Received Pronunciation? What amount of variation between different 'steps' on the cline should be allowed?

The problem of which sub-varieties should be included is far from trivial. Parakrama (1995: 42–3) finds that the notion of a standard fails to account properly for the post-colonial situations and should at least be widened. He quotes Kandiah's opinion (pp. 186–7) that

> from an internal point of view, there can, in [the New Englishes], be no mistakes, violations or rules and so on; *everything* belongs. But, the only state of affairs in which there can be no mistakes is one in which there *are* no rules governing conduct.

Parakrama's comments on this quotation stress the difficulty of describing these situations on the basis of old schemata: these new varieties push the concept of 'rules' to their limits. They 'are profoundly subversive of received notions that model *all languages* on the basis of certain "well-formed rule-governed systems" (such as Standard English, for instance) since they bring each of these categories to crisis' (p. 187).

In both Kandiah's (1995: xix–xx) and Parakrama's (1995: 5) opinions, the New Englishes are a kind of reality that is disruptive of the whole notion of standardisation as conceived so far. The transplantation of the concept into situations where the social mechanisms to implement a standard are not yet active allows for a dramatic and unveiled emergence of the conflict, of the struggle for hegemony that the establishment of a standard implies, and which is normally hidden or disguised as consensus.

4 The role of language planning and of education systems in attitude-building in ESL countries

Colonisers usually pursue some form of language planning,[5] especially through a school system, aimed at spreading their own language to the detriment of local languages, to increase insecurity and dependence in the natives, and to undermine nationalistic feelings.

During the colonial period, British settlers often created school systems modelled on their own, aimed particularly at the formation of a restricted class of educated natives who could interact with the central government, while the education of the people at large was neglected. The kind of language planning enforced in that period, then, was characterised by a utilitarian elitism with specific political aims. The typical traits of such language planning include a rigorous adherence to the British Standard, also as a means to construct social differences (Fasold 1984; Phillipson 1992; Leith 1983: 186; Pennycook 1994: 9–10, 110–11).

Although the pressures created by the imposition of this model were very effective, reactions started to be felt, especially after independence was regained (for most former colonies, this means between the late 1940s and the 1960s). This entailed the development of what has been called *schizoglossia* (Kandiah 1981), i.e. the co-existence of contrasting language attitudes: on the one side, the British model is still considered the yardstick of excellence, and the use of ('good') English is the best passport to modernity (i.e. westernisation) and to all sorts of advantages and comforts; on the other side, English is rejected as a symbol of dependence. The use of English is materially advantageous, and thus cannot be eliminated but, nationalistic arguments go, let it at least be enriched with local features, no longer seen as mistakes but as a sign of the appropriation of the language and of its adaptation to the new context. The 'New English' thus receives its legitimisation to be used by a free people in a free country, and the old external norms lose prestige in favour of new, local models.[6]

Some surveys carried out on students in the 1970s and early 1980s testify to this shift in attitudes. Thus, Schmied (1985: 1990) reports that the British norm is still the model in most textbooks and other educational material in East Africa, but that acceptance of 'non-standardisms' seems to be related to the degree of attachment to a local variety of English, and so is lower in Tanzania, where English is receding to the status of a foreign language, than in Kenya, which is a more typical ESL community. The same incidence of historical and political factors was found in Asia in a survey (Shaw 1981): Indian students seemed happier than Singaporean students to accept a local model, whose attitudes appeared profoundly divided, or than Thai students, who were almost totally in favour of the British model. These results mirror the various degrees of strength of the connection with the British Empire in the respective countries. A different survey carried out in Singapore (Teck 1983) showed high sensitivity to the medium of education and to the variables related to social class and gender, but matched-guise experiments showed that the evaluation of the British Standard as 'more pleasant', 'correct' etc. was still as high as 86 per cent, while the English spoken by Chinese-educated speakers was 'tolerated' only by informants of similar background, generally belonging to the lower classes. Information about the stigma attached to close imitations of the British standard by informants of other surveys is given in Kachru (1986: 22–5).

The influence of the British model has been stronger on written than on spoken English. Written language is easier to standardise because it is in fact more uniform, lends itself better to being transmitted via schooling, through the literary language and other formal channels, and it is also easier to reinforce; conversely, the spoken language, the language of face-to-face interaction, tends to split into several varieties more easily and is subject to fewer constraints (Cooper 1989: 138). There is, however, a widespread feeling that the English-based school system of the various ESL countries has been responsible for the development of local educated varieties – not only, though mainly, in the written language. This has produced new standards which appear 'bookish' and not very 'conversational' (Kachru 1983c: 41–2), if not 'monostylistic', i.e. flattened on the more formal level. There is not much space, in these varieties, for colloquialisms and other features typical of the spoken language, especially when exposure to other media in English (popular literature, TV programmes etc.) has been scant (Gonzales 1982: 222).

The problematic question of styles in education is emphasised by Platt (1983: 221–3), whose opinion is worth quoting at length:

> 1. If we teach only a formal style of the target variety, there is the possibility that no informal style will develop within it . . . The options then are to use a formal variety, even in informal situations and therefore appear over-formal and stilted or to drop down the lectal scale . . . 2. Teaching a range of styles from formal to informal may seem a far more attractive option, in fact the only feasible one . . . [but] pupils will continue to hear the more basilectal and mesolectal varieties outside the classroom . . . So, unless pupils were segregated it could take several generations for stylistic variation *within* the acrolect to develop by these means, if at all.

These shifts in attitudes are of course very slow, since the force of the prescriptive tradition is still considerable, especially where divisions are sharp and deep; yet this shift is perceptible. The progressive detachment from the British model anticipates a new awareness and a new pride about one's own form of English, about its correctness, dignity and worthiness to be considered a full-fledged variety in its own right, which can be used on all occasions and can serve as a future standard: gradually, linguistic insecurity and schizoglossia start to recede (Richards 1982: 228; Nihalani, Tongue and Hosali 1979: 205). In several publications that aim at a description of a 'New English', a programmatic bias can be found (Sridhar 1989: 56; Sahgal 1991: 303–4; Tay and Fraser Gupta 1983: 177–81), no longer in the direction of adherence to British English, but towards the affirmation of a local model (see e.g. Wong 1982 for alternatives to the 'native speaker' as basis for a norm):

> This leads us to the inevitable conclusion that we have to develop our own norms of acceptability instead of seeking every now and then the opinion of native speakers who . . . are not unanimous in their pronouncements. We do not want our whole vocation to be an endless imitation of the Queen's English. (Mehrotra 1982: 171)

This attitude can be compared with that expressed, for example, by Gonzales (1983), who recognises the existence of a Philippine English, but does not agree with its 'legitimization at par with American, British, Australian, Canadian and other varieties of English in formerly colonized countries', and recommends, for teaching aims, adherence to the American standard.

Overall, however, it would seem that the shift in attitudes has been recognised by linguists working on the 'New Englishes', who have repeatedly suggested that these new varieties can become new language models. Can we then conclude that linguists have been the 'champions' of the New Englishes, trying to defeat old prejudices? This would score a point in favour of the 'neutrality' and 'political correctness' that linguistics, especially sociolinguistics, tend to ascribe to themselves. As will be seen in the next section, however, this is unfortunately not always true.

5   Ambiguity in linguistic meta-discourse on new varieties

The fact that, in some ESL communities, local varieties have been established as new standards, and native-like variants have become the object of contempt or derision, certainly does not mean that the kind of prejudice we reviewed is on its way out altogether, especially since ambiguous attitudes are not confined to the public at large, but show up in specialists' statements as well. In particular, the deeply conflictual nature of language issues is often ignored. Parakrama (1995: x–xi) claims the right to employ a non-standard variety of Lankan English to highlight more effectively the 'struggle for hegemony':

> I done shown Standard spoken English as standing up only for them smug-arse social élites. And it ain't really no different for no written English neither. The tired ways in which the standardized languages steady fucked over the users of other forms had became clear when we went and studied them (post)colonial Englishes . . . these non-standard stuff is therefore 'natural' resistance and a sensitive index of non-mainstream against-hegemony. Persistent mistakes and bad taste fuck the system up because they cannot be patronized if you dont accept the explaination, so they fail your ass at the university and say you need remediation like its the pox.

Or, to take a more 'standardised' explanation by the same author (pp. xii–xiii):

> These standards are kept in place in 'first world' contexts by a technology of reproduction which dissimulates this hegemony through the self-represented neutrality of prestige and precedent whose selectivity is a function of the politics of publication. In these 'other' situations, the openly conflictual nature of the language context makes such strategies impossible. The non-standard is one of the most accessible means of

'natural' resistance, and, therefore, one of the most sensitive indices of de-hegemonization.

Before being linguists, we are first of all speakers and members of our own speech communities, and are therefore exposed to the absorption of all its prejudices and shibboleths. Getting rid of 'linguicism' (Phillipson 1992) is almost as difficult as getting rid of racism, and this is evident in some statements which, far from representing purely descriptive and objective analyses, show that the alleged 'neutrality' of the linguist is often indeed just a chimera (Williams 1992).

For some, Extraterritorial Englishes can become acceptable only if they remain adherent to the native standard. See, for instance, the discussion over the possibility of defining a 'standard Filipino English' (Tay 1991: 523–4), or the following statement by Jibril (1982: 83):

> There is evidence . . . that Nigerians do not place a high premium on acquiring close imitations of native accents of English, and that consequently they do not modify their accents significantly even after living in Britain or America for up to eight years; or if they do, they do not disown their original Nigerian accent but rather use it whenever they speak to their fellow Nigerians. Indeed the cultural climate in Nigeria at the present time discourages any tendency towards a perfect, native-like accent, though there is no corresponding aversion to *impeccable* written English.

The use of the adjective *impeccable*, which I have italicised in the text, shows that value judgements can be passed also in apparently unobtrusive, but no less harmful, ways.

Similarly, Mehrotra (1982: 153) does claim that ' "English English" and [Indian English] are each an efficient and fairly stable variety existing in its own right . . . and each therefore must be described . . . in its own terms', but then reports, without any visible criticism, opinions to the effect that the 'best' Indian variety is 'comprehensible' and 'acceptable' throughout the English-speaking world, and 'would very nearly pass as English English', or that 'at its best Indian writing in English *compares not unfavourably* with the best writing in Australia, Canada, or even in the United States and England' (p. 155, my italics).

Still in the late 1970s, note the cautious and non-committal position taken by Nihalani, Tongue and Hosali (1979: 3–4, 7): 'For brevity's sake, we shall refer to IVE [= Indian Variant(s) of English] as a variety of English without entering into the discussion about whether or not Indian English exists'; 'When comprehensive descriptions of the English used in India come to be written, as they will, questions of a prescribed standard will also have to be solved. Until then, we have hesitated to do more than describe.'

One of the loci of the discussion was the debate over the 'Teaching English as a Foreign Language Heresy' (reviewed in Parakrama 1995: 16–21), started in

1968 by Prator, who maintained that the choice of local standards for TEFL is demagogic and possibly undermines international intelligibility, giving priority to issues of nationalism over the principle that native inputs and standards should always be preferred in teaching. The Indian linguist B. B. Kachru contradicted these arguments in various publications (see a summary in Kachru 1986: 100–14), and, against the 'heresy' denounced by Prator, put forth the several 'sins' of educators like him, accusing him of ethnocentrism and imperialism. But even Kachru himself, as pointed out by Parakrama (1995: 52ff., 57–8), is not immune from prejudice, since for him, in the choice of a 'high' variety, the myth of the *native* speaker is simply to be substituted by that of the 'educated' speaker. The acceptance of any such dichotomy, Parakrama maintains, implies that some are 'worse' speakers than others; the 'educated norm' is no more neutral than other parameters, and does not assume a real, democratic idea of the polycentricity of the standard, but still hides a praise of uniformity.

Several metaphors and images have been put forth to reinforce this idea. One of the most common is the plant simile:

> In conclusion, a new variety of English may be likened . . . to a transplanted tree. This tree has developed and reached full maturity in the linguistic environment of multilingualism. Its historical roots can be traced back to either of two parent varieties – British or American English. Its sociolinguistic roots are firmly founded on its multifaceted uses . . . Its cultural roots consist of an impressive body of literary works . . . Being a vigorous and healthy tree, it has several branches with many more smaller branches. These are its varieties. (Llamzon 1983: 105).

This image is revealing because the new varieties, like small branches on a tree, are not granted autonomous, independent life from the parent plant. It is another example of how prejudiced views can be coated in apparently 'modern' or 'democratic' attitudes.

One of the best-known linguists representing this tendency is R. Quirk. See, for example, the following statement (Quirk 1983: 13):

> we need to ask ourselves who benefits if we encourage the institutionalizing as norms of certain types of language activity that could alternatively be seen as levels of achievement. It may temporarily comfort an individual to be told that his English is a communicatively adequate basilect; . . . it may, above all, seem comfortingly democratic. But will it serve the individual's own needs when he or she looks for a better job? . . . Will it serve democracy's goal of the individual's mobility within a coherent free society?

The reasons why Quirk downplays the importance of the new varieties are at least dubious, even if we keep to the 'official', not deeply ideological, reasons. As emerges from Sridhar's analysis (1989: 50–1), Quirk's position is based on the following assumptions:

(1)   that there is 'a relatively narrow range of purposes for which the non-natives need to use English',
(2)   that the indigenous languages are the primary vehicle for self-expression and the sustaining of traditional cultural values, and
(3)   that the arguments for not imposing a standard variety on all speakers may be right for the native English-speaking community but are not necessarily 'exportable' to ESL situations.

The first assumption is of course contradicted by the ample evidence for use of English in a wide range of functions. The second one is apparently true, but if we look at the numerous books and articles produced in English it is clear that English plays a very important role for the discussion of local events, besides being increasingly used for creative writing. The justification of the third assumption is not clear: if the argument is that these countries need an international form of English for technology transfer etc. it is not very strong, because standard forms of indigenous varieties of English have proved to be internationally intelligible. If it means that there is a global standard of English to which all national/regional varieties should tend, then it is something that affects the evolution of whole national languages, and not just varieties of English.

In conclusion, we seem to be still a long way from an acceptance of variation that is not only a form of lip-service paid to abstract 'scientific' principles, but something that has an incidence on our teaching and on our way of seeing things. The whole idea of one 'standard' (= good) form and other non-standard/dialectal/mixed (= bad) forms should be downplayed if only in the wake of the findings relative to the 'New Englishes', so that less monolithic views of language phenomena and of language behaviour can find their way into western culture. Until these prejudices are discarded by professional linguists, it will be very difficult even to start eradicating them from teaching practices and from public opinion, and until the latter process is under way, the new varieties of English will remain what they are now, second-class forms of expression employed by (though this is not said aloud, of course) second-class speakers.

Notes

1 Some early opinions about American English, for instance, are reported by McCrum et al. (1987: 235ff., and by Bailey (1992: 151–6, 239ff.). These give a taste of the Anglo-American language rivalry, but comments about other varieties are no more tolerant: see McCrum et al. (1987: 293–4) and Bailey (1992: 130–3) for eighteenth and nineteenth-century comments on other Extraterritorial Englishes.

2 'When the speakers of transplanted English were esteemed, their language was likewise highly valued (often for having an ancient "purity", since lost at home). When the speakers were scorned, their English was regarded as debased, vulgar, and un-polished.' (Bailey 1992: 123). This is in agreement with the strong tendency to associate morality with quality of speech in the eighteenth and nineteenth centuries,

when 'polite speech' was the model and 'vulgar speech' was an index of moral degeneration (Blake 1996: 244–5).
3 A cline ranges from the subvarieties that are closer to the native standard and are associated with the higher functions, to those forms that are further from the standard, i.e. colloquial forms that often present considerable simplification and reduction of grammatical markers.
4 This is a most undesirable consequence of the influence of the unilinearity and the tendency to privilege uniformity that is part of the ideology of the standard, and that often emerges in historical linguistics.
5 'Language planning refers to deliberate efforts to influence the behaviour of others with respect to the acquisition, structure, or functional allocation of their language codes.' (Cooper 1989: 45).
6 It must be noted that Kachru (1986: 134) considers this process typical of all kinds of Extraterritorial English-developing communities (i.e. both first- and second-language Extraterritorial Englishes). See also Abdulaziz (1991: 394–401).

References

Abdulaziz, M. H. 1991. 'East Africa (Tanzania and Kenya)', in Cheshire (ed.) 1991, pp. 391–401.

Akere, F. 1982. 'Sociocultural constraints and the emergence of a standard Nigerian English', in Pride (ed.) 1982, 85–99.

Avis, W. S. 1973. 'The English Language in Canada', in T. A. Sebeok (ed.), *Current Trends in Linguistics*, 14 vols., The Hague: Mouton, vol. X, pp. 40–74.

Bailey, R. W. 1982. 'The English Language in Canada', in Bailey and Görlach 1982, pp. 134–76.

1992. *Images of English. A Cultural History of the Language*, New York: Cambridge University Press.

Bailey, R. W. and M. Görlach (eds.) 1982. *English as a World Language*, Ann Arbor: University of Michigan Press.

Bamgbose, A. 1982. 'Standard Nigerian English: Issues of Identification', in Kachru (ed.) 1982, pp. 99–111.

Barry, M. V. 1982. 'The English Language in Ireland', in Bailey and Görlach (eds.) 1982, pp. 84–133.

Blake, N. F. 1996. *A History of the English Language*, London: Macmillan.

Bliss, A. J. 1984. 'English in the South of Ireland', in Trudgill (ed.) 1984, pp. 135–51.

Carver, C. M. 1992. 'The Mayflower to the Model-T: The development of American English', in Machan and Scott (eds.) 1992, pp. 131–54.

Chambers, J. K. 1991. 'Canada', in Cheshire (ed.) 1991, pp. 89–107.

Cheshire, J. (ed.) 1991. *English Around the World. Sociolinguistic Perspectives*, Cambridge University Press.

Cooper, R. L. 1989. *Language Planning and Social Change*, Cambridge University Press.

Crystal, D. 1987. *The Cambridge Encyclopedia of Language*, Cambridge University Press.

Das, S. K. 1982. 'Indian English', in Pride (ed.) 1982, pp. 141–9.

Delbridge, A. 1990. 'Australian English Now', in C. Ricks and L. Michaels (eds.), *The State of the Language. 1990 Edition*, London: Faber and Faber.

Dillard, J. L. 1992. *A History of American English*, London and New York: Longman.

Douglas-Cowie, E. 1984. 'The sociolinguistic situation in Northern Ireland', in Trudgill (ed.) 1984, pp. 533–45.

Eagleson, R. D. 1982. 'English in Australia and New Zealand', in Bailey and Görlach (eds.) 1982, pp. 415–38.

Fasold, R. W. 1984. *The Sociolinguistics of Society*, Oxford: Blackwell.

Fodde, L. 1994. 'Noah Webster's Dictionaries: Attempts to create an American Language', in D. Hart (ed.), *Aspects of English and Italian Lexicology*, Rome: Bagatto Libri, pp. 114–23.

Fraser Gupta, A. 1986. 'A standard for written Singapore English?', in *English World-wide* 7, 75–99.

Gibbons, J. 1987. *Code-mixing and Code Choice. A Hong Kong Case Study*, Philadelphia: Multilingual Matters.

Görlach, M. 1985. 'Lexicographical problems of New Englishes and English-related Pidgin and Creole languages', in *English World-wide*, 6, 1–36.

1987. 'Colonial lag? The alleged conservative character of American English and other "colonial" varieties', in *English World-wide* 8, 41–60.

1988. 'English as a world language – the state of the art', in *English World-wide* 9, 1–32.

Gonzales, A. 1982. 'English in the Philippines Mass Media', in Pride (ed.) 1982, pp. 211–26.

1983. 'When does an error become a feature of Philippine English?', in Noss (ed.) 1983, pp. 150–72.

Greenbaum, S. (ed.) 1985. *The English Language Today*, Oxford: Pergamon Press.

Gumperz, J. J. 1978. 'The sociolinguistic significance of conversational code-switching', in *RELC Journal* 8, 1–34.

Gunn, J. 1992. 'Social contexts in the history of Australian English', in Machan and Scott (eds.) 1992, pp. 204–29.

Harris, J. 1991. *Ireland*, in Cheshire (ed.) 1991, pp. 37–50.

Iacuaniello, F. 1991. *Lo Scots come simbolo di identità politica e culturale*, degree thesis, Napoli.

Jibril, M. 1982. 'Nigerian English: an introduction', in Pride (ed.) 1982, pp. 73–84.

1986. 'Sociolinguistic variation in Nigerian English', in *English World-wide* 7, 47–74.

Kachru, B. B. 1978. 'Toward structuring code-mixing: an Indian perspective', in B. B. Kachru and N. S. Sridhar (eds.), *Aspects of Sociolinguistics in South Asia*, special issue of *International Journal of the Sociology of Language* 16, 27–46.

1982, 'Meaning in deviation: toward understanding non-native English texts', in Kachru (ed.) 1982, pp. 325–50.

1983a. 'Meaning in deviation: toward understanding non-native English texts', in Noss (ed.) 1983, pp. 21–49.

1983b. 'Models of New Englishes', in J. Cobarrubias and J. A. Fishman (eds.), *Progress in Language Planning*, Berlin: Mouton, pp. 145–70.

1983c. *The Indianization of English*, Delhi: Oxford University Press.

1985. 'Standards, codification and sociolinguistic realism: the English language in the outer circle', in Quirk and Widdowson (eds.) 1985, pp. 11–30.

1986. *The Alchemy of English*, Oxford: Pergamon Press.

Kachru, B. B. (ed.) 1982. *The Other Tongue. English Across Cultures*, Urbana-Champaigne, University of Illinois Press (2nd edn Pergamon Press, Oxford, 1983).

Kahane, H. 1982. 'American English: from a colonial substandard to a prestige language', in Kachru (ed.) 1982, pp. 229–36.

Kandiah, T. 1981. 'Lankan English schizoglossia', in *English World-wide* 2, 63–82.

1995. 'Centering the periphery of English: towards participatory communities of discourse', foreword to Parakrama 1995, pp. xv–xxxvii.

Knowles, G. 1997. *A Cultural History of the English Language*, London: Arnold.

Lanham, L. W. 1985. 'The perception and evaluation of varieties of English in South African Society', in Greenbaum (ed.) 1985, pp. 242–51.

Lass, R. 1987. *The Shape of English*, London: Dent.

1990. 'Where do Extraterritorial Englishes come from?', in S. Adamson et al. (eds.), *Papers from the Fifth International Conference in English Historical Linguistics*, Amsterdam: John Benjamins, pp. 245–80.

Leith D. 1983. *A Social History of English*, London: Routledge and Kegan Paul.

Leitner, G. 1984. 'Australian English or English in Australia – linguistic identity or dependence in broadcast language', in *English World-wide* 5, 55–85.

Llamzon, T. A. 1983. 'Essential features of new varieties of English', in Noss (ed.) 1983, pp. 92–109.

1986. 'Life cycle of New Englishes: restriction phase of Filipino English', in *English World-wide* 7, 101–25.

Loveday, L. 1982. *The Sociolinguistics of Learning and Using a Non-Native Language*, Oxford: Pergamon Press.

Machan, T. W. and C. T. Scott (eds.) 1992. *English in its Social Context. Essays in Historical Sociolinguistics*, Oxford University Press.

Mazzon, G. 1992. *L'inglese di Malta*, Napoli: Liguori.

McCrum, R. et al. 1987. *The Story of English*, London: Faber and Faber/BBC Books.

Mehrotra, R. R. 1982. 'Indian English: a sociolinguistic profile', in Pride (ed.) 1982, pp. 150–73.

Mencken, H. L. 1941. *The American Language*, New York: Knopf.

Moag, R. 1982a. 'English as a foreign, second, native and basal language: a new taxonomy of English-using societies', in Pride (ed.) 1982, pp. 11–50.

1982b. 'The life cycle of non-native Englishes: a case study', in Kachru (ed.) 1982, pp. 270–88.

Nihalani, P., R. K. Tongue and P. Hosali 1979. *Indian and British English. A Handbook of Usage and Pronunciation*, Delhi: Oxford University Press.

Noss, R. B. (ed.) 1983. *Varieties of English in Southeast Asia*, Singapore: Singapore University Press.

Orkin, M. M. 1971. *Speaking Canadian English*, London: Routledge and Kegan Paul.

Parakrama, A. 1995. *De-Hegemonizing Language Standards*, London: Macmillan.

Pennycook, A. 1994. *The Cultural Politics of English as an International Language*, London and New York: Longman.

Phillipson, R. 1992. *Linguistic Imperialism*, Oxford University Press.

Platt, J. 1983. 'The relationship between sociolects and styles in established and new varieties of English', in Noss (ed.) 1983, pp. 213–27.

Platt, J., H. Weber and M. L. Ho 1984. *The New Englishes*, London: Routledge and Kegan Paul.

Prator, C. 1968. 'The British heresy in TESL', in J. A. Fishman, C. A. Ferguson and J. Das Gupta (eds.), *Language Problems of Developing Nations*, New York: John Wiley and Sons, pp. 459–76.

Pride, J. B. 1982. 'The appeal of the New Englishes', in Pride (ed.) 1982, pp. 1–7.

Pride, J. B. (ed.) 1982. *New Englishes*, Rowley Mass.: Newbury House.

Pringle, I. 1985. 'Attitudes to Canadian English', in Greenbaum (ed.) 1985, pp. 183–205.

Quirk, R. 1983. 'Language variety: nature and art', in Noss (ed.) 1983, pp. 3–19.

Quirk, R. and H. Widdowson (eds.) 1985. *English in the World*, Cambridge University Press/The British Council.

Richards, J. C. 1982. 'Rhetorical and communicative styles in the new varieties of English', in Pride (ed.) 1982, pp. 227–48.

Sahgal, A. 1991. 'Patterns of language use in a bilingual setting in India', in Cheshire (ed.) 1991, pp. 229–307.

Sato, C. J. 1991. 'Sociolinguistic variation and language attitudes in Hawaii', in Cheshire (ed.) 1991, pp. 647–63.

Schmied, J. 1985. 'Attitudes towards English in Tanzania', in *English World-wide* 6, 237–69.

1990. 'Language use, attitudes, performance and sociolinguistic background: a study of English in Kenya, Tanzania, and Zambia', in *English World-wide* 11, 217–38.

Sey, K. A. 1973. *Ghanaian English: An Exploratory Survey*, London: Longman.

Shaw, W. D. 1981. 'Asian student attitudes towards English', in L. Smith (ed.), *English for Cross-Cultural Communication*, London: Macmillan, pp. 108–22.

Sridhar, K. K. 1989. *English in Indian Bilingualism*, Delhi: Manohar.

Strevens, P. 1982. 'The localized forms of English', in Kachru (ed.) 1982, pp. 23–30.

Tay, M. 1982. 'The uses, users and features of English in Singapore', in Pride (ed.) 1982, pp. 51–70.

1991. 'Southeast Asia and Hong Kong', in Cheshire (ed.) 1991, pp. 319–32.

Tay, M. and A. Fraser Gupta 1983. 'Towards a description of Standard Singapore English', in Noss (ed.) 1983, pp. 173–89.

Teck, G. Y. 1983. 'Students' perception and attitude towards the varieties of English spoken in Singapore', in Noss (ed.) 1983, pp. 251–77.

Trudgill, P. 1986. *Dialects in Contact*, Oxford: Blackwell.

(ed.) 1984. *Language in the British Isles*, Cambridge University Press.

Trudgill, P. and J. Hannah 1985. *International English*, 2nd edn, London: Edward Arnold.

Williams, G. 1992. *Sociolinguistics. A Sociological Critique*, London: Routledge.

Wong, I. F. H. 1982. 'Native-speaker English for the Third World today?', in Pride (ed.) 1982, pp. 261–86.

6 Metropolitan values: migration, mobility and cultural norms, London 1100–1700

DEREK KEENE

Ideas of language entwine with those which shape the identity of peoples, territories, cities and states. Historians of medieval and early modern England have recently made much play with these themes, recognising the complexity of the issues and the fact that appeals to a 'language' as a basis for the social or political identity of a group can themselves transcend linguistic diversity.[1] Of all European countries, that of the English is the one with the deepest and most continuous historical roots. Thus notions concerning the English language and the significance of its 'standard' forms are deeply embedded in our sense of the past and in our attempts to order the present. In Britain, perhaps more than anywhere else, elements from a carefully constructed history of the nation have been, and are being, used to explain the evolution of the language itself. Thus, technical linguistic explanations of change should be linked to the best possible understanding of the economic, social and political forces which may have influenced it, but should also be aware of the agendas which underlie the writing of the history that they draw upon.

After the Norman Conquest, when the standard language of the Old English state was rejected in favour of Latin and the addition of French made England even more of a multilingual kingdom than it already was, it was recognised that the vernacular comprised many forms of speech which, along with differences in law and custom, marked strong regional cultures. Use of English spread into south Wales and Ireland, and extended further within Scotland. This resulted from warfare and the imposition of new forms of lordship, but even more from the spread of commerce and the foundation of towns.[2] By the late thirteenth century, English was distinctively associated with ideas of national identity, while the term 'tongue' itself seems sometimes to have been synonymous with 'nation'. Perhaps the single most powerful and visible force in shaping this political geography was London, the capital of the state and thus of English itself. Symbols of the political and linguistic subjugation of Wales and Scotland were ritually displayed in London. A notable case concerned the Scot, William Wallace, whose head, following his trial and execution in London in 1305, was set on London Bridge: the now silenced head of the rebel who was said during his raids of the northern counties to have slaughtered all who used the English tongue.[3] Yet London was also the English city where the greatest number of languages and language types, of both regional and overseas origin, were spoken and intermingled. It is generally acknowledged that out of this intermingling one or more types of London English emerged, which formed part of the input to Standard English. The processes involved are far from clear. Some authorities have attributed a special significance to the geographical pattern of migration to the largest and most dynamic city in the land. Others have given particular weight to the influence of a mercantile or civic élite or to London's authority as a national seat of government and justice, particularly as expressed in the bureaucratic production of texts.[4] London's role in the standardisation of English, however, was certainly more complex than this. The purpose of this paper is to provide a historian's account of factors which seem to be relevant to linguistic evolution, especially as they are evident in the economic and social interactions between London, other towns, and the country as a whole.

The account is descriptive rather than explanatory in character. Moreover, its author is a historian of cities who, though aware that the processes of social and linguistic interaction are closely allied, is, like most historians, more familiar with issues concerning names and vocabulary than with the markers that linguists commonly use to chart linguistic change. When the paper draws on the evidence of language, the emphasis is on vocabulary. Above all the focus is on the centrality and dominance of the city, and the increasing force of metropolitan culture. Essential to these topics are the exchange of goods and services between London and its wider hinterland and the flow of people to and from the city. A central question here is the degree to which the hinterland – as a productive territory and as a set of social cultures – shaped London or was itself shaped by the impact of the city. The paper assumes, on common sense grounds, that these exchanges and flows played an important part in the evolution of language in London and elsewhere. How the language itself evolved is a matter for linguists to decide, although the explanation of that process will certainly involve an effective marriage of historical and linguistic understanding. An important key to the discussion lies in the definition of the spaces, envisaged as social and temporal as well as purely territorial phenomena, within which these events took place. Which districts were close to London in terms of measured distance, time, or cost? Which were at a greater remove? How did London's influence manifest itself in places far away? In what ways did places once distant from the capital become more closely related to it? Likewise, what types of space within the city may have been associated with distinctive language types? Considerations of space also have a methodological relevance, since in studying medieval cities, for which there is relatively little direct evidence of interaction between individuals, the topography of residence and trades often provides vital clues as to the principles which underlie wider social phenomena. Thus an understanding of spaces may throw new light on the verbal and social exchanges which shape the language.

Since its foundation by the Romans London has been in essence a city of commerce and exchange.[5] Whatever pomp there may have been elsewhere in Britain, London was the place where the real business was done. Location has been the key. London had ready access to Continental flows of goods and information which mingled between the Rhine and the Seine, and could readily participate in the commerce of the North Sea and the English Channel. It was equally well positioned for internal trade: as the focal point of a road network which transmitted news quickly and provided the sinews of political control; and as the heart of a system of water transport which both penetrated deep inland via the Thames valley and, through coastal shipping, brought the city into close contact with large parts of eastern and southern England. Differences in transport costs were important in shaping the nature of contact. Livestock and people could walk or ride relatively cheaply to London along more or less straight lines, and the final price of valuable commodities such as spices or textiles could sustain their carriage over many miles by pack-horse or cart. Bulkier goods, however, such as corn, firewood, and building materials, could not economically be carried far by land and so the more circuitous routes of water transport played a crucial part. Thus, in terms of routine commercial contact, some 'distant' towns on the east and south coasts were 'closer' to London than land-locked areas only a few miles from the city (Figure 6.1). Exchanges between London and these places also generated linear patterns which are likely to have been as apparent in language and vocabulary as they were in material culture, reflecting fellowships of the road or those of the shout or ship.

Such interactions could be complex. In the mid-thirteenth century, for example, Winchelsea was said to be a port of special interest to Londoners, who doubtless used it in order to profit from cross-Channel trade and fishing as well as for access to local supplies of corn and fuel. At a later date Londoners were very active in Southampton, from which they sent imported goods overland to London and other centres where they had commercial and industrial interests. Coventry was one of those centres. Some families were active in both towns, supplying materials for the Coventry textile industry and a link to the metropolitan market for its cloth. In the late fourteenth century a Coventry friary church contained heraldic reminders of several leading citizens of London.[6] Moreover, the hinterland of Coventry played an important part in raising livestock destined for London. At the same time, London merchants with Norfolk origins or connections maintained a close interest in the routes between Norwich and London, and appear to have been regular visitors to towns and churches along the way. Regional contacts were even apparent in the internal geography of London. City churches dedicated to St Botolph, for example, which reflect contacts between London the great fair and port of Boston during the eleventh and early twelfth centuries, stood on the bank of the Thames, where goods shipped from Boston would have been landed, or outside the three city gates opening on to the most direct roads to Lincolnshire and the Wash.

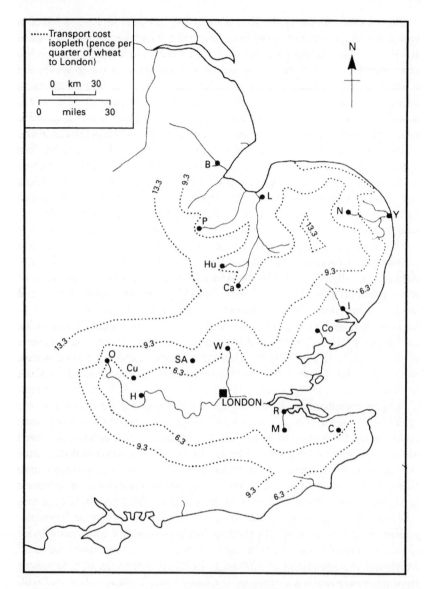

Figure 6.1 Transport costs to London *c*.1300. Each isopleth line indicates the cost of carrying a quarter of wheat from places on that line to London by the cheapest means available, including costs of cartage, shipping, and handling. The value 6.3 pence represents the cost from Cuxham, Oxfordshire (Cu), a village which regularly supplied grain to London via the local market at Henley on Thames (H). The map thus indicates the region most closely in contact with London through trade in heavy goods. It is derived from B. M. S. Campbell, J. A. Galloway, D. Keene, and M. Murphy, *A Medieval Capital and its Grain Supply: Agrarian Production and Distribution in the London Region* c. *1300* (Cheltenham: Historical Geography Research Series no. 30, 1993), Figure 7, where a fuller explanation is given.

As well as being the predominant site of English commerce, London contained the largest concentration of manufactures. That reflects the scale of the city's internal market, its concentration of élite demand, and its ready access to raw materials and markets elsewhere. By the fourteenth century the quality products of London workshops were distributed throughout the land, from Devon to Durham. London industry showed a remarkable capacity to innovate, adopting new ideas from elsewhere and organising systems of production which sometimes extended far beyond the city. Pottery manufacture in Essex and Surrey, for example, responded to innovations from London, while the specialised cutlery industry of the small town of Thaxted (Essex) was heavily dependent on London, where some of its products were finished to the highest standard. The precise and powerful languages of craft could thus forge distinctive links between London and the provinces, reinforcing those of trade.

How dominant was London? Estimates of population, wealth and trade provide some indication from the seventh century onwards, when London re-emerged as a busy centre. London was always by far the largest English city, and the degree of its primacy within the political, linguistic and territorial unit of which it was part was unique in Europe, notably by comparison with France and Germany. Between the Norman Conquest and the early fourteenth century, when the medieval city reached its peak in size, London's share of the English population rose from one to two per cent, at which level it remained until soon after 1500 (Figure 6.2). Later in the sixteenth century, and in the seventeenth, London's population grew again, this time at an explosive rate. Thus by 1700, when England's population had regained its level of 400 years before, one in ten English people lived in London and perhaps one in six visited London during their lifetimes, so that the metropolis came to have powerful unifying effect on all aspects of national life and served as a forcing house for change as never before.[7] In purely demographic terms, such a degree of metropolitan dominance has not been experienced since. Figures for trade and finance tell an even more dramatic story. In 1018, for example, London contributed £10,500 to the great payment to the Danes, representing 13 per cent of the national total and reflecting the strategic and political as well as the economic significance of the city. At about the same time, when the English coinage was produced at more than forty minting towns, London and Southwark together were responsible for almost half the output. In the early fourteenth century London contained about 2 per cent of the taxed wealth of the kingdom, rising to 12 per cent by the 1520s, while in the 1660s it produced about half the ordinary revenue available to government. Over the thirteenth century London's share of England's exports overseas doubled, to 35 per cent. Between the late fifteenth and the late sixteenth century its share rose from almost 60 to almost 90 per cent, while in 1700, following some growth at provincial ports, London accounted for 80 per cent of imports and 70 per cent of exports and re-exports.

Over the whole of this period England had a primate urban system, dominated by a single city. In the earlier Middle Ages, the second-ranking cities

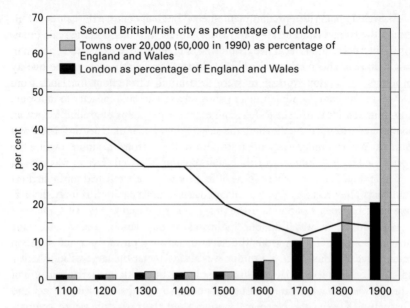

Figure 6.2 The population of London and other cities as a percentage of the population of England and Wales, 1100–1900.

were relatively dynamic by comparison with later and served as distinctive centres within a loosely integrated system of regional economies and cultures. With the rapid growth of the metropolis in size and wealth a more integrated system was established, in which London interacted directly with many provincial districts, and to some degree exercised a monopoly of urban culture. The two centuries after 1700 provide a striking contrast. In that period, fuelled by an expanding commercial and industrial empire, London continued to grow at a great rate, but now other towns also grew, some of them for the first time since the thirteenth century and others as new industrial centres. There was a sharp increase in the urbanised proportion of the population and a clearly hierarchical and integrated urban system emerged, in which London played a central role. One striking feature of this change was that, as the national market articulated by London came to bear on local resources and skills, regional identities became more pronounced, following the growth of second- and third-order provincial towns associated with specialised products and ways of life.[8] This three-stage model for the evolution of the English urban system provides a framework which helps to explain the changing character of regional cultures and their interaction with the metropolis, and may be of comparable value for understanding linguistic change.

The impact of medieval London is demonstrated by the way in which its citizens turned up elsewhere and threw their weight about, especially during the early part of the period when London was in one of its most dynamic phases by comparison with other European cities. In the 960s, for example, Londoners formed the most prominent group of non-local visitors to the shrine of St Swithun at Winchester, the political and cultural focus of the English kingdom. At Bury St Edmunds fair in the 1180s they affirmed that their city was of Roman origin and a former metropolis and that in consequence they did not have to pay the abbot's tolls. At the same time they had a trading colony in Genoa and were active, for commercial as well as religious reasons, in the reconquest of Portugal from the Moors. In the thirteenth century there were many Londoners among the burgesses of Dublin, while in Paris, now the greatest city in western Europe and a style-setter for the English capital, Londoners were prominent among the 'English', who represented one of the largest groups of Parisian taxpayers with an identifiable territorial origin. The Londoners' commercial power is demonstrated by the effects of their abrupt withdrawal of trade from Winchester fair soon after 1300.

London, however, lay on the periphery rather than at the heart of the commercial focus of northern Europe. By 1300 that focus was in the southern part of the Low Countries, where there was a marked concentration of major cities and big towns, all bigger than any English town apart from London (Figure 6.3). London, in fact, was on the margin of a region of intensive exchange, land exploitation and settlement which straddled the southern part of the North Sea and the English Channel, and included not only Flanders, Artois and Picardy, but also parts of East Anglia, northern and eastern Kent, and a coastal strip extending into Sussex. Most of the insular, and some of the continental, parts of that region were closer to London in terms of transport costs (cf. Figure 6.1) than districts to the south and west of the city. There was a constant interchange of people and goods between London and the Low Countries, and the languages of the two territories were similar. In the fourteenth and fifteenth centuries the concentration in the southern Netherlands of both European trade and the political authority of the Burgundian state became ever more marked. That was one of the principal factors which underlay the relative prosperity of London at the end of the Middle Ages and contributed to the shift in the concentration of national wealth from the Midlands into the counties of southeastern England between the fourteenth and the sixteenth centuries.

These commercial and demographic patterns were at variance with the early political geography of southern England, in which the heartlands of the kingdoms of Kent, Wessex and Mercia were distant from London. The city thus occupied a marginal position in relation to dominant cultures and presumably also to the languages associated with them. Nevertheless, it was already apparent in the seventh century that the rulers of those kingdoms had as one of their objectives the control of London. The kings of Mercia had particular success, and for much of the eighth and ninth centuries London, on an axis of power extending from the Midlands to eastern Kent, was the principal Mercian city. For these rulers, as for later English kings, London could provide access to markets overseas, money, weapons and fighting men, along with the legitimation

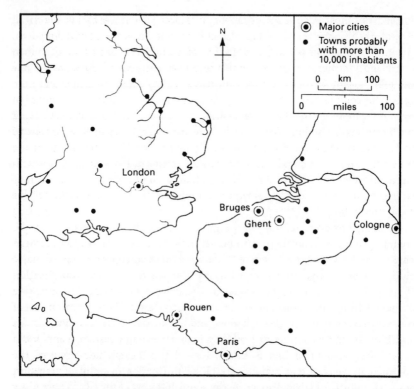

Figure 6.3 Major towns in England and neighbouring parts of the Continent *c*.1300.
Derived from Campbell *et al.*, *Medieval Capital*, Figure 1 (see caption to
figure 6.1 above).

of authority before a vast assembly of subjects. Even in the unified kingdom of
England which grew out of Wessex, in which the literary language of Winchester
was adopted as a political and cultural unifier,[9] London, on the margin of the
Danelaw, was acknowledged as a primary force. For Cnut London made sense as
the strategic capital of a North Sea empire, while Edward the Confessor, with his
patronage of Westminster, made a significant investment in London's infra-
structure as an emergent English capital which looked towards Flanders. The
Norman conquest, however, interrupted what may have been a trend, for within
the Anglo-Norman realm, with its peripatetic system of government, London,
although it was the English city where the king spent most time, lay at the eastern
limit of the territory within which he habitually moved. Moreover, Rouen was
equally significant for the monarch, and Winchester, centrally located on an axis
of power extending from Northampton to Rouen, was to remain an important
focus of government until the late twelfth century. The crucial break with
traditional structures, and perhaps the essential foundation of the modern
English state took place in the late thirteenth century under Edward I. From

then on, despite the occasional attractions of York as an outpost against Scotland, London has been the seat of the settled organs of government and law.

In this way two important sources of wealth and power came together at one place: the long-established commerce and manufactures of the city, and the extensive and unchallenged authority of the English Crown as the source of justice, peace and economic regulation. Increasingly, English people resorted to London to pursue their cause at law and to participate in councils and other political assemblies. This increased the temporary population of the capital and brought profit to its landlords and food markets. It also enhanced the city's standing as a centre for fashionable consumption, luxury manufactures, and finance. Thus, at the end of the thirteenth century, London, which had long been recognised as the chief city of the realm, came to be acknowledged as the prime focus of English identity and civilisation, and as the capital in something like the modern sense of that term.

London's force as a setter of national standards was already apparent by the late tenth century, when London gained precedence over Winchester as the place whose system of measurement was to be observed throughout the realm, while in the early eleventh century London's court set the standard for weighing precious metals. In later centuries, and especially after 1700 when London had achieved a commanding role, standardisation in such matters came to be perceived as a national project. London's management of its internal affairs was also influential from an early date. In the twelfth and thirteenth centuries, the city's customary practices, initially in association with those of Winchester, served as the principal model for the privileges which the Crown granted by charter to other towns. In the later Middle Ages London usages and vocabulary came to be adopted elsewhere. At Norwich, for example, a whole London terminology of local government replaced an earlier local system: aldermen for 'twenty-four citizens', wards for leets, and guildhall for toll-house.[10] Likewise, the chapmen and linendrapers of twelfth- and thirteenth-century Norwich and Winchester came by 1400 to be known as mercers, the London term for dealers in fine textiles which itself was probably adopted from Paris. Such terms embodied a sense of fashion and status, evident in the London practice of describing as chapmen those traders who came up to the city from the provinces but who back home were known as mercers or merchants.

As the discussion will have made clear, London's influence did not spread evenly or become weaker simply with distance from the city. It often followed linear patterns and was articulated through a hierarchy of provincial centres and lesser towns. Thus some relatively distant towns might be more closely integrated with the metropolis than were isolated villages much closer in. The urban hierarchy, with its widely-spaced towns in the second rank after London, emerges very clearly from the distribution of the larger towns as indicated by the poll tax contributions of 1377 (Figure 6.4). This evidence can be used to measure 'urban potential', a value which represents the capacity of any individual town to interact with others and thereby identifies those areas of the country

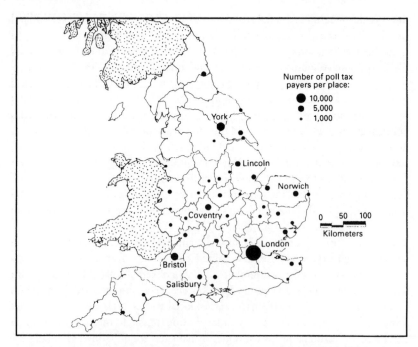

Figure 6.4 Principal English towns, 1377. Towns with one thousand or more payers of poll tax (and so with perhaps a minimum of 2,000 inhabitants) are shown. In the absence of returns for 1377, the 1381 figures have been used for Scarborough and Southwark, while Chester, St Albans, Reading, Romney and Sandwich have been assumed to have had one thousand taxpayers each. In some cases the recorded figures have been adjusted so as to allow for extra-jurisdictional areas. The map was compiled by Dr. J. A. Galloway as part of the 'Market networks in the London Region c.1400' project, funded by the Leverhulme Trust, at the Centre for Metropolitan History. Source: C. C. Fenwick, 'The English Poll Taxes of 1377, 1379 & 1381: a critical examination of the returns', PhD thesis, University of London (1983).

where exchange and interaction between individuals is likely to have been most intense (Figure 6.5). The urban potential model may be useful to linguists in their investigation of the relations between regional language types. In this exercise the population values of seaports (including London) has been doubled so as to take account of the effect of water transport in enhancing commercial activity. An unweighted exercise produces a very similar picture, although one in which Coventry, Leicester, and Northampton appear as part of a region of relatively high interaction associated with London. Both versions of the exercise, however, emphasise the unique power of London as a pole of attraction, and the degree to which the zones of high potential extended to the north and east of the city rather than to the south and southwest. One problem with the exercise is that it is impossible systematically to take account of the towns in the

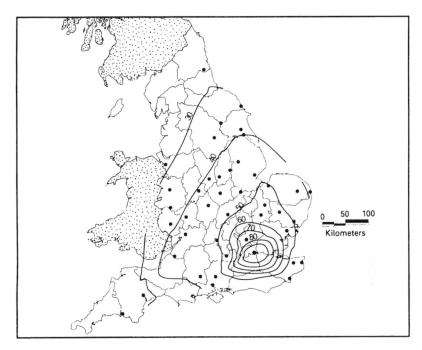

Figure 6.5 Urban potential in England, 1377. This map indicates the potential for interaction at the principal English towns by means of a value for each town (expressed as a percentage of the maximum value encountered) which takes account of the population of each place (see Figure 6.4) and its distance as the crow flies from all other towns covered by the exercise. In this case the population values of seaports (including London) were doubled, so as to take account of the transport advantages they enjoyed. The spread of values is expressed by means of isopleth lines. The method closely resembles that described in J. de Vries, *European Urbanization, 1500–1800* (London: Methuen, 1984), pp. 154–8, where the formulae used are given. An exercise which does not weight the values of the seaports produces a very similar picture, although one in which the isopleth lines for values of 60 and below lie further from London to the north and north-west. The exercises were undertaken by Dr. J. A. Galloway (see caption to Figure 6.4).

Low Countries which undoubtedly had a strong influence on the system. Had that been done, the zone of high potential would probably have been even more curtailed on the south, west and north, and more extensive to the east, where it would have included north and east Kent.

These relationships can also be mapped in terms of the debts owed to Londoners which were the subject of cases in the central Court of Common Pleas at Westminster during the years around 1400 (Figure 6.6). Londoners were active as traders and financiers throughout the land, and this analysis may provide as clear an overall picture of their regional connections during the later

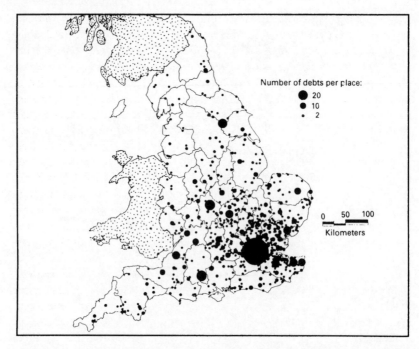

Figure 6.6 Residences of debtors to Londoners, *c*.1400. The exercise is based on a
sample of 7,806 cases from the Common Plea Rolls (Public Record Office,
CP40) for the Michaelmas terms in 1384, 1404 and 1424. In particular, it
concerns those 1,409 debts owed to Londoners by individuals whose place
of residence is identified. The sample was drawn from cases laid in Beds.,
Berks., Bucks., Essex, Herts., Kent, London, Middx., Northants., and
Surrey, but since London plaintiffs laid their pleas in London the exercise
presents a reliable picture for England as a whole. Moreover, there was
evidently an association between the significance of provincial centres and
their credit relationship with the capital (cf. Figure 6.4). The exercise was
undertaken by Dr. J. A. Galloway and Dr. M. Murphy as part of the
'Market networks' project (see Figure 6.4).

Middle Ages as can be obtained. By far the most numerous group of debtors
were other Londoners, demonstrating the scale and intensity of business there
(as well as the accessibility of the Court), but debtors from provincial towns such
as Canterbury, Salisbury, Bristol, Northampton, Coventry, York, Norwich and
Colchester also formed distinctive groups. The smaller places with close connections to London were densely distributed in the counties to the north and
immediately east of London, and along the Thames valley and the road to
Dover, reinforcing the picture derived from the 'urban potential' exercise.

Migration to London was another way in which the city interacted with its
hinterland. So unhealthy were medieval cities that they could not maintain their
populations, let alone increase them, without a large flow of immigrants. In the

case of London, that state of affairs did not begin to change until the late eighteenth century. It has been estimated that in the late sixteenth and in the seventeenth centuries London absorbed (and to a considerable degree destroyed) the whole of the 'natural increase' of the people of England. In earlier centuries London's impact was less drastic. Another feature of migration to centres of wealth is that its rate often increases when the mean level of incomes falls. That dynamic certainly underlay much of London's sixteenth-century growth and was probably also important in the period before 1300. By contrast, when the mean standard of living was rising, as in the later fourteenth and early fifteenth centuries, migration to London was associated rather with the search for opportunity and the practice of skill rather than with that for marginal employment or charitable relief. These two types of migration, sometimes characterised as subsistence migration and betterment migration, presumably could have very different linguistic outcomes since their practitioners differed sharply in their status within London and interacted with the mass of Londoners in very different ways.

Actual patterns of migration were extremely complex and cannot be fully reconstructed. They can be crudely mapped from the evidence of locative bynames, which indicate, roughly for the century or so before 1350, the places from which a significant sample of the urban population had come. This evidence does not always provide a precise and literal indicator. For example, the prosperous London mercer, Simon of Paris, actually came from Necton in Norfolk.[11] He may have adopted the byname from his master, which was a common practice. But even the master may not have originated in Paris, for he could have adopted the name on account of the Parisian associations of the mercer's trade: 'Paris thread' was one of the characteristic commodities offered by the Cheapside mercers, of whom Simon was one.[12] The Norfolk connection was also important since many London mercers are known to have come from Norfolk and handled the light textiles produced in the county, for which there was a big demand in London. Migration, commerce, fashionable consumption and naming could thus intersect. There are also other problems with the material, including the likelihood that many people with locative bynames in London were named after the substantial settlement nearest their place of origin rather than the place itself. Moreover, it is only possible to measure the distribution of the places of origin and not the numbers of people they may have contributed, so that we remain ignorant of the proportions of London's population overall which came from different parts of the country. The broad pattern, however, is significant. By this measure London had by far the most extensive catchment area for population, and its suburban settlements of Westminster and Southwark drew areas which were similarly extensive (cf. Figure 6.7). Of provincial towns only Winchester's migration field resembled London's, while the others drew much more heavily on their immediate vicinity. Distance of migration was closely related to the size and wealth of towns, but also to their political significance and perhaps to the possession of a major fair, as was the case with Winchester and Westminster. What we know of the origins of late thirteenth-century lawyers active in Westminster indicates that their pattern of migration to the capital resembled that of Londoners generally, and that was probably also true in the later Middle Ages. Thus there is unlikely to have been a 'Westminster language' which was distinct from that of the city, except possibly in the hermetic spaces of legal discourse.

Comparison between the migration regions of London, Winchester and Norwich (Figure 6.7) reveals significant features. As with the debt cases (Figure 6.6), London's close association with counties to the north and east and the sharp fall-off to the southwest of the city are clearly apparent. The latter may respect Winchester's dominance of its catchment area and the relative sparsity of population in that direction, as may also have been the case in the twelfth century when Winchester's strong association with the southwest was also apparent.[13] There was plenty of traffic on the road between Winchester and London in the later Middle Ages, much of it originating in the port of Southampton, but it seems not to have been of a type to promote migration. This state of affairs may have been similar in relation to the Dover road, which appears to have been much less significant for migration to London than for the commercial links indicated by debt cases.

The extension of London's migration field far into northeastern England is striking. Economic contacts with that region seem to have been mediated through urban centres such as York, Beverley and Newcastle (Fig. 6.7). By-names were drawn from a much wider range of places, although that apparent contrast may reflect the impossibility of estimating the contribution of the larger places to migration. There was a similar pattern in East Anglia. Norwich's catchment area was notably compact and fell off sharply in the direction of London. The capital presumably exercised a stronger pull than Norwich in Essex, Hertfordshire and Bedfordshire. Unlike the pattern to the southwest, however, London's migration field subsumed that of Norwich. Several possible explanations may be offered. Before 1350 Norfolk was noted for its high population density and its intensive agrarian regime. It could supply more people to London than the more sparsely settled counties to the southwest of the capital. Populations in Essex, Hertfordshire and Bedfordshire were also relatively dense.[14] The high densities in northern and eastern Kent, on the other hand, even when combined with close commercial contact, do not seem to have precipitated substantial migration to London. The inhabitants of those parts of Kent may have found enough employment and other attractions to keep them in the locality, or they may have looked more to the Low Countries than to London. In Norfolk, by contrast, the village-based textile industry may not have been able fully to absorb the surplus of labour generated by the intensive agrarian regime, thus precipitating migration to London through networks associated with the marketing of the cloth. In this period too the outstandingly prosperous port of Boston lost much of its business to London, undermining the opportunities for marginal employment to be found in the East Midlands

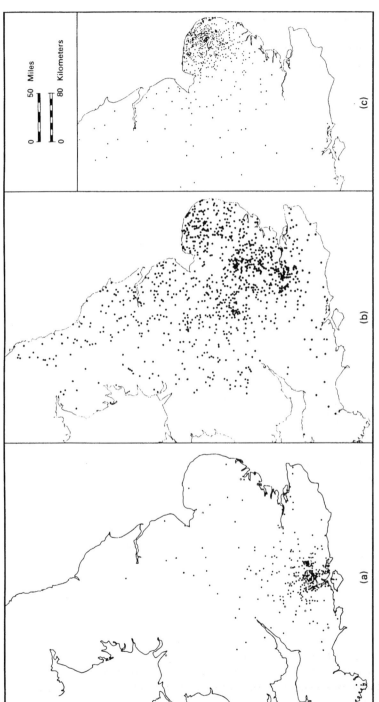

Figure 6.7 The migration fields of Winchester, London and Norwich, c. 1300. The maps show the places from which residents of the three cities derived their bynames. Such locative bynames can indicate commercial and other forms of contact, as well as patterns of migration. For these issues, see P. McClure, 'Patterns of migration in the late Middle Ages: the evidence of English place-name surnames', *Economic History Review*, 2nd series 32 (1979), pp. 167–82; D. Keene, *Survey of Medieval Winchester* (Oxford: Clarendon Press, 1985), pp. 371–9; G. Rosser, *Medieval Westminster, 1200–1540* (Oxford University Press, 1989), pp. 183–6; M. Carlin, *Medieval Southwark* (London and Rio Grande: Hambledon, 1996), pp. 144–8. a. Winchester: derived from Keene, *Medieval Winchester*, Figure 45, which is based on the bynames of property-holders alive before 1350 (circles represent the places from which later property-holders, up to c. 1550, are known to have come). b. London: derived from P. H. Reaney, *The Origin of English Surnames* (London: Routledge and Kegan Paul, 1967), pp. 345–51 and Figure IV, which is based on the bynames of Londoners in the period 1147–1330; the bulk of the material, however, dates from c. 1300. c. Norwich: derived from Reaney, *English Surnames*, pp. 332–7 and Figure III, which is based on Norwich bynames in the period 1285–1350.

generally. In the case of Norfolk, therefore, the mechanisms of subsistence and betterment migration may have operated interdependently.

This evidence for migration and for London's position within the economic and political geography of the kingdom only partially squares with the explanation for dialect shift in London which Ekwall has discussed so carefully.[15] For example, given the clear significance of commercial contacts with Kent, it seems possible that contacts or migration at the level of the mercantile élite were less significant than the mixture of mercantile and labour market contacts which operated to the north and northeast of the city. Furthermore, the regional attributions adopted in discussions of dialect shift may not always be appropriate, and terms such as 'Southern' and 'Home Counties' do not always match the apparent realities of medieval life. London's contacts with the Midlands (Mercia), for example, were already important before 850. Subsequently the city was far from remote from the Danelaw, while in the twelfth century, London's intense connections with its hinterland probably lay to the north and east rather than to the south and west. Unfortunately, we are unlikely to be able to reconstruct London's migration field for any period significantly earlier than that around 1300, which was one in which important changes in London pronunciation (or scribal renderings of it) were already taking place. It is clear, however, that in considering the forces which may have influenced linguistic change attention should be given to possible differences in the effects of contacts between London and its hinterlands as indicated by the evidence for migration, commercial contact and population density. Moreover, the connection between metropolitan and provincial labour markets was probably a crucial element in the equation.

Some late medieval changes certainly indicate that the impact of London on local labour markets could precipitate migration to the capital. In the late fifteenth century, in the two city companies (the skinners and the tailors) for which counts have been done, 46 per cent of 155 apprentices came from the northern counties and fewer than half as many from London and the Home Counties, in sharp contrast to the early fourteenth century, when apprentices seem predominantly to have come from counties close to the city and the northern counties may have contributed less than 10 per cent.[16] This may simply reflect the extension of London's influence and the drift of resources towards the southeast, but the change was probably also associated with the way in which the capital had drawn off the business of northern towns and so directly undermined local opportunities for employment and apprenticeship. The population of London may not have been expanding at that period, except on the impoverished periphery, but its overall level of business certainly was and that would have attracted northern youngsters. The mid sixteenth-century picture, to judge from the record of 1,055 men who took up the freedom of the city between 1551 and 1553, was different again. The largest proportion, 31 per cent, was once more contributed by London and the Home Counties; the northern counties still contributed a substantial share which, however, had fallen to 30 per cent; and that from East Anglia and Lincolnshire, which may have been over 20 per cent in the early fourteenth century, had fallen to seven per cent.[17]

Different trades promoted different patterns of migration. In the fourteenth century and later the mercers, cutlers, cornmongers, maltmen, butchers, tanners, and woodmongers of London each had different sets of regional connections which reflected the distribution of the rural resources and systems of production that they drew upon.[18] It may thus have been possible to recognise certain trades, and the city spaces associated with them, according to distinctive language types. A typical, if extreme, case is provided by the London butchers, the origins of whose apprentices during the 1580s can readily be mapped (Figure 6.8). At that date the pull of the London meat market was greater than it had been before, but the picture was probably not much different in the fifteenth century. The contrast with the overall pattern of migration to London around 1300 (Figure 6.7b) is striking and reveals, for example, a strong association with one region notable for livestock-rearing and -marketing in the Midlands and another less extensive one in Wiltshire and Somerset, together with a connection to long-distance droving routes extending further to the north and west. The absence of intensive contact with the counties immediately to the north and east of London and with East Anglia is important. The contrast may reflect an overall decline in migration from East Anglia, but that cannot provide the full explanation since the concentration of butchers' apprentices from the Midlands had no counterpart among the late fifteenth-century apprentices of the skinners and tailors, and the record of the freedom of the city indicates that many citizens came from the Home Counties.

Most adult Londoners were born outside the city: in the eighteenth century the outsiders may have been as many as two-thirds of the total. It is impossible to estimate the proportion for earlier periods, although London's rate of growth and the overall rate of mortality suggests that it was highest in the second half of the seventeenth century. We can be more certain, however, about those born outside the realm, who in the late Middle Ages represented, on the latest estimates, about 10 per cent of a total of perhaps 50,000 Londoners. Most of these alien immigrants were known as 'Dutch' by virtue of their language and came from the northern Netherlands and the lower Rhineland: they were people for whom at that time London offered safety and employment but as a preferred destination probably came second to Bruges or Antwerp.

Population exchange with London was not a one-way process. Within ten miles or so of the city many came and went on a daily basis, especially the country women who sold produce in the markets. Successful migrants often maintained business and social contact with their places of origin, paying frequent return visits. Moreover, many who went to London failed. About 60 per cent of a sixteenth-century sample of 44,169 London apprentices, for example, failed to complete their terms.[19] Some of those presumably entered the

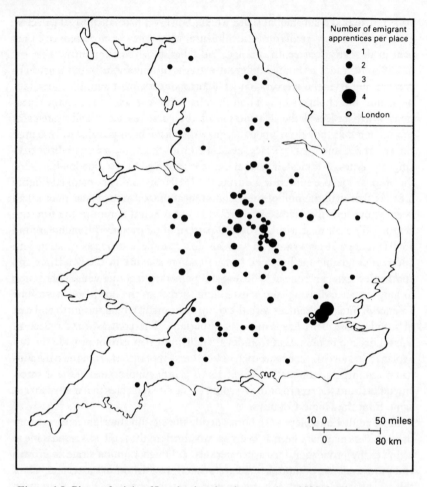

Figure 6.8   Places of origin of London butchers' apprentices, 1585–9. The map reveals
the distinctive pattern of migration and contact associated with cattle
rearing and marketing. It is based on material in P. E. Jones, *The Butchers of
London* (London: Secker and Warburg, 1976), Appendix V.

London market for unskilled or partially skilled labour, some died, but others
returned to the country. In these ways London knowledge and culture, and
perhaps London language too, was fed back to the regions.

Within London the population was highly mobile.[20] The pattern of occu-
pancy in a sample of about twenty houses in a relatively stable and prosperous
central district in the fifteenth century shows that on average rent-payers moved
house every two to three years, and perhaps 70 per cent of them occupied their
homes for two years or less. Most of these moves were over very short distances
within the same street, and the longer ones were characteristic of the wealthier
householders, who moved least often. These patterns of movement were asso-

ciated with individual houses and with craft districts whose status and characteristics endured over many centuries. This physical and social framework, em-
bodying networks of credit and of political responsibility at many different
levels, was an important element in the city's capacity to survive episodes of
crisis. This essential stability, as several historians have recently observed,
presents a marked contrast with the high rate of social turnover. Physical and
social communities and neighbourhoods probably reinforced and were reinforced by distinctive linguistic practice. This was most obvious in the case with
foreign immigrants designated as 'aliens'. Thus on the waterfront in the fourteenth century mixed-language place-names, such as *Steelyarde* (for the Low
German *Stahlhof*), *Stielwharf*, and *Stielwharfgate* came to be established in the
vicinity of the German merchants' guildhall,[21] suggesting that there was a high
degree of linguistic exchange between the Germans and their neighbours, while
a short distance upstream there was a marked, but less enduring, concentration
of French, Gascons and Spaniards engaged in the wine trade.[22] In the fifteenth
and sixteenth centuries the German merchants established an enclave for
themselves, while in certain marginal areas, especially in Southwark and on the
east side of the city, there were large numbers of poor immigrants from the Low
Countries who apparently formed recognisable language communities. Some of
these areas seem also to have served as 'zones of transition' for the reception of
alien immigrants, and have continued to do so to the present.[23]

What forms of language these different ethnic and craft groups used to
communicate in doing the business of London; whether standard London
languages existed or not; and, if they did exist, who owned them and endowed
any of them with status as a national standard, are questions for linguists to
assess. Historians can help by indicating ways in which economic, social and
political contexts may have had a bearing on the process. London is likely to
have had an influence in the emergence of Standard English not primarily as a
site of government and power but rather as an engine of communication and
exchange which enabled ideas and information to be distributed and business to
be done across an increasingly extensive, complex and varied field. Key processes to consider would include the establishment of fellowship, trust and
norms which fostered understanding and an ability quickly to conclude deals in
acknowledged and repeatable ways. In the speech of modern economists, such
forms of standardisation would have reduced transaction costs. It is no coincidence, therefore, that some of the earliest evidence for the force of London in
processes of standardisation concerns matters of measurement which were vital
to trade. Another useful concept from the world of economics concerns integration between markets – between London and other places, and around certain
focal points within the city – leading to uniformity in prices, products and
practice. Integration could be a spontaneous process, but it could also be
facilitated by a framework imposed by state authority, the king's peace as it was
called in the earlier Middle Ages. The search for peace, with a view to promoting harmony, exchange and prosperous cities, was a profound influence on

those who wielded power. Several episodes in English history show that a standard language was perceived as an instrument of peace and rule. As linguists and historians we must hope that the emergence and identification of that standard do not pass all understanding.

Notes

1 For recent surveys, see T. Turville-Petre, *England and the Nation: Language, Literature and National Identity; 1290–1340* (Oxford University Press, 1996); S. Foot, 'The making of Angelcynn: English identity before the Norman Conquest', *Transactions of the Royal Historical Society*, 6th series, 6 (1996), 25–47; R. R. Davies, 'The peoples of Britain and Ireland, 1100–1400: iv, language and historical mythology', *Transactions of the Royal Historical Society*, 6th series, 7 (1997), 1–24.

2 For Scotland, see D. Murison, 'The Scottish language', in D. Daiches (ed.), *The New Companion to Scottish Culture* (Edinburgh: Polygon, 1993), pp. 298–300; G. W. S. Barrow, *The Anglo-Norman Era in Scottish History* (Oxford: Clarendon Press, 1980), pp. 30–60; G. W. S. Barrow, *Scotland and its Neighbours in the Middle Ages* (London and Rio Grande: 1993), pp. 105–26.

3 W. Stubbs (ed.), *Chronicles of the reigns of Edward I. and Edward II.*, 2 vols. (London: Rolls Series, 1882–3), vol. I, pp. 90–1, 141.

4 Laura Wright, 'About the evolution of standard English', in Elizabeth M. Tyler and M. Jane Toswell (eds.), *Studies in English Language and Literature: 'Doubt Wisely', Papers in honour of E.G. Stanley* (London: Routledge, 1996), pp. 99–115.

5 For surveys of recent writing on Roman, medieval and later London, see *The London Journal* 20.2 (1995). See also D. Keene, 'Medieval London and its region', *London Journal* 14.2 (1989), 99–111; 'Small towns and the metropolis: the experience of medieval England', in J.-M. Duvosquel and E. Thoen (eds.), *Peasants and Townsmen in Medieval Europe: Studia in Honorem Adriaan Verhulst* (Gent: Snoek-Ducaju and Zoon, 1995), pp. 223–38; and 'London, 600–1300' and 'South-eastern England 600–1540', in *The Cambridge Urban History of Britain*, I: *The Middle Ages* (Cambridge University Press, forthcoming).

6 S. L. Thrupp, *The Merchant Class of Medieval London* (Ann Arbor: University of Michigan Press, 1962; reissue of 1948 edn), pp. 326, 341, 358, 367, 372; C. Tracy, 'Choir-stalls from the 14th-century Whitefriars church in Coventry', *Journal of the British Archaeological Association* 150 (1997), 76–95; A. F. Sutton, *A Merchant Family of Coventry, London and Calais: the Tates, c.1450–1515* (London, The Mercers' Company, 1998).

7 The classic account of this development is E. A. Wrigley, 'A simple model of London's importance in changing English society and economy 1650–1750', *Past and Present* 37 (1967), 44–70; reprinted in P. Abrams and E. A. Wrigley (eds.), *Towns in Societies: Essays in Economic History and Historical Sociology* (Cambridge University Press, 1978), pp. 215–45.

8 For these issues, see Keene, 'Small towns and the metropolis', n. 1.

9 H. Gneuss, 'The origin of standard Old English and Aethelwold's school at Winchester', *Anglo-Saxon England* 1 (1972), 63–83; W. Hofstetter, 'Winchester and the standardisation of Old English vocabulary', *Anglo-Saxon England* 17 (1988), 139–61.

10 W. Hudson (ed.), *Leet Jurisdiction in the City of Norwich during the XIIIth and XIVth*

centuries (London: Selden Society, vol. 5, 1892 for 1891), p. x.

11 E. Ekwall, *Two Early London Subsidy Rolls* (Lund: Gleerup, 1951), p. 299.

12 For these issues, and for London mercers who dealt with Paris merchants, see A. F. Sutton, 'The Mercery Trade and the Mercers' Company of London, from the 1130s to 1348', PhD thesis, University of London (1995), esp. Appendix 3.

13 M. Biddle (ed.), *Winchester in the Early Middle Ages: an edition and discussion of the Winton Domesday* (Oxford: Clarendon Press, 1976), Fig. 3.

14 For population densities, see R. Smith, 'Human resources', in G. Astill and A. Grant (eds.), *The Countryside of Medieval England* (Oxford: Blackwell, 1988), pp. 188–212.

15 E. Ekwall, *Studies in the Population of Medieval London* (Stockholm: Almquist and Wiksell, 1956).

16 Thrupp, *Merchant Class of Medieval London*, pp. 209–11, 389–92. Ekwall's conclusion concerning the early fourteenth century resembles Thrupp's: *Studies in the Population of Medieval London*, pp. xi–xii.

17 Figures recalculated so as to fit Thrupp's regional categories, from S. Rappaport, *Worlds within Worlds: Structures of Life in Sixteenth-Century London* (Cambridge University Press, 1989), pp. 78–9.

18 Cutlers: Keene, 'Small towns and the metropolis'. Cornmongers: B. M. S. Campbell, J. Galloway, D. Keene and M. Murphy, *A Medieval Capital and its Grain Supply: Agrarian Production and Distribution in the London Region c.1300* (Cheltenham: Historical Geography Research Paper Series, 1993). Mercers: A. F. Sutton, 'The early linen and worsted industry and the evolution of the London Mercers' Company', *Norfolk Archaeology* 40 (1989), 202–25. Tanners: D. Keene, 'Tanners' widows, 1300–1350', in C. M. Barron and A. F. Sutton (eds.), *Medieval London Widows, 1300–1500* (London and Rio Grande: Hambledon, 1994), pp. 1–28. Woodmongers: J. A. Galloway, D. Keene and M. Murphy, 'Fuelling the city: production and distribution of firewood and fuel in London's region, 1290–1400' *Economic History Review* 49 (1996), 447–72.

19 Rappaport, *Worlds within Worlds*, pp. 311–15. The proportion of tailors who in the fifteenth century failed to complete their term was even higher: see M. P. Davies, 'The Tailors of London and their Guild, c1300–1500', DPhil thesis, University of Oxford (1994).

20 Cf. J. P. Boulton, 'Residential mobility in 17th-century Southwark', *Urban History Yearbook 1986*, 1–14; D. Keene, 'A new study of London before the Great Fire', *Urban History Yearbook 1984*, 11–21.

21 D. Keene, 'New discoveries at the Hanseatic Steelyard in London', *Hansische Geschichtsblätter* 107 (1989), 15–26; D. Keene, 'Du seuil de la Cité à la formation d'une économie morale: l'environnement hanséatique à Londres, 1100–1600 après J.C.' in J. Bottin and D. Calabi (eds.), *Les étrangers dans la ville* (Paris: Maison des Sciences de l'Homme, forthcoming 1999); W. Kurzinna, 'Der Name "Stahlhof"', *Hansische Geschichtsblätter* 17 (1912), 429–61. For the earliest record of these names (in 1384), see *Calendar of Inquisitions Miscellaneous*, vol. IV (London: H.M. Stationery Office, 1957), no. 275.

22 The house-name *La Riole* (preserved in the modern parish-name St Michael Paternoster Royal) denotes the presence of Gascon wine merchants from La Reole by 1232: M. D. Lobel (ed.), *The City of London from Prehistoric Times to c.1520* (Oxford University Press: The British Atlas of Historic Towns III, 1989), p. 84. There had been a market in French wines in the vicinity, probably since the eleventh century:

Keene, 'New Discoveries', p. 18. For French and Iberians in the neighbourhood c.1300, see Ekwall, *Subsidy Rolls*, pp. 181–6.

23 These issues, concerning London and other towns, are addressed in the English contributions to Bottin and Calabi (eds.), *Les étrangers dans la ville*. See also Carlin, *Medieval Southwark*, pp. 149–67.

Part two

Processes of the standardisation
of English

7 Standardisation and the language of early statutes

MATTI RISSANEN

1 Introduction

The rise of standard language is closely connected with increasing literacy and the wide distribution of written texts representing various genres with various functions. In the present paper I shall discuss the influence of a highly specific genre, statutory texts, on the early development of the written English standard in Late Middle and Early Modern English. My survey begins with the reintroduction of English in the fifteenth century; unfortunately space does not permit a discussion of the role played by Old English legal texts in the developing standards before the Norman Conquest.

Discussion of the rise of the standard has so far mainly concentrated on the gradual fixation of English orthography and the loss of variant spellings. This is quite natural as spelling variants, at least to a certain extent, give information on dialectal pronunciations. Furthermore, the monumental *Linguistic Atlas of Late Mediaeval English* has given great impetus to the systematic study of spelling in fifteenth-century English.

It is obvious, however, that the time has come to shift the focus of interest from spelling variants to other linguistic features. As Laura Wright points out in her insightful article about the evolution of Standard English:

> Most of all, we cannot claim to have identified and understood a process of standardisation until we have treated not only spelling, but also morphology, vocabulary, phonology, and syntax. The evolution of the written sentence is one of the most central developments of standardisation, along with the process of making external contexts explicit. Until we have understood the development of such constituents, the story of the evolution of Standard English remains to be told. (1996: 113)

I will first briefly discuss the more general aspects of standardisation from the point of view of syntax and lexis, refer to the role played by different genres, categories or types of text in the process of standardisation, and try to place statutory texts in this picture. Finally, I will compare the use of a few syntactic and lexical features typical of early statutes with their occurrence in texts representing other genres.

2   On standardisation

It has been frequently pointed out, for example in many of the papers in this volume, that it is difficult to give a definition of a standard or the process of standardisation which would be equally valid both for a discussion of present-day varieties of language and for a historical approach which emphasises the rise and development of the written standard. Furthermore, an appropriate definition may vary according to whether the study focuses on spelling or on other linguistic features.

An adequate basis for our attempt to define standardisation from a dynamic diachronic point of view can be found in Milroy (1992: 129), on whom the following list is based, although the wording and typographical organisation is slightly altered:

(i)   The main linguistic symptom of standardisation is invariance.
(ii)   The effect of standardisation is to make a language serviceable for communicating decontextualised information-bearing messages over long distances and periods of time.
(iii) The standard is imposed through its use in administrative functions by those who have political power.
(iv)   Once it spreads from administrative into other functions, the standard acquires what we usually call 'prestige', in the sense that those who wish to advance in life consider it to be in their interests to use standard-like forms.

All these features are relevant to the discussion of the relationship of the language of the statutes to the process of standardisation.

The role played by the Chancery Standard in the establishment of English spelling has been thoroughly discussed in earlier literature and needs little comment in this context. As the language of the fifteenth-century statutes is just a further deregionalised and decontextualised version of Chancery Standard, it was probably influential in the standardisation of spelling.[1] But the standardising effect of documents and statutes is less obvious when we are dealing with questions of syntax and lexis. Spelling is wholly a matter of written language; in addition, it is independent of meaning. For this reason, it is easy to adopt a relatively invariant model for spelling from a genre which is highly restricted in topic and style, such as statutory texts. The development of standard forms and expressions in the fields of syntax and lexis is a more complicated procedure and to attribute this development solely or mainly to the influence of the language of officialdom would be an oversimplification.

If we try to map the routes of syntactic and lexical standardisation, we must look at genres, sub-genres, and text types much more extensively. In Late

Middle English, in the second half of the fourteenth and the fifteenth century, we can distinguish at least the following macro-genres or types of writing which should be taken into account in the discussion of the development of the standard.

(i)   Statutory texts (documents and laws)
(ii) Religious instruction (sermons, rules, Bible translation, etc.)
(iii) Secular instruction (handbooks, educational treatises, etc.)
(iv) Expository texts (scientific treatises)
(v)   Non-imaginative narration (history, biography, travelogue, diary, etc.)
(vi) Imaginative narration (romance, fiction, etc.)

It is no coincidence that this list fairly closely corresponds to the division into the so-called prototypical text categories in the Helsinki Corpus, which cut through the history of English writing. These categories are of course broad and generalised and consist of several genres or text types. Furthermore, even texts included in one and the same genre are often heterogeneous in regard to their linguistic features. This is, of course, because genres can only be defined and specified by extralinguistic criteria.

In his pioneering article M. L. Samuels gives the following four groups of texts as probable sources of the written standard (1989 [1963]: 64–80; cf. also Sandved 1981; Benskin 1992):

Type 1   Wycliffite manuscripts, etc. (religious instruction, secular instruction, non-imaginative narration)
Type 2   The Auchinleck MS, etc. (imaginative narration, religious instruction)
Type 3   Chaucer, etc. (imaginative narration, secular instruction, religious instruction, expository, statutory)
Type 4   Chancery standard (statutory)

When these groups have been referred to in later literature, it has sometimes been forgotten that they consist of a variety of genres and texts. In fact, all the six text categories mentioned above are included in Samuels' types. The short titles of the categories are given in brackets after each group. Although spelling was probably most strongly influenced by Type 4, it is obvious that we should not overlook the three other types, or even other sources, in our search for the roots of the standardisation of the syntactic constructions or lexical items in Late Middle and Early Modern English.

We could divide genres and text groups into the following three groups according to their role in the process of standardisation:

1. Texts producing syntactic or lexical variant forms that will gradually become elements of the standard
2. Texts contributing to the spread of these forms over regional and register borderlines

3.   Texts contributing to the establishment of these forms as elements of the standard

This classification echoes James and Lesley Milroy's model for the actuation of change in their *Journal of Linguistics* article (1985) and later writings, in which they specify innovators and early adopters, although with reference to spoken language and not written. The social dimension of course plays an important role in the pattern outlined above. The texts producing forms that tend to become standardised must have prestige: Bible translations, religious treatises, or secular writings by eminent authors from Chaucer onwards are likely candidates. The introduction of loan words forms an important part of this process. Texts belonging to this innovator category have, by definition, wide distribution in manuscripts or early printed editions, and this certainly contributes to the spread of the innovations over dialect boundaries. But more important still, from the point of view of the standardisation process, is the diffusion of innovations from their original genre of writing to others. Here it would seem that instructive texts, which are often more objective and less author-involved than religious or imaginative writings, are in a key position. And finally, such texts as statutes and official documents, associated with power and authority, play a role in establishing the form or word as part of the standard.

This outline of the introduction, spread and establishment of forms in the written standard is necessarily hypothetical and based on generalisations. One of the problematic points is the lack of homogeneity between individual texts within a single genre. This concerns both the linguistic features of the texts and their discoursal, pragmatic and attitudinal aspects of composition. In spite of this, the scheme set out above might help us to a better understanding of the complicated paths of standardisation, particularly as a number of important types of writing in English, such as religious instruction, prose romance, medical instruction and science, travelogue, prose history and handbooks of household affairs, began to show genre-distinctive features in the fourteenth and fifteenth centuries.

3   Characteristics of the language of administration

The first Acts of Parliament written in English appeared at the end of the fifteenth century. Their language was most obviously based on the writings produced by the Chancery and other state offices in the course of the century.

The language of laws and statutes is characterised by neutrality and generality; it avoids subjective and personal attitudes and strong regional marking. To ensure correct and unambiguous transmission of information it must be conservative in its choice of structure and lexis and hostile to stylistic variation. It aims at maximum disambiguation in its text and discourse structure. The text is generalising in the sense that its system of references should cover all and only the referents which form the topic of the statement. These aims may make the language complex and repetitive, but they also make it innovative in some aspects of syntactic and lexical usage. Finally, the statutes represent anonymous authority and power. To emphasise this, they often develop a special, slow-moving style which sounds artificial but may also create collocations and patterns, often formulaic, which are easily borrowed by other genres and, occasionally, even by spoken language.

All in all, it seems that in spelling the standardising model offered by documents and statutes had a strong influence on other genres of writing; in the case of syntax and lexis, on the other hand, laws and documents adopted forms from other genres, decontextualised and deregionalised them, and thus marked these forms as part of the standard.

4   The language of the early statutes: some examples

After this attempt to place the language of law in the story of early standardisation, I shall discuss a few syntactic and lexical features of Late Middle and Early Modern English legal texts. My evidence comes from the Helsinki Corpus, which contains a number of samples of statutes dating from the fifteenth, sixteenth and seventeenth centuries. The edition, a collection called *The Statutes of the Realm*, was published in the nineteenth century, but the texts are reproduced faithfully and keep the original spelling.[2] The samples representing each Helsinki Corpus subperiod are a little over ten thousand words in length, too short for far-reaching conclusions, but sufficient to show the trends in usage and development within a genre which represents a narrow code and whose expression aims at a maximum degree of invariance.[3]

The following extract dating from c.1490 shows a number of features typical of early statutory text:

AN ACT FOR DYVERS PRIVILEGES TO BE GRAUNTED TO PERSONS BEING IN THE KINGES WARRS.

Where by the grace of Almyghty God the King oure Soverayn Lord intendeth in his most Royall person to take his viage Royall in to the lond of Fraunce ageyn his auncient enmyes of **the same** Realme, accompanyed in **the seid** Viage with gret multitude of the most honorable actif persons and true subgettes of **this his Realme** of Englond, **aswell** for the defence of his most noble person **as** for the defence of theym self and of all the inhabitantes within **this his seid Realme** of Inglond to the high **laude fame and preyse** of the King oure Soverayn Lord and of all thoes which **shall accompany** hym in **the seid** Viage either by see or lond: **Wherfor** the King oure Soverayn Lord by thadvyce and assent of the lordes spirituelx and temporelx and the Commens of this present parliament assembled and by auctorite of **the same, enacteth ordeyneth and establissheth** that every person of what condicion or degre he **be of being or herafter shalbe** in oure **seid** Soverayn Lord the Kinges Wages beyonde the See or on the See at his pleso*ur* have the pr*o*teccion of *p'fectur'* or *moratur' cum clausa volum'*; And that **the seid** pr*o*teccion be allowed in all the King*es* Courtes and other Courtes where **the seid** pr*o*teccions **shalbe** pleded or leyed for any of **the seid** p*er*sons in all plees; plees of Dowre in the Writte of Dowre unde *nichil h'et, quare impedit* and assise of darreign pr*e*sentment except. **Provided that** this acte be **not available to eny person for any entre** syn the first day of this pr*e*sent parliament. (c.1490, *The Statutes of the Realm* II, 550)

The most conspicuously typical features of the language of law are marked with boldface: the phrases *the same* and *the said* for increasing cohesiveness and referential accuracy; the compact anaphoric expression *this his (seid) Realme* (typical of early law text; cf. Kytö and Rissanen 1993), the link *as well (. . .) as*, the repetitive *laude, fame and preyse*, the future auxiliary *shall*, the link *wherfore*, the universalising formula *be of being or hereafter shalbe*. In view of the influence of the language of law on the standard, attention can also be called to the link *provided that*, the compound adverb *hereafter*, and last but not least to the avoidance of double or universal negation in *not available to eny person for any entre*.

In the following, four of the features mentioned above will be subjected to closer scrutiny: (1) the choice of the future auxiliary (*shall/will*); (2) multiple negation; (3) the link *provided (that)*; and (4) compound adverbs of the type *hereafter*.

4.1   Shall/will

The development of the future auxiliaries *shall* and *will* is one of the most discussed questions in the history of English syntax (see e.g. Mustanoja 1960: 489–95; Fischer 1992: 263–5). *Shall* seems to develop the 'neutral' future indication earlier than *will* in Middle English; it was particularly favoured in the second and third persons and in formal styles. The curious person-based dichotomy in the use of these auxiliaries developed in the Southern Standard in the course of the sixteenth and seventeenth centuries and was codified by grammarians from the seventeenth century on.

Variation in the use of future auxiliaries was dysfunctional in the language of law, particularly in view of their inherent semantic implications. The aim of neutrality and generality favoured the choice of a single auxiliary to indicate the neutral future, and in this context the natural choice was *shall*, which was the more depersonalised of the two and frequently used when obligation was involved. This is one of the features for which the language of law could well have established the standard form but failed to do so.

Table 1 gives figures of the occurrence of *shall* and *will* in auxiliary function in Late Middle English statutes and in a number of other genres and texts dating from the fifteenth century.[4]

Table 1. *Shall* and *will* as future auxiliaries in the Helsinki Corpus, ME4 (1420–1500), absolute figures.

	shall	*will*
Laws	51	14
Handbooks	161	19
Scientific texts	53	1
Caxton's Preface	29	3
Sermons	173	35
Romances	104	72
Reynard the Fox	54	37
Plays	200	150
Private letters	77	79

The genres are clearly divided into two groups: laws, handbooks, scientific treatises and Caxton's prefaces strongly favour *shall* as the future auxiliary. These would seem the kind of text most likely to establish the standard form. But texts representing more personalised, contextualised and private genres, such as romances, fiction (*Reynard the Fox*, printed by Caxton), miracle and morality plays and private correspondence, have a much higher percentage of *will*; in private letters, *will* is as frequent as *shall*. Sermons show a proportionally higher frequency of *shall* than the laws, but distinctly lower than the other '*shall*-genres'.

At this stage, the person of the subject does not influence the choice of the auxiliary. The semantic implications of obligation or volition certainly affected the choice in many instances, the former in law texts and the latter in the texts with strong author involvement or personal affect, but it is easy to find examples of neutral future with *shall* in law texts and of *will* in more imaginative texts, as shown by (1) and (2):[5]

(1)   Provided alwey that no Capteyn be charged by this acte for lakke of his noumbre reteyned as is above seid whoes Souldeours **shall happe** to dye or other wise dep*ar*te not in the defaute of the Capteyn; (1488–91, *The Statutes of the Realm* [STAT2] 550)

(2)   How be hit the barge is comyn with þe said stuff as þis nyght at vij of clocke: and Syr, soo hit **will be** the morne or I can receyvyd hit. (1476 Letter by Elizabeth Stonor [ESTONOR] 19)

It is only to be expected that the use of *will* in the earliest laws should be contextually restricted. No less than eight out of the fourteen instances occur in the formula *will sue*, as in example (3):

(3)   the Kyng therof to have the on halfe and the fynder that can prove it and **will sue** it in the Kyng*es* Eschequer the other halfe; (1488–91, *The Statutes of the Realm* [STAT2] 527)

The documents included in Fisher, Richardson and Fisher (1984), dating between 1417 and 1455, also show a prevalence of *shall*, although the frequency of *will* is somewhat higher than in the statutes, about one third the frequency of *shall*.

Table 2 shows the tendency to adopt *shall* as the sole auxiliary of the future in the law texts in the next two centuries:

Table 2. *Shall* and *will* as future auxiliaries in statutory texts in the Early Modern English sub-corpora of the Helsinki Corpus, absolute figures

	shall	*will*
EModE1 (1500–1570)	97	15
EModE2 (1570–1640)	248	8
EModE3 (1640–1710)	246	6

The figures are dramatic. Most of the few examples with *will* are, once again, contextually marked, 17 out of 29 representing the formula *will sue* mentioned above.[6] In four instances, *will* occurs with other auxiliaries (*can shall or will testifye*), and in most of the others it is intentional (*if he will receyve or accepte it*). Thus, if law texts had been allowed to determine the usage of the standard, *shall* would probably have developed into the unmarked future auxiliary. The development followed other lines, however, as can be seen in Table 3, which shows the distribution between the two auxiliaries in the second and third Helsinki Corpus subperiods of Early Modern English (1570–1640 and 1640–1710):

Table 3. *Shall* and *will* as future auxiliaries in certain text types in EModE2 and EModE3 in the Helsinki Corpus (1570–1640 and 1640–1710), absolute figures

	EModE2		EModE3	
	shall	*will*	*shall*	*will*
Handbooks	89	60	33	95[1]
Scientific texts	38	36	10	29
Official letters	25	19	13	41
Sermons	50	53	20	48
Fiction	29	49	65	84
Comedy	57	80[2]	61	45[3]
Private letters	48	88	43	79

[1]Excluding 7 instances of *I'll*.
[2]Excluding 4 instances of *'ll*, with various subject pronouns.
[3]Excluding 76 instances of *'ll*, with various subject pronouns.

Even in handbooks, scientific texts and official letters, the proportion of *will* is high in EModE2 and in the more speech-like and subjective genres, including the sermons, it is the majority variant. The figures for EModE3 show that this development continues towards the end of the seventeenth century. Perhaps surprisingly, in the case of this syntactic feature, the development of the standard followed the natural, spoken expression; it was influenced by change from below rather than by change from above.[7]

4.2   Multiple negation

In the development of negative expressions legal texts may have offered an early model that resulted in the avoidance of multiple or universal negation in Late Middle and Early Modern English.

In Late Middle English, multiple negation was still accepted and universal negation was only gradually becoming obsolete, possibly with the loss of *ne*. In the fifteenth century, the *not . . . no* construction (example 4) was still the rule (see e.g. Fischer 1992: 284), but in the Helsinki Corpus samples of legal texts this combination does not occur even once, while the combination *not . . . any* (example 5), can be found no less than eight times. In other contexts, such as are exemplified in (6) and (7), multiple negation occurs even in the statutes, but the use of *any* is more common than in the other genres.

(4)   But grant me þat ʒe be **not** wrothe wyth **no** man þat I brynge wytt me into yowr presens. (c.1500, *Siege of Jerusalem* [SJERUS] 88)

(5)   Provided that this acte be **not** available to **eny** *per*son for **any** entre syn the first day of this *pre*sent parliament. (1488–91, *The Statutes of the Realm* [STAT2] 550)

(6)   . . . to ordeyne and establissh . . . that **no** bocher **nor** his *ser*vaunt slee **no** man*er* best within the seid house called the Skaldyng house, (1488–91, *The Statutes of the Realm* [STAT2] 528)

(7)   Wherfor the Kyng oure So*ve*reign lorde . . . hath ordeyned establisshed and enacted that **no** fyner of Golde and Silver, **nor** parter of the same by fyre or water, fromhensforth alay **no fyne Silver** nor Golde, **nor none** sell in **eny** other wise **ne** to **eny** other parsone or parsones but only to thoffycers of myntes chaunges and Goldsmythes within this Realme, (1488–91, *The Statutes of the Realm* [STAT2] 526)

Note the use of both *no* and *any* in (7).

The same trend can be seen in sixteenth-century texts: the *not . . . no* type is avoided in the statutes while it is still an accepted minority variant in other text types. This is not surprising, since the tendency towards disambiguation and clarity of expression probably resulted in the avoidance of double negation in legal texts well before the normative grammarians started arguing about two negatives making one affirmative.

4.3   Provided (that)

The language of law needs links which show relations between concepts in an unambiguous and, at the same time, economical way. The conditional subordinator *provided that*, meaning 'on the condition that', 'if' (example 8), may well have been introduced into the standard by the language of law.

(8)   Except and **provided that** yt be ordyned by the seid auctorite, that the le*tt*res patentes late made by the Kyng to Thomas Lorde Dacre of Maister Foster of the seid forest, stand and be goode and effectuell to the same Thomas after the teno*ur* and effecte of the same le*tt*res patentes, the seid Acte not withstondyng.

    Provided also that this acte extend not ne be p*r*ejudiciall to Henry Erle of Northumberlond, of or for eny graunt le*tt*res patentes or confirmacion made by the Kyng oure Sov*er*eigne Lorde to the seid Erle. (1489–91, *The Statutes of the Realm* II [STAT2] 532)

The first examples of this link are recorded by the *MED* from the 1420s. All early examples are formulaic and occur in documents and statutes. The Helsinki Corpus evidence clearly points to the introduction of this word into the standard through administrative language.[8]

Table 4. *Provided that* in the Helsinki Corpus

ME4 (1420–1500)

Laws	10

EModE1 (1500–70)

Laws	18
Trials	1[1]

EModE2 (1570–1640)

Laws	12
Handbooks	2[2]
Official letters	1

EModE3 (1640–1710)

Laws	24
Handbooks	1
Scientific texts	2
Philosophy	1
Fiction	3

[1]In a quotation from a statute.
[2]Both examples occur in Markham's *Countrey Contentments*, dating from 1615.

Provided (that) seems not to be established outside the administrative domain before c.1600. There are nine examples in Shakespeare, two without *that*, as in the following:

(9)   If I come off and leave her in such honour as you have trust in, she your jewel, this your jewel, and my gold are yours, **provided** I have your commendation for my more free entertainment. (*Cymbeline* I, 4: 151)

By the end of the seventeenth century, *provided* has found its way even into highly colloquial contexts:

(10)   The Rival cruelly vext; got a red hot iron, and comes again, tell her he had brought her a Ring, **provided** she would give him another kiss; (1684–5, *Penny Merriments* [PENNY] 159)

4.4   Compound adverbs

It is not surprising that the tendency toward compact anaphoric referentiality favoured the use of compound adverbs formed by *here* or *there* and a preposition (*hereby*, *therewith*, *thereto*, etc.). In her very thorough study Aune Österman (1997) has shown that these adverbs increase in number and frequency from Old English to the seventeenth century, after which there is a rapid decrease. One reason for their waning popularity may be that they represent, in a way, an untypical structural development in English: from analyticity to syntheticity. The only compound that has really become a grammaticalised part of English is *therefore*.

In the language of law, however, these compounds offered a welcome means of cohesive reference, more compact than the ordinary prepositional phrase. Even in the Late Middle English laws they are very common, as can be seen in Table 5. The figures per 10,000 words given in brackets show that these compounds are much more frequent in the statutes than in other genres both in Late Middle and Early Modern English.

Table 5. Compound adverbs formed with *there-/here-* and a preposition in Late Middle and early Modern English in the Helsinki Corpus. (Figures per 10,000 words in brackets.)

	Statutes	Other texts
ME4 (1420–1500)	68 (60)	621 (31)
EModE1 (1500–70)	77 (65)	503 (28)
EModE2 (1570–1640)	84 (71)	461 (26)
EModE3 (1640–1710)	126 (96)	191 (12)

In Early Modern English, there is an interesting difference between the development in legal texts and other genres. While there is a dramatic drop in the frequency of these compounds in general (see also the table in Österman 1997:

194–8; 200), the number of tokens and, incidentally, the number of types, increases in the statutes. It seems likely that the language of administration favoured the adoption of compound adverbs in the standard. Gradually, however, the general analytic trend, which favours prepositional phrases at the cost of accidence or derivation, stops this development in genres other than the statutes, in which compound adverbs continued to have a referential-cohesive function.

Unfortunately, space does not permit a discussion of the influence of legal language on semantically meaningful lexis. Although its narrow code restricts the role played by this genre, it is obvious that laws and documents were of importance in fixing terminology and special vocabulary as parts of the standard. Most of the early laws dealt with trade and other features of everyday city and country life. The definition of items and concepts was important, and a terminology with fine distinctions was probably established and distributed by administrative texts. The following extract dealing with cloth-making, which dates from 1511–12, illustrates the occurrence of special terms in the statutes:

AN ACT AGAYNST DECEYPTFULL MAKING OF WOLLEN CLOTH.

. . . the Wolle whiche shalbe delyv*e*red for or by the **Clothier** to any p*e*rsone or p*e*rsones for **brekyng kembyng cardyng** or **spy*n*nyng** of the same the delyv*e*re therof shalbe by even just and true **poise** and weight of **haberdepois** sealid by auctorite not excedyng in weight after the rate of xij pounde Wolle **seymed** above oon quart*e*r of a pound for the **waste** of the same wolle and in noon other maner; And that the **breker** or **kember** to delyv*e*r agayn to the seid Clothier the same Woll so **broken** and **kempt** and the **carder** and **Spynner** to delyv*e*r agayn to the same Clothier yerne of the same Woll by the same even just and true **poise** and weight the **wast** thereof excepted without any part therof concealyng or eny more oyle water or other thyng put therunto deceyvably. (1511–12, *The Statutes of the Realm* [STAT3] 28)

5   Concluding remark

It is obvious that the the language of law is of considerable importance not only in the standardisation of spelling but also in the development of syntactic features and grammaticalised lexis. Without the slightest doubt, any discussion of the rise of Standard English which does not pay due attention to early statutory texts will tell us only part of the story.

Notes

1 But cf. the discussion of the variability of certain spellings in the statutes and other types of text in Late Middle and Early Modern English in Rissanen 1999.

2 The following extracts from *The Statutes of the Realm* are included in the Helsinki

Corpus: Vol. II (1488–1491; 11,240 wds), 524/10–535/42; 549/6–555.13. Vol. III (1509–1543; 11,790 wds), 8/1–9/33; 26/28–29/61; 31/49–32/19; 33/43–34/33; 906/1–907/57; 909/48–911/14. Vol. IV (1588–1604; 11,780 wds), 810/12–811/30; 852/11–853/55; 857/1–859/63; 1026/1–1027/35; 1028/1–1029/10; 1058/10–1058/47; 1060/23–1061/56. Vol. VII (1695–1699; 13,180 wds), 75/1–77/20; 97/20–98/32; 210/22–211/49; 454/27–460/7; 586/10–587/51.

3 Reference is also made to the corpus consisting of the letters and documents in Fisher, Richardson and Fisher (1984). This corpus of some 70,000 words is stored in an electronic form by the University of Virginia computing centre; it is available through the Oxford Text Archive and the WWW.

4 Only the forms *shall* and *will* (with various spellings) are included in these figures, not the forms *should* and *would*.

5 The capitalised titles in square brackets refer to the abbreviations as given in the Manual of the Helsinki Corpus (Kytö 1996: 167–230).

6 There is one instance of the type *will and shall sue*. There are only four examples of *shall sue* in these samples.

7 An analysis of the usage with various subject pronouns would sharpen the picture of the development but is outside the scope of the present survey. It might be pointed out, however, that the rather high proportion of *shall* in fiction and comedy in EModE3 may be due to a gradually developing tendency to favour this pronoun with first-person subjects.

8 The formulaic *provided that* can also be found in the documents in Fisher, Richardson and Fisher (1984). There are altogether seven instances, all dating from the 1450s.

References

Benskin, Michael 1992. 'Some new perspectives on the origins of standard written English', in *Dialect and Standard Language in the English, Dutch, German and Norwegian Language Areas*, ed. J. A. van Leuvensteijn and J. B. Berns, Amsterdam: North Holland, pp. 71–105.

Blake, N. F. 1996. *A History of the English Language*, Basingstoke and London: Macmillan.

Fischer, Olga 1992. 'Syntax', in *The Cambridge History of the English Language*, ed. Norman Blake, Cambridge University Press, pp. 207–408.

Fisher, John F., Malcolm Richardson and Jane L. Fisher 1984. *Chancery English*, Knoxville, Tennessee: University of Tennessee Press.

Kytö, Merja 1996. *Manual to the Diachronic Part of the Helsinki Corpus of English Texts* 3rd edn, Helsinki: Department of English, University of Helsinki.

Kytö, Merja and Matti Rissanen 1993. ' "By and by enters [this] my artificiall foole . . . who, when Jack beheld, sodainely he flew at him": Searching for syntactic constructions in the Helsinki Corpus', in *Early English in the Computer Age: Explorations Through the Helsinki Corpus*, ed. M. Rissanen, M. Kytö and M. Palander-Collin, Berlin and New York: Mouton de Gruyter, pp. 253–66.

Milroy, James 1992. *Linguistic Variation and Change*, Oxford and Cambridge, Mass.: Blackwell.

Milroy, James and Lesley Milroy 1985. 'Linguistic change, social network and speaker innovation', *Journal of Linguistics*, 21.2, 339–84.

Mustanoja, Tauno F. 1960. *A Middle English Syntax*, Helsinki: Société Néophilologique.

Österman, Aune 1997. 'There compounds in the history of English', in *Grammaticalization at Work: Studies of Long-term Developments in English*, ed. Matti Rissanen, Merja Kytö and Kirsi Heikkonen, Berlin and New York: Mouton de Gruyter, pp. 191–276.

Rissanen, Matti 1999. 'Language of law and the development of Standard English', in *Writing in Non-Standard English*, ed. Irma Taavitsainen, Gunnel Melchers and Päivi Pahta, Amsterdam and Philadelphia: Benjamins, pp. 189–204.

Samuels, M. L. 1989 [1963]. 'Some applications of Middle English dialectology', revised in *Middle English Dialectology: Essays on some Principles and Problems*, ed. Margaret Laing, Aberdeen University Press, pp. 64–80. Originally published in *English Studies* 44, 81–94.

The Statutes of the Realm, vols. II–IV, VII, 1963 (1816–20), London: Dawsons.

Sandved, Arthur O. 1981. 'Prolegomena to a renewed study of the rise of Standard English', in *So meny people longages and tonges: philological essays in Scots and mediaeval English presented to Angus McIntosh*, ed. Michael Benskin and M. L. Samuels, Edinburgh: Middle English Dialect Project, pp. 31–42.

Wright, Laura 1996. 'About the evolution of Standard English', in *Studies in English Language and Literature: 'Doubt wisely', Papers in Honour of E.G. Stanley*, ed. M. J. Toswell and E. M. Tyler, London and New York: Routledge, pp. 99–115.

8   Scientific language and spelling standardisation 1375–1550

IRMA TAAVITSAINEN

1   Aim and outline of this study

The aim of this article is to assess spellings in scientific writing c.1375–1550 in relation to the incipient standardisation of spelling in some Central Midlands text types and the spread of the national standard spelling system. I approach the topic from a sociolinguistic point of view, taking into account the sociohistorical setting of the time and its nationalistic language policy. The language of science formed a new register in English during this period, widening the functions of the vernacular to the prestige area of learning; the conventions of writing science were transferred from authoritative Greco-Roman models. The vernacularisation process started in the latter half of the fourteenth century and continued to the seventeenth century.[1] Thus it coincides with the process of language standardisation, as the period from 1400 to 1660 was concerned with the establishment of a written standard throughout the country (Blake 1996: 12).

    This article claims that the form of the new register of scientific writing was a conscious choice, both distinct and influential. This language variety is known as the Central Midland Standard in the literature, and it has mainly been associated with Wycliffite writings. In the present paper it will be referred to as the Central Midland spelling system in scientific texts, as this is a more precise label for the features considered here. The empirical part of this study proves that Central Midland spellings were widely disseminated in scientific writing and continued in use in the late fifteenth century. The process of the spread of the national standard in this register differs somewhat from the pattern established in other fields of writing. The new discoveries pose new questions about the relation between scientific language and the Wycliffite variety, and about the place of origin of the Central Midland spelling system. They are discussed at the end, but remain to be answered in further studies.

2   Vernacularisation processes of scientific writing

The general language policy of late medieval England may provide the key to the vernacularisation of scientific writing. It seems to have been part of the same nationalistic policy that promoted the use of English in administration and literature. According to the current view, the use of the vernacular was promoted by conscious Lancastrian policy; the aim was to enforce their power against the French, so that English became the language of administration (Fisher 1992). The role of literary language in establishing the position of English was parallel: the creation of a national literature was part of the Lancastrian promotion of English nationalism against the French. The development of a literary canon can be regarded as an essential credential of English as a written language (Blake 1996: 176). Chaucer's role in transferring literary influences and establishing this canon has been recognised, and it is also significant that he wrote the *Astrolabe* (1391), and perhaps the *Equatory* (c.1393),[2] which meant the introduction of the scientific register into his writings.

The language varieties of education and science are often the result of nationalistic movements and are considered a prerequisite for a full repertoire of language.[3] The creation of a learned register involves a conscious effort and a nationalistic language policy, e.g. as proclaimed in the following:

> Aristoteles bokes and oþere bokes also of logyk and philosofy were translated out of Gru into Latyn. <Also atte> prayng of K<yng> Charles, Iohn Scot translatede Seint Denys hys bokes out of Gru ynto Latyn. <Al>so holy wryt was <tran>slated out of Hebre<w> ynto Gru and out of Gru into Latyn and <þanne> out of Latyn y<n>to Frensch. þanne what haþ Engly<sch> trespased þat hyt myȝt noȝt be translated into Englysch? Also Kyng Alured, þat foundede þe vnyuersite of Oxenford, translatede þe beste lawes into Englysch tonge and a gret del of þe Sauter out of <Latyn> into Englysch, and made Wyrefryth, byschop of Wyrcetre, translate Seint Gregore hys bokes Dialoges out of Latyn ynto Saxon. Also Cedmon of Whyteby was inspired of þe Holy Gost and made wonder poesyes an Englysch nyȝ of al þe storyes of holy wryt. Also þe holy man Beda translatede Seint Iohn hys gospel out of Latyn ynto Englysch. . . . þanne Englysch translacion ys good and neodfol. (Trevisa, *Dialogue Inter Dominum et Clericum*, MS Cotton Tib. D Vii, ff. 1v–2, ed. Waldron 1988: 292–3)

The above quotation from the *Dialogue between the Patron and his Clerk* is prefixed to the translation of *Polychronicon*, which was completed in 1387. It appears that Thomas Berkeley and Trevisa had a fully fledged language policy with an ambitious goal, comparable to that of King Alfred. This was the underlying motivation for undertaking the translations of *Polychronicon* and later *De Proprietatibus Rerum* (completed in 1398/9).

The vernacularisation process of scientific writing in late medieval Europe was an outcome of such nationalistic aims and took place in a larger frame, as a pan-European phenomenon, with parallel developments in several countries (see *Early Science and Medicine* 1998). It started in England in the latter half of the fourteenth century, perhaps c.1375, and a good number of scientific manuscripts survive from the early period. Medicine led the way, but texts of other branches of science were translated as well; Trevisa's translation of the most important contemporary encyclopaedia was an important achievement. Most medical texts were translations or adaptations mainly from Latin sources, – Lanfrank's and Chauliac's texts, for example, are learned translations, with transferred features (see Taavitsainen and Pahta, 1998) – but there were also new compositions in English. The field of surgery is especially prominent in this respect, as three of the four most eminent surgeries produced in England were written in the vernacular and only John Arderne wrote in Latin (Voigts 1989: 390).[4] The scope of written English widened to encompass academic treatises and surgical texts as well as guidebooks to health; remedies had a longer vernacular tradition. In contrast to scientific and medical texts, religious writing had a continuity with earlier periods, though biblical translations in prose were new, and were roughly contemporary with the first scientific texts in English.

3   External evidence of medical book production and local language

The mode of book trade and manufacture in fifteenth-century London was quite different from that practised in monastic scriptoria (Christianson 1989: 96). Secular copying flourished, and there is sociohistorical evidence of a specialised production of medical and scientific codices in London. The Delta scribe produced five manuscripts in prose in the early fifteenth century, four of which are scientific or medical (Voigts 1989: 384, Doyle and Parkes 1978). In the mid-fifteenth century for example, John Multon, of the dynasty of London stationers and Roger Marchall, with Cambridge connections, worked there (Voigts 1989: 379, 382, 385; Voigts 1995; Getz 1990: 259–60). A large number of texts is associated with Multon, but only one manuscript, now Trinity College Cambridge MS R.14.52, consists of medical and scientific texts (Gross 1996: 116–17; Pahta 1998: 123–6).[5] Another group of manuscripts produced in London or Westminster at this time comprises eight medical, alchemical and astrological manuscripts; six of them form the so-called 'Sloane' group.[6] They are so similar that it appears that an individual or a group co-ordinated and controlled their subject-matter and presentation (Voigts 1989: 384–5; 1990: 37).

Another, linguistically more northern centre of scribal activity in medical writing in the fifteenth century has been identified by McIntosh (1983). Manuscripts that show strong similarities are surgical, mostly copies of Chauliac's and Arderne's works, but not wholly limited to them (see below). The evidence for their distribution comes solely from their linguistic features. The dialect of these manuscripts is Central Midland, but the exact location has not been verified (see below), and we do not have external evidence of their place of origin.

London is by far the most important area for the development of writing standards in the Late Middle English period. It was the place of origin of the emerging national standard in the fifteenth century, and before it some other forms of London English (Samuels' Types II and III) were important. There were various language varieties within the area and the Midland component in London English was considerable. The influence of the Central Midlands has been explained by various sociohistorical factors such as immigration into the metropolis and good transport and communication connections (Samuels 1989 [1963]: 74). It has been stated that the direction of change in the London population was from East Anglian to Central Midland in the fifteenth century and that the dialects of the capital converged markedly on the Central Midland type (Blake 1996: 173; Benskin 1992: 92), although this story is questioned in other papers in the present volume and elsewhere (see Wright 1996).

The various text types within the London area as identified by Samuels in 1963 can be associated with particular scribes and scriptoria (Samuels 1989 [1963], Fisher 1977). What Samuels called the 'Central Midland Standard', his Type I, has, according to Blake, the best claim to be the first literary standard after the period of French and Latin dominion (Blake 1996: 169). It has proved difficult to localise texts written in this or other Central Midland dialects (see below). In his seminal article Samuels associates his 'Central Midland Standard' with London (Samuels 1989 [1963]: 67).

The role of printing in spreading the form of a London-based standard, not necessarily identical with that of the Chancery, may have been important (Blake 1996: 11). The use of printing provided prescriptive norms and can be correlated with the contemporary growth of vernacular literacy, meaning the ability to read. A survey of the locations of printed medical books follows the common pattern.[7] The great majority are from London; the university towns of Oxford and Cambridge are the only other locations of printing.

4   'Central Midland Standard' and the national standard

A standard language of this period can be characterised as a taught language, which means that different writing systems that were amalgamated from different dialect forms developed an existence of their own; the systems were taught to scribes and copyists no matter what their own dialect was (Blake 1996: 172–3). Other definitions of a standard language emphasise a wider geographic area than where the language form originated, describing it as a model considered worthy of imitation by people outside the geographical area or social group within which the variety arose (Sandved 1981: 31), with maximal variety in function and minimal variation in form (Leith 1983: 32–3). Fixed spelling, lexicon and grammar, and the use of a set of established rules that signals competence have been given as criteria (Smith 1996: 65); others look simply for uniformity of usage (Milroy 1992: 158). All these definitions imply that standard language is achieved by education, which has prestige value. The nature of the process has been described as a selection of variant forms and a gradual abandonment of local and regional usage (Sandved 1981: 32).

Before and simultaneously with the rise of the national standard, there were language forms that were less obviously dialectal. The most important was the Central Midland spelling system, based on the dialects of Northamptonshire, Huntingdonshire, and Bedfordshire, but not localisable to any one place (Samuels 1989 [1963], *LALME* vol. I: 40). It was claimed to be readily understandable over large areas of the country, as Trevisa (or Higden) claims of the Midland type of language: 'men of myddel Engelond . . . vnderstondeþ betre þe syde longages, norþeron and souþeron, þan northeron and souþeron vnderstondeþ eyþer oþer' (Trevisa, *Polychronicon*),[8] although whether this was ever actually true is questionable. There were enough writings using this spelling system to provide a model, and sufficient prestige to exert an influence on scribes' writing habits in a larger area. It was current before 1430 and continued to be written till the later fifteenth century (Samuels 1989 [1963]: 68; Blake 1996: 170).[9] It is a distinct, well-defined spelling system and thus different from the 'colourless' system, which forms a continuum in which the local elements are muted (*LALME* vol I: 47). The main bulk of writing that uses it are Wycliffite tracts and other religious and devotional treatises, and it has been speculated that it was probably due to the negative values associated with Lollardism that it lost its position and never developed into a national standard spelling system (Burnley 1989: 24–5). In a footnote to his 1963 article, Samuels lists the main categories of manuscripts in this language form and mentions secular works, including the following medical writings: Lanfrank's 'Cirurgerie' in Bodleian Library MS Ashmole 1396, and two scientific manuscripts, British Library MS Royal 17.A.III and British Library MS Sloane 73, both containing various anonymous medical tracts. Twenty years after Samuels' article McIntosh pointed out a cluster of mainly surgical manuscripts in Central Midland dialects (McIntosh 1983). No attention has been paid to these remarks and their implications, or to the Central Midland texts of scientific register in *LALME* that escape definite localisation.

The spread of the national standard spelling system involved various stages of abandoning local variants in favour of other forms in more widespread use, which although still native to the local dialect were common currency over wider areas (Samuels 1981: 43). Such 'colourless' regional spelling was common in the fifteenth century by the side of the more dialectal varieties, so that many locations had two written systems, a local register used in texts for local use, and an upper, more neutral register of the 'colourless' type for writings intended for a wider use or more exalted public (*LALME* I: 47). Administrative language is usually taken as indicating the degree to which the processes of development towards the national standard had spread by 1550. Some other types of writing, such as private letters (e.g. Gómez-Soliño 1981, Raumolin-Brunberg and Nevalainen 1990) and literary texts (Blake 1997), have been studied, but scientific language has not been considered in this connection. The language of science belongs to an upper register of language use, and can be claimed to be just as prestigious as administrative or literary language, especially as the Middle English period is characterised by the absence of a fully institutionalised standard variety. It is possible that the spread of the national standard may have taken place at different rates in different genres of writing.

5   LALME: Central Midland counties and scientific writings

The area of origin for the Central Midland spelling system has been identified as Northamptonshire, Huntingdonshire, and Bedfordshire (Samuels 1989 [1963]: 67). These three counties show a predominance of religious writings in the source list for the *Linguistic Atlas of Late Mediaeval English* (*LALME*). In Bedfordshire, the majority of the analysed materials are religious, including several Wycliffite tracts, but the medico–alchemical MS Sloane 73 (see above) is also included. In Huntingdonshire, Wycliffite materials predominate, so that at least eight of the twelve are Wycliffite texts, the contents of three manuscripts are not stated, and one is 'a gospel harmony'. The additional materials show the same bias. Northamptonshire sources seem to be more varied, though it is difficult to say precisely as the contents of all manuscripts are not given. Wycliffite and other religious texts predominate, but additional materials include 'A Treatise of Surgery' by St William of Tonke in MS Sloane 563, with a note on its language being rather mixed but containing elements from this county; its linguistic profile is not given.

The difficulties with the Central Midland materials have been recognised in the introduction to *LALME*: the spellings of a manuscript may be Central Midland, but the local origin escapes identification, and the spelling system was adopted by writers from areas far beyond the Midlands. These conclusions rest on a large number of witnesses and, as it appeared that little could be gained by investigating more material of the same type, such writings were passed over as regards the *LALME* sources. As a result the materials are distorted (*LALME* I: 40). This statement is given in connection with 'literary manuscripts'. The only other parallel category is 'documents', so the former may well include medical and scientific texts, which, however, are usually classified as non-literary.

Thus scientific writing is an understudied and neglected area, and the sources of *LALME* in general contain relatively few medical and scientific texts.[10] In view of the characterisation of the Central Midland spelling system as containing features of various Midland counties, the neighbouring regions should also be considered, especially as Leicestershire and Rutland features seem to be frequent in medical manuscripts (see below).

6   Spelling features of the Central Midlands and the spreading national standard

In view of the hypothesis that the Central Midland spelling system should be more firmly associated with scientific texts, I decided to test its spread empirically in our computer-readable Corpus of Early English Medical Writing (see below). For this purpose I established a list of features typical of this language form. Samuels's article (1989 [1963]) gives the following items as core features of 'Central Midland Standard': *sich* 'such', *mych* 'much', *ony* 'any', *silf* 'self', *stide* 'stead', *ʒouun* 'given', and *siʒ* 'saw'. It has been stated that this orthography should be fairly uniform and admit relatively little internal variation (Samuels 1989 [1963]; Sandved 1981: 40; Benskin 1992: 84). A closer examination of *LALME* materials reveals variation in these items. The only 'Linguistic Profile' (as it is termed in *LALME*) of a scientific manuscript in a dialect of the three core counties is that of MS Sloane 73 (LP 4708 Beds), the *Book of Quinte Essence*.[11] The core items show the following forms in it:

> Sloane 73, LP 4708: *siche* (*sich*), *myche* ((*miche, mych*)), *ony, silf, stide, stede, ʒouen, ʒeuen, ʒeven, ʒouen, siʒen* (pt-pl)

Thus besides the core forms, the variants MICH(E, STEDE, ʒOUEN, ʒEUEN, ʒEVEN, ʒOVEN should be taken into account in this register, and these variants should also be assessed. Some of the items occur in the above form in the two Linguistic Profiles of scientific writings given from Leicestershire, but on the whole there is more variation. These Linguistic Profiles include the following forms:

> Yale University Medical Library, Foulton MS (Gynaecology) LP 432: *syche, sych* (*such*), *mych* (*myche*) ((*muche, mykull*)), *ony, selfe, styd*. This manuscript has been edited, and it is included in our corpus, "Wymmen"; see below.

> Takamiya 59. (Guy de Chauliac's Chirurgery). LP 767: *siche, any* (*eny*), *miche* (*myche*), *selfe, silfe* ((*selffe*)), *giffen* (*geffen, geven, ʒeuen*), *sawe*. The edition of the text is based on another manuscript, see below.

These variants should also be considered. In addition, I decided to supplement the list with some other features of Linguistic Profile 4708 in order to build a more extensive basis for this pilot study. I selected the following items: *ech(e, aftir, ʒit, ʒitt, þoruþ, þorouʒ, aftirward, eyr(e, eir(e* 'air', *bitwix, brenn, bisy, iʒe, yʒe* 'eye', *fier, heed, lyue, moun* (pl. 'may'), *puple, peple, renn,* and *togidere*. They are common in the Central Midland counties, but otherwise their occurrence is limited.

Of the variant forms that in the earlier literature have been noticed as significant for the spread of the 'Chancery Standard' spelling system (Blake 1997; Fisher 1996; Benskin 1992), I chose three core forms that in the Central Midlands deviate from the Chancery Standard: *such, much,* and *any*. Some Central Midland forms were absorbed into mainstream London or Westminster usage, but these three were not. The forms *sich, mich,* or *ony*, whenever they occur, point to either an immigrant from Central Midlands, or a writer looking directly to the Central Midlands for his model (Benskin 1992: 92).

7   Material of this study: the Corpus of Early English Medical
      Writing

The material of the empirical part of this study comes from the Corpus of Early
English Medical Writing under analysis at the English Department of the
University of Helsinki. Its first part, 1375–1550, contains c.500,000 words.[12]
The selection is nearly complete, but final proofreading is lacking. We try to
include as wide a range as possible and include all editions of Middle English
medical writing known to us and available to us. In our selection of material we
have to rely on editions; unfortunately most of the manuscripts mentioned by
McIntosh and Voigts remain unedited. Various levels of writing are represented, from academic treatises to remedybooks. As the underlying traditions and
vernacularisation processes of these types are very different (see Voigts 1984,
Taavitsainen and Pahta 1997 and 1998), I decided to focus on the more learned
writings of prestige, with surgical texts in the forefront. A glance through the
source materials of *LALME*, and an initial search of the recipes and remedies in
our Corpus proved that remedybooks have a very different pattern of distribution, which is best dealt with in another study (forthcoming).

   Only two Linguistic Profiles of manuscripts included in our Corpus are
given in *LALME: The Book of Quinte Essence* in British Library MS Sloane 73
and the Linguistic Profile of 'Wymmen' in Yale Medical Library MS 47. The
LALME source list gives locations of some texts but detailed analysis is lacking. Other information about the origin of texts can be gleaned from the
introductions of editions, but older editions do not include this information, or
some of it may be outdated. Trevisa's work has been edited from British
Library Add. MS 27944. The date of the manuscript is probably c.1410 and it
is in 'standardised southwestern dialect with southern admixtures, copied
verbatim from its exemplar in London or Westminster' (Seymour 1988: 12).
More recent editions rely on the *LALME* method, but as several manuscripts
are from the middle of the fifteenth century, the spread of the national standard may make their localisation difficult or impossible. For instance, the
language of Gilbertus Anglicus is dated c.1460 and described as 'late transitional English of the southeast Midlands that can best be described as standard
English' (Getz 1991: 64). There may be external facts that connect text to
places, e.g. *The Commonplace Book of Robert Reyne of Acle* from the end of the
fifteenth century is from Norfolk, but its date is very late for the language to
exhibit dialectal features. The zodiacal lunary is edited from the Guild-book of
the Barber-Surgeons of York, and in spite of its late date, 1486, it is written in
genuine dialect with some standardised features (Taavitsainen 1994). The date
is important as peripheral forms were often replaced by more common ones,
the result being 'colourless' or levelled regional spelling. Unfortunately we do
not have the exact dates or localisations of most texts. The great majority must
be from after 1430, when the influence of the spreading national standard
started to be felt away from London. Because of such vagueness, this study

must be taken as indicative only, and much work remains to be carried out in the future.

8 Occurrences of Central Midland and national standard spellings

The results of the lexical searches are given here according to the special fields of medicine; texts may easily have influenced others in the same field, according to medieval practices. A short title of the work is given first (see the appendix for the editions), the manuscript is stated next with possible information about the dialect and date and the source of information. The lexemes of interest for the spread of the Chancery Standard spelling system are given in bold. Instead of the *LALME* notation system, absolute frequencies are more accurate for the present purpose; they are indicated in brackets. Point one lists the Central Midland spellings of Samuels' core list and the corresponding Chancery Standard (CS) spellings thereafter. Point two lists additional items selected from the Linguistic Profiles mentioned above.

Surgery 1375–1475

Lanfrank's 'Cirurgie'. MS. Bodleian Library Ashmole 1396. 'Central Midland Standard' (Samuels 1963).
1) **sich (2), myche (19), ony (13)**, silf
2) ech, aftir, aftirward, eyr, eir, fier, heed, renne, moun, togidere

Lanfrank's 'Chirurgia parva'. Wellcome MS 397. SEML or SCML (Asplund 1970).
1) stede, selfe; CS: **suche (11), muche (24), eny (15)**
2) eche, aftir, ʒit, brenn, eyr, moun, renn

Arderne's 'Fistula'. British Library MS Sloane 6. Rutland (*LALME*).
1) **sich(e (52), syche (1), sych (1) mych(e (47), mich (38), ony (2)**, stede, selfe, giffen; CS **such(e (20), much (3), any (73)**
2) eche, aftir, aftirward, brenne, bisy, lyue, puple, renne

Chauliac's 'Cyrurgie'. Paris, Bibliothèque Nationale MS Anglais 25.
1) stede; CS: **suche (4), eni (1)**
2) eche, heed, renn

Chauliac's 'Ulcers'. New York, Academy of Medicine MS 12. English possibly of NE Leicestershire or SW Lincolnshire, but seems to contain an element from further South in Leicestershire (*LALME*).
1) **sich (18), sych (2), mych (21)**, selfe, giffen; CS: **any (8)**
2) brenn, renne

Chauliac's 'Wounds'. *Ibid.*
1) **sich (15), sych (2), mych (20), mich (1)**, selfe, stede, giffen;

CS: much (1), any (10)
2) lyue, moun

'Morstede's Surgery'. British Library MS Harley 1736. Date 1446 (MS).
1) syche (4), myche (9), selfe; CS: muche (2), any (9)
2) eyre

Anonymous surgery in Wellcome MS 564.
1) sich(e (15), myche (4), ony (9), silf, ȝeuen
2) ech, aftir, aftirward, ȝitt, þoruȝ, eir, yȝe, bitwixe, heed, moun, peple, renn, togidere

Mondeville's surgery. Wellcome MS 564.
1) sich(e (23), myche (15), ony (22), stide, ȝeuen
2) ech, aftir, aftirward, ȝitt, þoruȝ, þorouȝ, bitwixe, yȝe, brenn, fier, heed, moun, togidere

Surgery 1475–1550

de Vigo's 'Chirurgerye'. Printed in 1543.
1) stede, selfe; CS: such(e (17), much(e (13), any (6)
2) eche, brenn, heed, renn

Anatomy 1375–1475

(The anonymous surgery in Wellcome MS 564 contains an anatomy part.)

Chauliac's 'Anatomy' (edition from 1964). New York, Academy of Medicine MS 13. Perhaps northern Northamptonshire, Central Midlands (Wallner 1996: 12).
1) sich (1), mych (4), selfe
2) 0

Chauliac's 'Anatomy' (edition from 1995). Glasgow University Library, Hunter MS 95. SEML (Wallner 1996: 12).
1) myche (1), selfe, stede, ȝeuen; CS: suche (1), eny (2)
2) eche, aftir, aftirward, ȝit, þoruȝ, eire, heed, yȝe, renne

Special treatises 1375–1475

Gilbertus Anglicus. Wellcome MS 537. Transitional English of the southeast Midlands (Getz 1991).
1) siche (2), myche (8), ony (5), silf; CS: suche (30)
2) eche, aftir, aftirward, (bitwixte), fier, heed, moun, renne

'Liber Uricrisiarum' 1. Huntington MS HM 505 (third quarter of the fifteenth century; Henry Daniel's translation from 1379, with Rutland associations.

Hanna 1994).
1) siche (1), myche (1), silf; CS: suche (1), any (1)
2) ech, aftirward, eyr, brenn, renn

'Liber Uricrisiarum' 2. Wellcome MS 225. The dialect is predominantly Northern with some East Midland forms (Jasin 1983, see appendix under 'Liber
Uricrisiarum' 2).
1) ony (12)
2) ȝit, eyre, renn

Epilepsy. British Library MS Royal 17.A.viii and Bodleian Library MS Rawlinson A. 393.
1) CS: such(e (3), much(e (8), any (1)
2) ȝit, brenn

Woman's Guide. British Library MS Sloane 2463.
1) ony (11), stede; CS: such(e (37), eny (2)
2) eche, thorouȝ, eyre, eir, brenn, heed, renn

'Wymmen'. Yale Medical Library MS 47 (ex dono Fulton). LP 432, Leicestershire (*LALME*).
1) syche (6), mych(e (29), mykull (1), ony (5), selfe; CS: muche (1)
2) brenn, renn

'Of Phlebotomie'. Cambridge, Gonville and Caius College MS 176/94 (SEML)
and MS 84/166. Nottinghamshire but some incongruous forms (*LALME*).
1) siche (2), mych(e (3), ony (2), geffen; CS: suche (1), any (2)
2) aftir, aftirwarde, brenn, heed, peple, renne

Reyne's 'Blood-letting'. Bodleian Library Tanner MS 407. Norfolk (*LALME*).
1) ony (1)
2) –

'Quinte Essence'. British Library MS Sloane 73. LP 4708 *LALME*.
1) sich(e (9), myche (20), miche (2), ony (8), silf, stide, stede; CS: such(e
    (2), much (5), any (3)
2) ech, aftir, aftirward, eyr, eir, bitwixe, brenn, fier, heed, renn, togidere, lyue,
    peple

Canutus Plague Treatise. British Library MS Sloane 404.
1) stede; CS: suche (12), any (7)
2) peple

Benvenutus Grassus. Glasgow, University Library MS Hunter V.8.6. Midland
dialect, more east than west, probably close to London (Eldredge 1996, see
appendix under Benvenutus Grassus).
1) mych(e (6), ony (9); CS: much(e (11), such(e (28), any (16)
2) eche, brenn, eyre, heede, peple, togiders

Special Treatises 1475–1550

Syphilis. British Library MS Sloane 389, ff. 147–53.
1) CS: **suche (1), any (3)**
2) peple

Herbals

'Agnus Castus'. Stockholm, Royal Library MS X. 90. Norfolk (*LALME*).
1) **myche (1), ony (31)**; CS: **such (2), much (1), any (1), eny (11)**
2) ech, eyre, brenn, heed, renn

'Macer'. Stockholm, Royal Library MS X. 91.
1) silf, stede; CS: **such (4), eny (10)**
2) eche, aftir, aftirward, 3it, eir(e, brenne, heed(e, peple, renn, togider

Encyclopaedias and Compendia 1375–1475

Trevisa. British Library MS Add. 27944. Standardised SW dialect with southern admixtures, copied *verbatim* from its exemplar in London or Westminster (Seymour 1988: 12).
1) **siche (5), myche (5), mich (2), ony (9)**, silf, stede; CS: **suche (115), any (9), eny (5)**
2) ech(e, aftir, 3it, eir, brenn, i3e, y3e, heed, lyue, renne

'Secretum', Ashmole. Bodleian Library Ashmole MS 396.
1) **ony (3)**, geven; CS: **such (7), much, any (9), eny (1)**
2) brenne, peple

'Secretum', Hispaniensis. Bodleian Library MS Rawlinson C. 83.
1) **ony (1)**, selfe; CS: **such(e (11), much (2), any (1)**
2) aftir, brenne, peple, renne

Encyclopaedias and Compendia 1475–1550

'Secretum', de Caritate.
1) **mych(e (28), ony (13)**
2) aftir, brenne, lyue, renne

'Secretum', Copland.
1) **ony (4), miche (9)**; CS: **such (22), any (5)**
2) eche, aftir, brenne, eyr, heed, lyue, moun, renne

Zodiacal Lunary. British Library Egerton MS 2572. The Guild-Book of the Barber-Surgeons of York. York.
1) **ony (13)**, selfe; CS: **such(e (5), any (3)**
2) heede, lyue, fier

Boorde's 'Dyetary'. Printed in 1542.
1)   selfe; CS: **such(e (28), much (2), any (53)**
2)   eche, eyre, heed, lyue

'Governal'. Printed in 1489.
1)   silf(e, sylfe, selfe; CS: **suche (13), any (4), eny (2)**
2)   eche, brenn, lyue, renne

'Elyot'. Printed in 1541.
1)   selfe; CS: **such(e (5), any (11)**

In a private discussion some ten years ago, Prof. Samuels mentioned the *ij* spellings of words like *lijf* as typical of the Central Midland spelling system, though such spellings can also be found in some other manuscripts. For example, MS Digby 88, a Leicester manuscript, has *ij* spellings which probably shows the influence of the prestigious Central Midland system (Taavitsainen 1988: 185). The spelling *ij* was found in the following words in the Corpus: *lijf*, *sijk, sijknes, wijsdom, lijknes* and *whijt*, in the following texts: *Quinte Essence*, Lanfrank's *Cirurgerie*, the anonymous surgery from 1392, Mondeville's surgery, and Gilbertus Anglicus. Of these the two first are explicitly given as Central Midland texts (see above), but the others have not been localised precisely.[13]

9   Focused use, standardised forms and medical writing

The Central Midland spellings pervade the present corpus material, which consists of nearly all edited texts of Middle English medical writing except remedybooks. For a full picture, the unedited medical manuscripts, especially those mentioned above, should also be consulted, but this was beyond the scope of this study. Some forms favoured by the Central Midland spelling system are fairly common and found over large areas of the country, and are thus native to several other counties as well, so they must be interpreted with caution.

Some patterns emerge. Most works in the above list show similarities to the Central Midland spellings. The influence of the Central Midlands is prominent in surgeries, anatomy texts and some of the special treatises e.g. in Gilbertus Anglicus. The bias towards Leicestershire and Rutland is evident, and thus the counties are not exactly the same as those mentioned by Samuels. A number of Chauliac and Arderne manuscripts come from this area: British Library MS Sloane 6 (see above) and Sloane 277 (Arderne's *Fistula*, North Leicestershire / North Rutland border) are similar in language; Sloane 1 (*LALME*: medica, North Rutland) and Takamiya 59 (see above) are close to one another; Sloane 563 (*LALME*: Hand D, possibly Rutland), Sloane 3666 (not in *LALME*) and New York Academy of Medicine 12 (see above) have affinities with both. This network was pointed out by McIntosh (1983: 243), and he concludes that wherever in the area they originated, they share so many characteristics that they must have been produced in a single scriptorium. In a note he lists further medical manuscripts which merit closer examination in relation to the above-mentioned groups.[14] Of these, Paris Bibliothèque Nationale MS Anglais 25 is included in this study, but it shows few of the features under scrutiny. In addition, McIntosh (1983: 244) refers to a number of other manuscripts that require detailed investigation, but does not specify them. Other medical material from Central Midland locations in *LALME* includes texts that have remained unedited.[15] They should be included in a future study. There seems to be ample material for a reassessment. Samuels' study and the *LALME* sources concentrate on Wycliffite tracts, and the Central Midland spelling system has previously been defined with religious manuscripts in focus. In light of the present study, the language of medical writing is not exactly the same as that of the Wycliffite texts. Several of the above manuscripts seem to escape precise location: the word 'possibly', a question mark, or some more detailed indication of the difficulty is given in connection with the localisation, which is also significant (see below).

The pattern of the spread of the national standard seems somewhat different from what would be expected on the basis of the earlier literature. The lexeme that led the spreading of the national standard was *such*, which gained ground rapidly and replaced the competing variants, so that by the 1420s the form *swich* seems to be recessive in London English (Blake 1997; Benskin 1992: 80); *swich* is not found in the present material at all. The typical Central Midland form was *sich*, which is clearly deviant from the Chancery use and London use of Type III. It seems to retain its position until fairly late; for example, Gilbertus Anglicus (c.1460) has it. Another lexeme with a deviant pattern is *any*. The Chancery English spellings are *any* and *eny*; *ony* is found in one document from 1388 only. The prevailing Central Midland spelling was *ony*. It has retained its position very well in this material as it is found even in the printed books. The third form selected for scrutiny here is *much*. The Central Midland spellings are *mych(e*, *mich(e*, which do not belong to Chancery English; they are found in Gilbertus Anglicus and Trevisa, and even late texts of the Secretum tradition have them. Further evidence for a deviant pattern in the spread of the national standard is suggested by the frequencies of other spellings which have been assumed to be typical of it. *Thees* and *þees* do not occur in the Corpus at all, *theyse* is found once in the *Governal*, *thorow* is found six times in Morstede, once in Benvenutus Grassus, and twice in Lanfrank's *Chirurgia Parva*, where *þorow* is also found twice (cf. Benskin 1992).

10   Trevisa's language policy, scientific writing and Wycliffite texts

The dialect features of Trevisa's translation of *De proprietatibus rerum* are most intriguing. He worked in Gloucestershire, a peripheral dialect area. No holograph or copy very near to the original is extant. The manuscript selected as the copytext for the edition is in a very different dialect, and although the preface states that it best preserves the original features and is a *verbatim* copy of its

London or Westminster exemplar (see above, p. 132), it shows Central Midlands characteristics. This relation to the Central Midland spelling system is striking in the above analysis. The influence of Trevisa's translations on the language policy of vernacularisation and the selection of the language type for this register seems crucial. The passage from the *Dialogue between the Patron and his Clerk* quoted above is undeniably peripheral in its linguistic features. In another text Trevisa ponders the mutual intellegibility of dialects, claiming a better position for the dialects of the Midlands in this respect. The dialect of the *Polychronicon* translation has been studied and its Gloucestershire features are explicit (see Waldron 1991); yet the most conspicuous dialect features of the above quoted *Dialogue* are not found in the translation itself, and there seems to be a curious shift towards more widely distributed forms (private discussion with Prof. Waldron).

Trevisa translated *De proprietatibus rerum* into English about ten years later than the *Polychronicon*. Trevisa may have modified his spellings in the Central Midland direction himself on purpose, to guarantee maximum intelligibility, 'for to make þis translacion cleer and pleyn to be knowe and vnderstonde' (Waldron 1988: 294), or the issue may be more complicated. Reaching an audience was central in his translation policy, and it could well be that the Midland type of language was a conscious choice to gain a larger readership.

The relation between the Wycliffite texts and the medical texts looks puzzling, but the key can be found in Trevisa's language policy and the sociohistorical evidence of his career. Trevisa spent about twenty years of his life in Oxford, and some of this period coincided with Wycliffe's stay there. Recent scholarship has found more evidence to suggest that Trevisa worked with John Wycliffe, Nicholas Hereford, and probably others on a translation of the Bible (Fowler 1995: 227; Lawler 1983; Fristedt 1953–73). This collaboration explains the connection and the use of the Central Midland spelling system in Lollard writings, and leads to conclusions about their mutual relations (see below). The choice of the spellings for Wycliffite texts could thus have been influenced by Trevisa.

11   The Delta scribe

No holograph manuscript is extant and so it is equally possible that someone else changed the spellings. One participant in the process of selecting or enforcing the Midland spellings as the variety of science could be the Delta scribe who copied both the *Polychronicon* text (Cambridge, St. John's College MS H.1 (204), British Library Add. MS 24194, and a third *Polychronicon* text, Princeton, MS Garrett 151) and Guy de Chauliac's *Cyrurgie*, now in Paris, Bibliothèque Nationale MS Anglais 25, on which the edition is based. The hand of the Delta scribe is very similar to that of scribe D who wrote British Library Add. MS 27944, which again is the base text of the edition of *Of the Properties of Things*. Evidence for the two scribes working in the same scriptorium or having a master–apprentice relationship is lacking. The most likely explanation would be that they were independent practitioners in the same neighbourhood (Doyle and Parkes 1978: 206–7; Voigts 1989: 384). Scribe D belongs to a group that was copying English works in the London area during the first quarter of the fifteenth century, and various links connect him with the workshop of Herman Schierre or Skereuyeren in London in Paternoster Row in c.1404 (Waldron 1991: 82; Christianson 1987: 50 and 1989: 96). It is interesting that the text shows Central Midland spellings. The translators and composers of surgical works had a model there, and it may be that the influence of prestige has been underestimated. It has been pointed out in the literature that the greatest progress was made in the field of surgery in this period, and these writings must have set a model for others to imitate. The creation of this upper register of science and medicine was the goal of the policy that Trevisa and his patron Thomas Berkeley had in mind.

12   Conclusions

The present study shows that the Central Midland spelling system was much more important in scientific writing than has been verified earlier. The register of scientific writing widened the functions of the vernacular to a new area of prestige. The influence of the Central Midland system seems to be pervasive in this register. It may be that Wycliffite writings took their model from scientific texts and not vice versa. Wycliffite texts circulated secretly; they were therefore not likely to exert an influence of this kind on scientific writing, whereas medical texts belonged to the more public, utilitarian sphere; their translation and composition was desirable, and official approbation was guaranteed.

The Central Midland element in London English has previously been explained by immigration, but it may rather be that other factors influenced it. The present material proves that much of the early scientific writing used the Central Midland spelling system, or had features of it. The research focus has been on religious texts, and theories of the 'Central Midland Standard' have been based on Wycliffite tracts. There is external evidence that some of the manuscripts with such features originated from the London area, the centre of secular book production, but in most cases the locations are unknown. An intriguing feature of medical texts analysed in *LALME* is that the co-occurrence patterns of dialectal spellings escape exact localisation. The case of scribe D proves that the possibility of London as the place of origin cannot be excluded, even if the dialect appears to be from the Midland area.[16]

As to the spread of the national standard, medical texts do not seem to follow the pattern established in administrative and literary writing, though the order of adoption seems to be the same. *Such* leads the process towards uniformity, in accordance with the earlier literature. There is more variation in the other items, and the variants favoured by the Chancery Standard spelling system are less prominent in scientific texts in the late fifteenth to early sixteenth century. An explanation can perhaps be found in the influence of prestige: scientific writing as an intellectual pursuit with learned connections versus administrative language with a different kind of power. The influences must have been conflicting. Thus there may have been two contrary forces working at the same time in the fifteenth century in scientific writing. The spread of the national standard spelling system in scientific writing seems to have been slower than in some other text types, presumably because of this prestige. Yet more work on more extensive materials, including unedited manuscripts, is needed for definite conclusions. Although the results of my study are tentative, they show how a variety not previously studied in detail can cast new light on one of the key questions in the history of English and indicate new topics for future studies.

Notes

I would like to thank Dr A. I. Doyle and Prof. Waldron for private discussions about the issues raised by this study at the Early Book Society Conference in Lampeter, July 1997, and Dr Jeremy Smith and Prof. Linda Voigts for their suggestions.

1 The dominant role of Latin in scientific writings lasted in England to the middle of the seventeenth century (Webster 1975: 267); Latin discourse forms served as models to vernacular texts. The dialect(s) of English used in fourteenth- and early fifteenth-century scientific writings have not been assessed. The present approach through the spelling forms is in accordance with the methodology used in *LALME*, and provides a good starting point for future studies on the spread of standardisation in other language features.

2 Scholars disagree on this issue. See Robinson 1991, Edwards and Mooney 1991, and Rand-Schmidt 1993.

3 Written language is a necessary precondition for a national standard language, and in most cases it is supported by a model of some outside language. Latin provided a guide as to what a standardised variety of English might be like (Blake 1996: 2). Prefaces are a good indicator of attitudes to the language as this topic is often explicitly treated in them. The inadequacy and rudeness of the vernacular are commonly mentioned (for a discussion of sixteenth-century materials, see McConchie 1997, ch. 2), but some more positive notes can also be found. The preface of Henry Daniel's *Liber uricrisiarum*, which is characterised as 'a schorte tretyce conteynynge fulle þe marowe of þis faculte', praises the contents and expresses a more positive and very emotive attitude towards the language: 'þe science is fair and wonderful, and also such a science is as it were propurly myche profitable vnto men . . . iwroten in þe tonge þat forsothe is ry3t dere to me' (MS Huntington HM 505, quoted from Hanna 1994: 189).

4 These are an anonymous surgery edited by Grothé, the surgery attributed to 'Thomas Morstede', though probably spuriously (see Getz 1990), and Roger Marchall's treatise, which remains unedited.

5 This is one of the most important scientific manuscripts of the period. An international project has been launched by M. Teresa Tavormina to study it in detail.

6 The following manuscripts from the 1450s and 1460s are included in this group: MSS Sloane 1313, 2567, 2948, and Sloane 2320, 1118 and BL Add. MS 19674. In

addition, other medical manuscripts are related to this group. See Voigts 1989: 384–5.

7 Of the c. 250 medical books printed in England between 1475 and 1640 only twelve were printed outside London: seven in Cambridge and five in Oxford. These figures are based on a list compiled by Dr Chris Whitty, which he kindly let us use for the Corpus work. I am not counting various editions here. Scotland had its own circulation. It has been estimated that 98 per cent of all English books were printed in London in this period (Görlach 1991: 13), which percentage is even higher than the proportion of London books in this material.

8 Trevisa gives a reason for selecting the Midland type of language for works aimed at a wider geographical distribution (see above) in a situation of emerging vernacular writing. It has been pointed out that it is not necessarily a central dialect that guarantees optimal intelligibility but one with political power and prestige (Görlach 1997: 16). This does not apply here as there was no prestige form of the vernacular at this time; the prestige form was Latin. Yet the spellings selected for scientific writing gained prestige, which is important for the present study.

9 Some of the evidence has been found untenable, but the main force of the original argument is valid (see Sandved 1981: 42).

10 A glance through the list of sources confirmed this impression. The bias is towards religious writing. Recipes have been included in several linguistic profiles, especially in Lincolnshire: LPs 277, 491, 501 and 908; surgical texts cluster to the Leicester-shire-Rutland area (see below). For the present study the other counties surrounding the three core ones would be of special interest. A search confirmed that Bucking-hamshire, Oxfordshire, Warwickshire, Peterborough, Ely and Cambridgeshire in-cluded no medical texts. No medical manuscripts of the London area are included in *LALME*.

11 MS Royal 17.A.III, also listed as a 'Central Midland Standard' manuscript, contains a lunary that I have edited (1989). Its spellings contained surprisingly few items from the list selected for this study, only *ony*, *bitwixe*, and *lyue*.

12 For details of the corpus plan see Taavitsainen and Pahta 1997. The coverage of the whole corpus extends to 1750. Its Middle English part is further divided into two periods: from 1375 to 1475, and from 1475 to 1550, with the introduction of printing into England (1476) as an extralinguistic criterion. We aim at a total of at least 1.2 million words. Shorter texts are included *in toto*, and in order to have representative material for pilot studies, we have at this point included extracts of c. 10,000 words from more comprehensive treatises. In the final version of the corpus we aim at including full texts whenever possible, as extracts are not sufficient for all our research purposes. The second part under compilation now reaches from 1550 to 1750, and the establishment of the Royal Society in 1660 serves as a dividing line there.

13 I also checked the Middle English part of the Helsinki Corpus for these spellings. *lijf* occurred 45 times: 34 times in the Wycliffite Bible, 6 times in Cursor Mundi; In MEII (1250–1350) it occurred three times in The Life of St. Edmund in the South English Legendary and twice in Kalex. Other words spelled with *ij* include *sijk*, *wijs* and *lijk*, and they occurred in the same texts.

14 MSS Sloane 374 (not in *LALME*), Sloane 505 (not in *LALME*), Sloane 965 (contains Chauliac's Anatomy). *LALME*: Northeast Leicestershire, possibly Rutland), Sloane 1721 (not in *LALME*), Sloane 2187 (not in *LALME*), Sloane 2464 (not in *LALME*),

Sloane 3466 (*LALME*: possibly Lincolnshire), Sloane 3486 (not in *LALME*), and British Library Add. 60577 (The Winchester Anthology of verse and prose. *LALME*: Hampshire).

15 They are: Sloane 7, medica, Hand A Derbyshire, Hand B Lincolnshire / W Midlands + more northerly features; Sloane 213, scientific, Hand A Nottingham-shire, Hand B mixture N and S Lincolnshire; Sloane 358 medica, N Midland language, Sloane 563 William of Tonke's Surgery, Northamptonshire; Sloane 610, medica Rutland, spellings mixed with elements of mid-Leicestershire and Southwest Lincolnshire.

16 According to *LALME* (I: 23), the dialect of the manuscript indicates the place where the scribe learned to write. This may, however, be too limited, since a language form could also be consciously adopted, as seems to be the case here.

References

Benskin, Michael 1992. 'Some new perspectives on the origins of standard written English', in *Dialect and Standard Language in the English, Dutch, German and Norwegian Language Areas*, ed. J. A. van Leuvensteijn and J. B. Berns, Amsterdam: North Holland, pp. 71–105.

Blake, Norman 1996. *A History of the English Language*, Basingstoke and London: Macmillan.

1997. 'Chancery English and the Wife of Bath's Prologue', in *To Explain the Present: Studies in the Changing English Language in Honour of Matti Rissanen*, ed. Terttu Nevalainen and Leena Kahlas-Tarkka, Mémoires de la Société Néophilologique de Helsinki 52, Helsinki: Société Néophilologique, pp. 3–24.

Burnley, David 1989. 'Sources of Standardisation in Later Middle English', in *Standard-izing English: Essays in the History of Language Change in Honor of John Hurt Fisher*, ed. Joseph B. Trahern, Jr., Knoxville: University of Tennessee Press, pp. 23–41.

Christianson, C. Paul 1987. *Memorials of the Book Trade in Medieval London: the Archives of Old London Bridge*, Cambridge: D. S. Brewer.

1989. 'Evidence for the study of London's late medieval manuscript-book trade', in *Book Production and Publishing in Britain 1375–1475*, ed. Jeremy Griffiths and Derek Pearsall, Cambridge University Press, pp. 87–108.

Doyle, A. I. and M. B. Parkes 1978. 'The production of copies of the *Canterbury Tales* and the *Confessio Amantis* in the early fifteenth century', in *Medieval Scribes, Manuscripts & Libraries: Essays Presented to N. R. Ker*, ed. M. B. Parkes and Andrew G. Watson, London: Scolar Press, pp. 163–210.

Early Science and Medicine 3.2 1998. Special issue: *The Vernacularisation of Science, Medicine, and Technology in Late Medieval Europe*, ed. William Crossgrove, Margaret Schleissner and Linda E. Voigts, Leiden: Brill.

Edwards, A. S. G. and Linne R. Mooney 1991. 'Is the *Equatorie of the Planets* a Chaucer Holograph?', *ChR* 26, 31–42.

Fisher, John H. 1977. 'Chancery and the emergence of standard written English in the fifteenth century', *Speculum* 52, 870–99.

1992. 'A language policy for Lancastrian England', *PMLA* 107, 1168–80; repr. in Fisher 1996.

1996. *The Emergence of Standard English*, Lexington: University of Kentucky Press.

Fowler, David C. 1995. *The Life and Times of John Trevisa, Medieval Scholar*, Seattle and London: University of Washington Press.

Fristedt, Sven L. 1953–1973. *The Wycliffe Bible*, 3 vols., Stockholm: Almqvist and Wiksell.

Getz, Faye 1990. 'Archives and sources: medical practitioners in medieval England', *Social History of Medicine* 3.2, 245–83.

Getz, Faye (ed.) 1991. [Gilbertus Anglicus] *Healing and Society in Medieval England: A Middle English Translation of the Pharmaceutical Writings of Gilbertus Anglicus*, Madison, Wis.: The University of Wisconsin Press.

Görlach, Manfred 1991. *Introduction to Early Modern English*, Cambridge University Press.

1997. *The Linguistic History of English. An Introduction*, Basingstoke and London: Macmillan.

Gómez-Soliño, J. S. 1981. 'Thomas Wolsey, Thomas More y la lengua inglesa estándar de su época', *Revista Canaria de Estudios Ingleses* 3, 74–84.

Gross, Anthony 1996. *The Dissolution of the Lancastrian Kingship. Sir John Fortesque and the Crisis of Monachy in Fifteenth-century England*, Stamford: Paul Watkins.

Hanna, Ralph 1994. 'Henry Daniel's Liber Uricrisiarum (Excerpt)', in *Popular and Practical Science*, 185–218.

The Helsinki Corpus of English Texts Helsinki: Department of English, University of Helsinki, 1991.

LALME. McIntosh, Angus, M. L. Samuels, Michael Benskin et al. *A Linguistic Atlas of Late Mediaeval English*, vols. I–IV, Aberdeen University Press, 1986.

Lawler, Traugott 1983. 'On the Properties of John Trevisa's Major Translations', *Viator* 14, 267–88.

Leith, Dick 1983. *A Social History of English*, London: Routledge and Kegan Paul.

Milroy, James 1992. 'Middle English Dialectology', in *The Cambridge History of the English Language*, vol. II, ed. Norman Blake, pp. 156–206.

McConchie, R. W. 1997. *Lexicography and Physicke: The Record of Sixteenth-Century English Medical Terminology*, Oxford: Clarendon Press.

McIntosh, Angus 1983. 'Present indicative plural forms in the later Middle English of the North Midlands', in *Middle English Studies Presented to Norman Davis*, ed. D. Gray and E. G. Stanley, Oxford: Clarendon Press.

Pahta, Päivi 1998. *Medieval Embryology in the Vernacular: The Case of De spermate*, Mémoires de la Société Néophilologique de Helsinki 53, Helsinki: Société Néophilologique.

Popular and Practical Science of Medieval England, ed. Lister M. Matheson, East Lansing, Mich. and Cambridge: Colleagues Press / Boydell and Brewer, 1994.

Rand-Schmidt, Kari Anne 1993 *The Authorship of the 'Equatorie of the Planetis'*, Cambridge: D. S. Brewer.

Raumolin-Brunberg, Helena and Terttu Nevalainen 1990. 'Dialectal features in a corpus of Early Modern Standard English?', in *Proceedings from the Fourth Nordic Conference for English Studies, Helsingør, May 11–13, 1989*, ed. Graham Caie et al., Copenhagen: Department of English, University of Copenhagen, vol. II, 119–31.

Robinson, Pamela 1991. 'Geoffrey Chaucer and the *Equatorie of Planetis*: The State of the Problem', *ChR* 26, 17–30.

Samuels, Michael 1989 [1963]. 'Some Applications of Middle English Dialectology', *English Studies* 44, 81–94; revised in Margaret Laing (ed.), *Middle English Dialectol-*

ogy: Essays on Some Principles and Problems, Aberdeen University Press, pp. 64–80.

   1981. 'Spelling and dialect in the late and post-Middle English periods', in *So meny people longages and tongues*, pp. 43–54.

Sandved, A. O. 1981. 'Prolegomena to a renewed study of the rise of Standard English', in *So meny people longages and tongues*, pp. 31–42.

Seymour, M. C. et al. (eds.) 1975–88. *On the Properties of Things: John Trevisa's Translation of Bartholomaeus Anglicus, De Proprietatibus Rerum*, 3 vols., Oxford: Clarendon.

Smith, Jeremy 1996. *An Historical Study of English: Function, Form and Change*, London: Routledge.

So meny people longages and tongues: philological essays in Scots and mediaeval English presented to Angus McIntosh, ed. Michael Benskin and M. L. Samuels, Edinburgh: Middle English Dialect Project.

Taavitsainen, Irma 1988. *Middle English Lunaries: A Study of the Genre*, Mémoires de la Société Néophilologique de Helsinki 47, Helsinki: Société Néophilologique.

   1989. 'Storia Lune and Its Paraphrase in Prose. Two Versions of a Middle English Lunary', *Neophilologica Fennica*, ed. Leena Kahlas-Tarkka, Mémoires de la Société Néophilologique de Helsinki 45, Helsinki: Société Néophilologique, pp. 521–55.

   1994. 'A zodiacal lunary for medical professionals', *Popular and Practical Science*, 283–98.

Taavitsainen, Irma and Päivi Pahta 1997. 'The corpus of Early English medical writing', *ICAME Journal* 21, 71–8.

   1998. 'Vernacularisation of medical writing in English: a corpus-based study of scholasticism', *Early Science and Medicine*, special issue, ed. William Crossgrove and Linda E. Voigts, 157–85.

Voigts, Linda E. 1984. 'Medical prose', in *Middle English Prose: A Critical Guide to Major Authors and Genres*, ed. A. S. G. Edwards, New Brunswick, N.J.: Rutgers University Press, pp. 315–35.

   1989. 'Scientific and medical books', in *Book Production and Publishing in Britain 1375–1475*, ed. Jeremy Griffiths and Derek Pearsall, Cambridge University Press, pp. 345–402.

   1990. 'The "Sloane Group": Related scientific and medical manuscripts from the fifteenth century in the Sloane Collection', *The British Library Journal* 16.1, 26–57.

   1995. 'A doctor and his books: the manuscripts of Roger Marchall (d. 1477)', in *New Science out of Old Books: Studies in Manuscripts and Early Printed Books in Honour of A. I. Doyle*, ed. Richard Beadle and A. J. Piper, Aldershot: Scolar Press, pp. 249–314.

Waldron, Ronald 1988. 'Trevisa's Original Prefaces on Translation: a Critical Edition', in *Medieval English Studies Presented to George Kane*, ed. Edward Donald Kennedy, Ronald Waldron, and Joseph S. Wittig, Cambridge: D. S. Brewer, pp. 285–99.

   1991. 'Dialect Aspect of Manuscripts of Trevisa's Translation of the *Polycronicon*', in *Regionalism in Late Medieval Manuscripts and Texts: Essays Celebrating the Publication of 'A Linguistic Atlas of Late Mediaeval English'*, ed. Felicity Riddy, Cambridge: D. S. Brewer, pp. 67–87.

Wallner, Björn (ed.) 1996. *An Interpolated Middle English Version of the Anatomy of Guy de Chauliac*, part II, Lund University Press.

Webster, Charles 1975. *The Great Instauration: Science, Medicine and Reform 1626–1660*, London: Duckworth.

Wright, Laura 1996. 'About the evolution of standard English', in Elizabeth M. Tyler and M. Jane Toswell (eds.), *Studies in English Language and Literature: 'Doubt Wisely', Papers in honour of E.G. Stanley*, London: Routledge, 99–115.

Appendix: Texts from the corpus of early English medical writing used in this study (1375–1550)

Surgery

Lanfrank's 'Cirurgie'. *Lanfrank's 'Science of Cirurgie'*, ed. Robert v. Fleischhacker, EETS, O.S. 102, London: Kegan Paul, Trench and Trübner, 1894.

Lanfrank's 'Chirurgia parva'. *A Middle English Version of Lanfranc's Chirurgia parva: The Surgical Part*, ed. Annika Asplund, Stockholm University, 1970.

Arderne's 'Fistula'. John Arderne's *Treatises of Fistula in Ano Hæmorrhoids, and Clysters*, ed. D'Arcy Power, EETS. O.S.139, London: Kegan Paul, Trench and Trübner and Henry Frowde, Oxford University Press, 1910.

Chauliac's 'Cyrurgie'. *The Cyrurgie of Guy de Chauliac*, ed. Margaret S. Ogden, EETS. 265, London: Oxford University Press, 1971.

Chauliac's 'Ulcers'. *The Middle English Translation of Guy de Chauliac's Treatise on Ulcers*, ed. Björn Wallner, Stockholm: Almqvist and Wiksell, 1982.

Chauliac's 'Wounds'. *The Middle English Translation of Guy de Chauliac's Treatise on Wounds*, ed. Björn Wallner, Lund: Gleerup, 1976.

Morstede's 'Surgery'. *Extracts from Morstede's 'Fair Book of Surgery'*, in *The Cutting Edge: Early History of the Surgeons of London*, ed. R. Theodore Beck, London: Lund Humphries, 1974.

Anonymous surgery in Wellcome MS 564. 'Le ms. Wellcome 564: deux traités de chirurgie en moyen-anglais', ed. Richard Grothé, dissertation, University of Montreal, 1982.

Mondeville's surgery. Wellcome MS 564. 'Le ms. Wellcome 564: deux traités de chirurgie en moyen-anglais', ed. Richard Grothé, dissertation, University of Montreal, 1982.

de Vigo's 'Chirurgerye'. Joannes de Vigo's *The Most Excellent Workes of Chirurgerye* (Facs.), Amsterdam and New York: Da Capo Press, 1968.

Anatomy

Chauliac's 'Anatomy' 1. *The Middle English Translation of Guy de Chauliac's Anatomy*, ed. Björn Wallner, Lund University Press, 1964.

Chauliac's 'Anatomy' 2. *An Interpolated Middle English Version of The Anatomy of Guy de Chauliac*, ed. Björn Wallner, Lund University Press, 1995.

Special treatises

Gilbertus Anglicus. *Healing and Society in Medieval England: A Middle English Translation of the Pharmaceutical Writings of Gilbertus Anglicus*, ed. Faye Marie Getz, The University of Wisconsin Press, 1991.

'Liber Uricrisiarum' 1. 'Henry Daniel's Liber Uricrisiarum (Excerpt)', ed. Ralph Hanna III, in *Popular and Practical Science*, 1994.

'Liber Uricrisiarum' 2. 'A Critical Edition of the Middle English Liber Uricrisiarum in Wellcome MS 225', ed. Joanne Jasin, dissertation, Tulane University, 1983.

Epilepsy. Excerpts from *Liber de Diversis Medicinis*, in 'Epilepsy: The Falling Evil', ed. George R. Keiser, in *Popular and Practical Science*, 1994.

Woman's Guide. *Medieval Woman's Guide to Health*, ed. Beryl Rowland, Kent, Ohio: The Kent State University Press, 1981.

'Wymmen'. The *'Sekenesse of Wymmen'*, ed. M.-R. Hallaert, in *Scripta 8: Mediaeval and Renaissance Texts and Studies*, ed. W. L. Braekman, Brussels: Omirel, UFSAL, 1982.

'Of Phlebotomie'. *A Middle English Phlebotomy*, ed. Linda E. Voigts and Michael R. McVaugh, Transactions of the American Philosophical Society 74, Part II, Philadelphia, 1984.

Reyne's 'Blood-letting'. 'Directions for Blood-letting', in *The Commonplace Book of Robert Reynes of Acle*, ed. Cameron Louis, New York and London: Garland, 1980.

'Quinte Essence'. *The Book of Quinte Essence or The Fifth Being; That is to say, Man's Heaven*, ed. Frederick J. Furnivall, EETS , O.S.16, London: Trübner, 1866/89.

Canutus Plague Treatise. 'A Translation of the "Canutus" Plague Treatise', ed. Joseph P. Pickett, in *Popular and Practical Science of Medieval England*, ed. Lister M. Matheson, East Lansing, Mich., 1994.

Benvenutus Grassus. *Benvenutus Grassus: The Wonderful Art of the Eye. A Critical Edition of the Middle English Translation of his 'De Probatissima Arte Oculorum'*, ed. Larry Eldredge, East Lansing, Mich.: Michigan State University Press, 1997.

Syphilis. 'An Early English Manuscript on Syphilis', ed. E. L. Zimmermann, in *Bulletin of the Institute of the History of Medicine*, vol. V, Baltimore: The Johns Hopkins Press, 1937.

Herbals

'Agnus'. *Agnus Castus: A Middle English Herbal*, ed. Gösta Brodin, Uppsala: Almqvist and Wiksell, 1950.

'Macer'. *A Middle English Translation of Macer Floridus de Viribus Herbarum*, ed. Gösta Frisk, Uppsala: Almqvist and Wiksell, 1949.

Encyclopaedias and Compendia

Trevisa. *On the Properties of Things: John Trevisa's translation of Bartholomæus Anglicus De Proprietatibus Rerum*, vol. I, ed. M. C. Seymour, Oxford, 1975.

'Secretum', Ashmole. The *'Ashmole' Version of the 'Secrete of Secretes'*, in *Secretum Secretorum: Nine English Versions*, ed. M. A. Manzalaoui, EETS 276, Oxford University Press, 1977.

'Secretum', Hispaniensis. *Johannes Hispaniensis' Regimen Sanitatis: The Booke of Goode Governance and Guyding of þe Body*, in *Secretum Secretorum: Nine English Versions*, ed. M. A. Manzalaoui, EETS 276, Oxford University Press, 1977.

'Secretum', de Caritate. *Johannes de Caritate's 'Þe Priuyté of Priuyteis'*, in *Secretum*

Secretorum: Nine English Versions, ed. M. A. Manzalaoui, EETS 276, Oxford University Press, 1977.

'Secretum', Copland. *Robert Copland's 'The Secrete of Secretes of Arystotle'*, in *Secretum Secretorum: Nine English Versions*, ed. M. A. Manzalaoui, EETS 276, Oxford University Press, 1977.

Zodiacal Lunary. 'A zodiacal lunary for medical professionals', ed. Irma Taavitsainen, in *Popular and Practical Science*, 1994.

Boorde's 'Dyetary' (1542). *Andrew Boorde's Introduction and Dyetary, with Barnes in the Defence of the Berde*, ed. F. J. Furnivall, EETS, E.S. X. (1973), Millwood, N.Y.: Kraus Reprint Co., 1870.

'Governal'. *Governal: In This Tretyse That Is Cleped Governayle of Helthe* (1489), The English Experience 192, Amsterdam: Da Capo Press, 1969.

'Elyot'. Elyot, Sir Thomas, *The Castel of Health*, London: T. Bertheleti; Facs. New York: Scholars' Facsimiles and Reprints, 1937.

9 Change from above or from below? Mapping the *loci* of linguistic change in the history of Scottish English

ANNELI MEURMAN-SOLIN

1 Introduction

The early history of some geographical varieties of English is in the process of being rewritten as a result of there now being a much wider range of texts available for tracing diachronic developments in greater detail than before. As compared with research based on the literary canon, studies extracting data from non-literary genres such as legal documents, handbooks, scientific treatises, narratives of a more private or informal nature, for instance diaries and autobiographies, and official and private letters, have provided evidence of a lower degree of uniformity and unidirectionality in patterns reflecting variation and change; in fact a high degree of heterogeneity and quite complex processes of change have also emerged in regional and local varieties used in relatively restricted areas. This is of course what compilers of diachronic computer-readable corpora have had as their working hypothesis. Moreover, with the new generation of carefully structured diachronic corpora (Nevalainen and Raumolin-Brunberg (eds.) 1996, Meurman-Solin forthcoming b, c), the application of some of the methods of modern sociolinguistics to diachronic data now seems possible and reasonable.

The case of the Scottish English variety is particularly interesting because of the varying social, cultural and political pressures created on the one hand by the local and regional interests, and on the other hand by England, and also by the two nations' somewhat different contacts with the Continent. Also, variables related to the varying importance of the regions as compared with the metropolitan area (Edinburgh), patterns of social stratification, and cultural traditions and achievements all highlight the idiosyncratic features of Scotland; thus correlations attested between linguistic features and extralinguistic factors of the above-mentioned kind in the history of Southern English have no immediate relevance to Scottish English.

At present, texts representing the history of Scottish English are available in computer-readable form in the Helsinki Corpus of Older Scots (HCOS), 1450–1700, and in the Corpus of Scottish Correspondence (CSC), 1540–1800.

The former consists of 850,000 words of running text and comprises short texts or text extracts of varying lengths; these have been classified into fifteen different genres (Meurman-Solin 1995a, b). The latter is in the process of being compiled; the focus at present is on sixteenth-century letters by male and female writers, and on women's personal letters, diaries and autobiographies dating from the seventeenth century. As less experienced writers, women are particularly important informants in the reconstruction of less formal and less edited language use.

The Helsinki corpora are structured by coding information about extralinguistic variables that characterise the texts and their authors (Kytö 1996). Variables of this kind can describe the texts only in very general terms. However, if variables such as 'genre' are interpreted as *summarising* complex sets of factors, rather than as labelling one particular conditioning factor, they can provide a useful tool for analysing linguistic variation and change (Meurman-Solin forthcoming d). The user of these corpora thus has the task of defining some of the variables in more detail, and of clustering the factors and subfactors in ways that reflect varying political, social and cultural aspects and settings.

In addition to considering the language-external variables coded into the HCOS and the CSC (particularly those that can be related to the social function of a text) the present study aims at redefining the concepts 'from above' and 'from below' by relating them to other dichotomies that may be relevant in the reconstruction of the past. The two concepts that polarise the main types of direction in language change have been applied in varying ways in post-Labovian literature. The classic use of 'from above' in the meaning 'originating on a conscious level of language use' perhaps appropriately describes the rise of the Scottish national norm in the second half of the fifteenth century and the later spread of its distinctive features to regions outside the Central Scots area (Meurman-Solin 1993a, 1997 a–c). More detailed studies of sixteenth-century letters have shown, however, that besides the Scottish English Standard, regional and local norms also continued to enjoy prestige (Meurman-Solin 1999, forthcoming b–c). 'From above' can thus refer to the influence of any norm in the hierarchical system of coexisting norms; 'from below' would then refer to the spread of a new feature from non-standardised language use to a specific established norm.

It will be proposed here that the above-mentioned concepts usefully highlight major diachronic developments, for instance with reference to the political and economic importance of a particular area and its position on scales such as 'centre' against 'periphery'. This dichotomy can be complemented by taking into account the possibility that, at the centre and on the periphery, there may be speech communities reflecting a high degree of geographical and socioeconomic mobility, or, in contrast, individuals or groups of individuals who live encapsulated in their isolation and therefore remain linguistically unaffected by changes taking place elsewhere (cf. Trudgill 1996). It is further assumed that, in the norm-setting and norm-changing processes as well as in the diffusion of norms geographical, economic and social mobility are more important than the variable 'social rank'. This is also because the different social ranks are internally relatively heterogeneous (Nevalainen 1996, Raumolin-Brunberg 1996, Meurman-Solin 1999, forthcoming a–c). Moreover, the different ranks are unevenly represented among informants in the text corpora, as the majority of sixteenth- and seventeenth-century writers belong to the nobility, the gentry or the clergy.

In Scotland, no explicit prescriptivist rules intensified pressure towards linguistic conformity in pre-1700 texts; rather, a national standard norm was widely adopted as a repertoire of linguistic practices that a growing number of literate people needed for their written communication. At the same time, a high degree of variation resulted especially in areas where people with multiplex social networks tended to use a mixture of features derived from several norms. It is assumed here that, if sufficient systematicity in the linguistic preferences of a mixed dialect of this kind can be identified in a wide range of data, it will be possible to specify the direction of change in terms of the incoming norm and the established norm. Also, when detailed chronological information is available about the introduction of new variants and their co-occurrence patterns with older ones, generalising labels such as 'from above' can be used to refer to trends which result from a consensus as regards the relative prestige of a particular norm in a hierarchical system of various norms.

In order to identify *loci* of change and to relate the concepts 'from above' and 'from below' to a number of relevant extralinguistic variables, the following dimensions will be discussed:

(1)   supranational – national – regional – local
(2)   formal – informal
(3)   competent and experienced writers (mostly men) – less competent and inexperienced writers (including women)
(4)   conservative genre – innovative genre
(5)   written idiom – spoken idiom

The hypothesis is that the concepts that specify these dimensions can be usefully related to the generalisations 'from above' and 'from below', for example by contrasting texts produced by the central government with those that have a function in the local administration; texts written to the general public with private records (the former often printed, the latter existing in a single MS); texts written for a wide audience with texts addressing a restricted group of readers; or texts written by people in tightly-knit speech communities with texts written by those whose social networks consist of weak ties.

The term 'supranational' here refers to the competing standards, the Southern English and the Scottish English Standard; rivalry on the 'national' level is mostly between Edinburgh, the centre of national administration, and the other, mostly urban centres in the country. The term 'regional' refers to the main dialect areas, such as East-Mid Scots or Mid-Northern Scots (Murison 1977, 1979), where 'local' norms can be identified. Level of formality is one of the variables coded into the Helsinki corpora; in principle, texts such as legal documents, official letters and sermons are labelled 'formal', while texts such as diaries and family letters are labelled 'informal'. In the case of male writers, the level of linguistic competence is evaluated by education and literary activities and production, and sometimes by age[1]; when no extralinguistic information is available – biographical data is difficult to obtain about less well-known letter writers – linguistic and stylistic criteria are used. In the present material, the majority of women writers have been categorised as less experienced writers. In addition to being related to types of speech communities and social networks, the dimension 'conservative' versus 'innovative' provides a general framework for assessing the model-imposing effect of genre conventions and, in contrast, innovative pressures in the evolution of genres (for further information on the conditioning of linguistic and stylistic competence, see Meurman-Solin forthcoming d). As regards the dimension 'spoken' versus 'written', the assumption is that, in addition to texts labelled 'speech-based' such as judicial depositions in records of trial proceedings, features reflecting the spoken idiom can be identified in less carefully planned texts and in unedited texts that have been produced in informal settings.

To sum up the general comments on the dimensions: since the majority of the writers in the two corpora, or in fact in any material extant from the medieval and the Renaissance periods in Scotland, belong to the upper classes, it is not relevant to try to describe the origin and direction of change only in terms of hierarchies related to the social status of individual writers. Rather, diachronic developments should be related to hierarchies that can be defined for instance with reference to the core area and the periphery in the application of a particular norm; to hierarchies between competing linguistic and stylistic norms; or hierarchies based on varying degrees of literacy and linguistic and stylistic competence. The general assumption then is that there are several co-existing norms, and this explains the multidirectionality of diachronic developments in the history of Scots.

2   Supranational – national – regional – local

Firstly, the dimension 'supranational – national – regional – local' can be related to the diverging and converging tendencies between the Southern English Standard and the Scottish English Standard in the history of the English language. Divergence from the Northern English dialect towards the Scottish English Standard is a de-anglicisation process, and the tendencies of convergence towards the Southern English Standard an anglicisation process. In this field of study, the term standardisation is used to refer to the rise of the Scottish English Standard as a result of a successful de-anglicisation process.

I have elsewhere (Meurman-Solin 1997b) illustrated the general trends reflected in the texts of the HCOS, assessed according to a set of features diagnostic of a differentiated Scottish English Standard (Meurman-Solin 1993a:

132–5). As regards the fifteenth-century prose texts in the Corpus, the intensification of differentiation can be exemplified by the difference between Gilbert Hay's Prose Manuscript in 1456 and John of Ireland's *Meroure of Wyssdome*, dating from 1490. From the point of view of identifying *loci* of change, it is significant that a time-lag in the adoption of distinctively Scottish features has been recorded in the Aberdeen records, which are, from the perspective of the national government, a text produced on the periphery. A similar time-lag has been attested in translations from French. Text category is also significant: the pace of differentiation is more rapid in texts representing religious instruction than in those representing secular instruction.

In a statistical analysis of this kind (see also Meurman-Solin 1997a), we can also see the rise of the Scottish National Standard, the situation in the sixteenth century when the Scottish English variety with its highly distinctive features developed into an internally relatively homogeneous all-purpose language. The peaks, i.e. texts where the percentage of distinctively Scottish variants is at least 80 per cent, are acts of Parliament, records of Stirling, official letters, and political pamphlets. These are texts whose social function is directly linked with wielders of political power in the Central Scots dialect area, the southeastern part of Scotland. Later in the sixteenth century and in the first decades of the seventeenth century, high percentages of Scottish features have also been attested in diaries and letters; this is also true of speech-based recordings of trial proceedings. As will be seen later in this study, a spread of this kind, a pattern of diffusion from public to private, is one of the dominant patterns of change in Renaissance Scots.

Anglicisation, the other supranational development, takes place in the seventeenth century when, for example as a result of the Union of the Crowns, tendencies to adopt English features intensified in the majority of written texts. There is a dramatic decrease of Scottish variants in the acts of Parliament dating from 1661 to 1686, whereas texts dealing with regional topics, such as the Aberdonian John Spalding's history of Scotland (c.1650), remain distinctively Scottish. This is not the case, however, with texts written for a wider audience, such as stories about witches in *Satan's Invisible World Discovered* (1685) by George Sinclair, or texts discussing a topic of general interest among professional people such as his *Natural Philosophy* (1672/1683).[2] Different localities show significant variation in the chronology of change, depending on whether they are at the centre of national administration, in its close proximity or on the periphery. I have shown (Meurman-Solin 1997a: 206–8) that the different social function of acts of Parliament on the one hand, and of the records of the different municipalities on the other, is an important conditioning factor, so that legal documents of nation-wide relevance regularly take the lead in both diverging and converging trends in Scottish English.

The spread of features of the national norm is considerably slower in the regional norms of legalese than in official letters representing the different areas. By the 1540s, marked features of the national norm such as *i*-digraphs have spread to autograph letters in the *Correspondence of Mary of Lorraine*, whatever the dialect area of origin of the different writers (Meurman-Solin forthcoming b).[3] As the title of the collection suggests, the majority of these letters are addressed to Mary of Lorraine, a public figure at the centre stage of national politics; the idiolects differ, however, as regards the relative proportion of national to regional or local features. Such differences may reflect the varying degrees of intensity and density of the contacts the different writers had with the centres of national administration (Wardhaugh 1992: 127–30, Chambers 1995: 71–3).

On the basis of evidence provided by these letters, it is also possible to claim that, in general, the diffusion of national features is more rapid in the east, from the Borders up to as far north as Dornoch in the Highlands, the seat of Dunrobin Castle. In contrast, writers originating from the west, i.e. the West Mid Scots and the South Mid Scots dialect areas, retain a higher frequency of features typical of their local or regional norm. Moreover, phonetic spellings that antedate some of the phonological or phonetic changes recorded by Aitken (1977, 1979) have chiefly been attested in the eastern areas (Meurman-Solin forthcoming b, c). Despite the shared feature of having contacts with Edinburgh, northern and western writers thus differ as regards their adoption of features of the national standard. It is necessary, however, to remember that there are also differences in how influential the various noble families of Scotland were in the Renaissance period; in the North, both the Gordons of Huntly and the Sutherlands of Dunrobin had a central role in the national political arena.

To sum up my comments on the first dimension, the *loci* of change can primarily be related to language-external variables such as the geographical area, the social function of the text in terms of vicinity to centres of political power and other public arenas, the audience of the text and whether it was printed or not, and, in letters, the participant relationship (see also Meurman-Solin 1993a: 137–48, 180–3).

When we look at the de-anglicising and standardising processes and later the anglicising tendencies in the history of Scottish English, our evidence seems to suggest that the direction of change is motivated from above, from the level of nation-wide central administration, and the time-lag in the diffusion of change is dependent on the geographical distance between the centre and the other regions. Trudgill (1996) discusses the differences in patterns of linguistic variation and change, and usefully distinguishes between isolated areas and areas on the periphery. Applied to the case of Scots, in isolated areas the local norm with all its anomalies and archaisms may be retained; such areas can be found for example in the southwest. On the periphery, processes of change attested in the central areas will take place, but there is usually a delay in the pace of change; a time-lag of this kind has been recorded for example in Aberdeen. However, a greater number of texts will have to be analysed in order to further specify the pace and direction of change in the different areas.

3   Level of formality

The second dimension, 'formal versus informal', can be related to the first, as all legal documents can be considered formal. To illustrate the direction of change from formal to informal in Scottish English, I would like to refer to general trends in *t/d* deletion and insertion (Meurman-Solin 1997c). In the morphology of verbs, in this case especially in the formation of past tense and past participle, variation and change in *t/d* deletion and insertion are at least partly conditioned by the writer's literacy or non-literacy in Latin; it seems relevant to examine whether the feature can be meaningfully related to level of formality in other respects as well. As presented in Meurman-Solin 1997c, examples of the following kind illustrate deletion in the word-class of verbs in the HCOS: *ac, accep, adieck, abstra(c)k, coac, contrak, convik, correk, direck/direk/derec/derek/ dereck, effek, instruk, restrik, subjeck, suspek, accep, attemp, corrup, excep/exsep, exemp, interrup,* and *temp.* There are also nouns, such as *ac, attemp, contrak, effec(k)/effek, precink, pressep, respeck, sanc;* adjectives, for example *dere(c)k, effecfull, strick, affecket/affecnot,* 'affectionate'; and adverbs, for example *coniunc-ly, -lie.*

Variants with deletion spread from the position before the morpheme *-it/-yt* to other morpheme boundaries and finally to other positions, so that, in late Middle Scots (1550–1700), the frequency of deletion in word-final position, also in word-classes other than verbs, increases as compared with earlier periods. The preposition *excep* is the most resistant variant with deletion. The infinitive *attemp* in a letter dating from 1701 is the only verb form with deletion in the subperiod 1640–1700 of the HCOS. It is significant here that the last examples have been attested in texts such as late sixteenth-century *Criminal Trials* (1570–91), labelled 'speech-based' in the HCOS, Patrick Waus' *Journal* (1587) and letters by Jane, Countess of Sutherland (1616–23). As could be assumed, the standardising trends thus take longer to reach texts that, for various reasons, reflect practices of spoken language. Moreover, it is noteworthy that the language of texts produced in informal settings is rarely checked or edited, and therefore remains unaffected by the regularising and uniformitarian trends.

Further evidence of direction of change is provided by hypercorrect variants such as *publict* for *public;* the variant with inserted *t* occurs in parliamentary acts and burgh records throughout the HCOS, and, on the basis of evidence from the period 1580–1610, it seems to have spread from formal texts to others. A transition period of this kind reflects an increased awareness of correct usage that, at the same time, leads to overadjustment to the norm in the form of hypercorrection. Together with the Latin influence (see below), evidence of this kind seems to suggest that, in the case of Scots, genres representing formal usage consistently lead the change, whether this is assessed by the dominance of deleted variants, the regularisation of the past tense and past participle morpheme, or the occurrence of hypercorrect variants.

In legal language, the use of verb bases ending in *-t* as past participles

(Meurman-Solin 1997c: 116, Table 1) has been shown to be particularly frequent in early sixteenth-century acts of Parliament (80 per cent), as compared with contemporary Stirling records (68 per cent), Aberdeen records (44 per cent) and official letters (54 per cent). In the period 1570–1640, the spread of the feature is reflected in Stirling records (80 per cent) and in Aberdeen records (62 per cent). Significantly, although absent in pre-1570 private letters, these forms have been attested in later private letters.

The more explicitly Latin verb bases ending in -at(e) or -ut(e) are mostly uninflected as early as the period 1500–70: 97 per cent of the total of past participles in acts of Parliament as compared with 42 per cent in the period 1570–1640. In Aberdeen records, which regularly reflect a time-lag in the adoption of national features, the percentages are 50 per cent and 100 per cent respectively. Verbs of this kind are relatively rare in informal texts, but it may be of interest that in post-1640 private letters 40 per cent of the past participle forms of these verbs are uninflected. The rule of deleting the morpheme -it/-yt is thus applied earlier and more categorically to the transparently Latin verbs than to other verbs ending in -t.

The morpheme -ed was substituted for -it/-yt earlier in official letters than in private letters (Meurman-Solin 1993a: 151–6). As there is evidence of a correlation pattern between this change and the decrease of uninflected past participle forms (Meurman-Solin 1997c: 120), it seems that the regularisation took place in genres in the same order in which the practice of uninflected past participles became a dominant feature in Scots, i.e. first prevalently in formal language use, then in texts whose social and cultural function motivates the use of the national norm, and finally in more informal writings. The insertion of t after th, as in baitht, 'both', faitht, strentht and witht, may also be a feature of formal registers, since in the period 1450–1500 it is conspicuously frequent in acts of Parliament; in fact 80 per cent of pre-1500 occurrences have been attested in this source (only 14 per cent in Peebles records, 3 per cent in Aberdeen records and 3 per cent in Dicta Salomonis). Among legal texts, those written far from the national administration retain the feature longer (compare the mean frequency 0.2/1,000 in sixteenth-century Peebles records, 2.4/1,000 in contemporary Aberdeen records). However, variants of this kind have not been attested in the post-1620 texts of the HCOS. Simultaneously with a decrease in statutory texts, variants with word-final -tht began to spread into some of the most distinctively Scottish texts of the sixteenth century, for instance Gau's Richt Vay to the Kingdom of Heuine (8.7/1,000), the Complaynt of Scotland (12.8/1,000) and Pitscottie's history (7.2/1,000). In addition, spelling variants of this kind have been recorded from a female writer's autograph letters dating from 1548–9 (Meurman-Solin forthcoming a); among the early seventeenth-century examples, we also find a woman writer using vitht/vytht in her private letters.

As illustrated in more detail in Meurman-Solin (1997c), the direction of change is again from above; the diffusion of variants in -tht is from national and local statutory texts to religious instruction, a political allegory, a history, official letters, and finally family letters. Geographically, the spelling practice seems to have been introduced into legal texts of the national administration, and to have then spread into records of the royal burghs on the periphery. During the last decades of the sixteenth century, a decrease has been attested in texts of the latter kind at the same time as an increase can be recorded in a narrative text.

4   Less experienced writers as informants

The third dimension that is related to the writers' linguistic and stylistic competence suggests that *loci* of change can be identified by analysing texts that have been written for instance by people who have received little or no official education, who have not been sufficiently trained in their written skills, or who are relatively ignorant of stylistic conventions. In the sixteenth- and seventeenth-century Scottish material, trained and experienced writers are mostly men; they tend to follow some system of orthography more or less consistently. In contrast, women tend more often to resort to spellings that reflect in various ways the pronunciation of the words. It appears that the linguistic competence of men usually allows them to distinguish between the spoken and the written forms of words, whereas women's skills in the area of written language are less developed; therefore women frequently use variant forms prevalent in their spoken language in their writing. Texts written by women can thus be assumed to be a richer source for reconstructing phonological developments and practices of the spoken idiom. In my experience, other sources for phonetic spellings are texts produced in tightly-knit speech communities such as records of local administrative or judicial bodies, and early letters of less educated and less experienced male writers.

In the approximately 850,000 words of running text in the HCOS, phonetic spellings are clearly clustered in women's writings, but there are a number of male writers whose letters show a mixture of established orthographic practices, also reflected in hypercorrect spellings, and of phonetic spellings. I have elsewhere (Meurman-Solin 1999) discussed phonetic spellings for instance in Patrick Waus' letters from school to his parents, dating from 1540. These spellings give evidence of the shortening of long vowels in environments specified by Aitken's Law (the 'Scottish vowel-length rule'; Aitken 1981) earlier than has been previously assumed. This can be illustrated by *mittine*, 'meeting', or the variant *mit* of the adjective *meet*, 'fit, appropriate', instead of the prevalent variants *mete* or *meit* in contemporary Scots. Variants of this kind have also been attested in other letters dating from the 1540s, so that, for instance in the *Correspondence of Mary of Lorraine*, we find Marion Haliburton, Lady Home, using *plis* for *ples(e)/pleis* and Alexander Gordon using *besyk* for *besek(e)/beseik*.

The restricted set of graphs available for a varying range of vowel or diphthong quality within the variational space of each phoneme often makes it difficult to draw definitive conclusions about the chronology of change. Aitken (1977: 7) suggests that /i:/ became /ei/ by c.1475, and /ai/ by c.1600. An earlier date can perhaps be suggested on the basis of variants such as Patrick Waus' *bay* for the prevalent *by*, 'to buy', as the graph can be assumed to reflect at least a lower quality of the vowel (/be:/), probably a diphthong (/bei/ or /bai/). There is overlapping in the variational space of Middle and Modern Scots realisations of Early Scots /e:/ (later /i:/, finally /i/), /ɛ:/ (later either /i:/ > /i/ or /e:/ > /e/), /a:/ (later /e:/, finally /e/) and /ai/ (later /ɛi/, finally /e:/). However, for example in the above-mentioned letters by Patrick Waus, it is possible to see a clear pattern in the choice of spelling variants. For instance, the writer's alternatives *beth* and *beath* (for the prevalent *baith*, 'both'), *ne*/*nene* and *nae* (for *na*, *nane*/*nain*), *schaik* for *sake*, but *stet* for *stat(e)* seem to suggest a systematic pattern of variation between a shorter and a longer realisation, /e/ and /e:/; in addition, *pement* for *payment* may suggest a compressed realisation of Middle Scots /ɛi/ (Early Scots /ai/) or a monophthongisation of the diphthong to /e:/.

The relatively high degree of systematicity in the choice of the variants supports the claim that the evidence provided by less competent writers can be considered relevant in identifying *loci* where new features were adopted earlier than elsewhere. In fact information of this kind is not available in other sources representing areas where the standard norm is in widespread use. Meurman-Solin (forthcoming b) shows that early adopters of innovative variants have been identified among writers originating from the Southern Scots dialect area and from areas north of the Forth. However, in the Edinburgh region, the core area of the East Mid Scots dialect, the majority of letter writers analysed so far are too well-trained to use phonetic spellings. It is therefore difficult to find direct evidence of phonological developments in areas of this kind, and further research is required in order to trace whether there is any indication of either conservative or innovative trends in the fixed standard norm or norms in these areas. At this stage it is assumed, however, that innovative variants of the above-mentioned kind are in fact used as part of the spoken idiom in the standard norm, even though this cannot be verified because of the absence of phonetic spellings. On the other hand, it can also be claimed that a well-established national norm may be more successful in resisting change than the regional or local norms applied in its close proximity. Momentum for change is perhaps especially strong in areas where, as a result of regular and frequent contacts, language users are most acutely aware of the requirements of successful communication. Among social aspirers, this may also trigger the use of hypercorrect forms. Further research will be necessary to identify for instance the motivating factors of the shortening of long vowels; these may then also serve to identify the *loci* where change originated. A further point of relevance is that, as a result of the intensive anglicisation of Scottish English especially during the latter half of the seventeenth century, letters by less competent writers remain virtually the only source of prose writing where phonological developments can be traced. For instance Elizabeth Ker's letters from the 1630s and 1640s confirm the monophthongisation of /ai/, later /ɛi/, heralded by Patrick Waus and others a century earlier; to suggest the pronunciation /e/, she consistently chooses the graph *e* both in words such as *hest* ('haste'), *sef* ('safe'), *shemless* ('shameless') and in *pens* ('pains'), *slen* ('slain'), *fell* ('fail'), *wet* ('wait').

Informants of this kind allow us to trace the diffusion of phonological and phonetic variants and to map *loci* of change in a system of various coexisting norms at a time when the majority of written texts have adopted the orthographic practices of the national norm. Findings based on the HCOS stress the importance of women's letters. Besides the mid-sixteenth-century examples commented on earlier (p. 163), for instance the shortening of /e:/ to /i/ has also been attested in Katherine Kennedy's letter written to her husband, Sir Patrick Waus, Lord Barnbarroch:

> Maist speciall, efter my maist hartle commendatioun, for sa meikill ye sall vit that the maist speciall causs that I stayit forge sa lang vas for the gettying of euery manis anser about the siluer, and now ye se your self quhat I am *indid* ['indeed'] sertane of bathe affeill and at hame. (1587, Katherine Kennedy, Lady Barnbarroch)

A similar variant also occurs in the following extract from a letter written by a northern writer at Dunrobin Castle:

> Bot I am glaid of the excuis they pretend, alledgeing that ye ar to *sik* ['seek'] ane support off thame at your hame cuming. (1616, Alexander Gordon)

However, all the later examples in the HCOS are from women's letters:

> Hee thought you had so much weitt as to gyd that; only simpelly to *kip* ['keep'] the peaces, and nott be ane disturber of itt. (1668, Margaret Hay)

> Dauet is busi skliting the turettes. I am only now uaiting for a litl more lyme, which is uery ill to be had; for John *nides* ['needs'] for Tarbet, who is *indid* ['indeed'] a uery good griue and becomed a uery frugale man. (c. 1690, Ann Sinclair)

> I doubt if your brother will get written this day, for he is out of toune; he has been very earnest with me to lett him goe to the academy here, which *indid* is very much commended; the master is a French refugie, and is call'd a cerious honest man. (c. 1695, Margaret Wemyss)

Some women have thus been shown to be among the early adopters of new variants, but women's linguistic behaviour is largely dependent on their place of origin and social contacts. As a member of a prestigious family in Edinburgh, Katherine Bellenden is competent to write an elegant letter in the Scottish Standard in 1543, whereas her contemporary Margaret Strowan, Countess of Erroll, still uses non-differentiated variants in her letter written in Perth. At the same time, Lady Home can be considered an early adopter of variants that have not been attested in Katherine Bellenden's or the Countess of Erroll's letters (for further information, see Meurman-Solin 1999, forthcoming a, b). Thus, women are a relatively heterogeneous group of informants; their idiolectal practices are an especially challenging area of study, also because it is usually quite difficult to reconstruct womens' lives to explain their linguistic choices with reference to language-external variables.

5   Written language – spoken language

Besides reflections of the spoken idiom in texts written by less competent or inexperienced writers, a few more general points can be added on *loci* of change specified in terms of written language versus spoken language. The assumption is that the differentiation of Scottish English from the Northern English dialect in the fifteenth century took place both in written and in spoken language. In contrast, the late sixteenth- and seventeenth-century anglicisation process was chiefly realised in written Scots and can be viewed as change on a more conscious level of language use; motivated by a political and socioeconomic unification process, an important number of features in a majority variety, i.e. Southern English, were substituted for those in a minority variety, i.e. Scots, at least in certain linguistic and/or extralinguistic environments. Also in the written medium, patterns of change during the anglicisation process were multidirectional (cf. Milroy 1992, Romaine 1984: 250–1), and ongoing corpus-based research will shed more light on them. However, the description of the spread of anglicisation to texts reflecting the spoken idiom may remain flawed due to scarcity of material and problems in its availability.

There is evidence that it was written language that played a central role in strengthening and intensifying processes of divergence and standardisation, the rise of the Scottish English Standard, in the fifteenth and sixteenth centuries. The role of printing is also relevant here: in my earlier research I have shown that it strengthened the establishment of the distinctive Scottish variety in the sixteenth century; however, in the seventeenth century, the printing of texts allowed their authors to reach wider audiences and anglicisation of the language was therefore required (Meurman-Solin 1993a: 137–48). It is no coincidence that the texts printed earliest represented genres such as handbooks, scientific treatises, pamphlets, travelogues and sermons, as these genres appealed to a more general readership. In contrast, absence of addressee-orientation (Meurman-Solin 1994 and forthcoming d) in genres such as the documentary public records (burgh records), regional histories and introvert private records (diaries and autobiographies) seems to mark texts that remain linguistically conservative.

As regards other evidence of the central role of written language in the rise of the Scottish Standard, there is a conspicuous increase in the degree of Scottishness in trials dating from the last quarter as compared with those dating from the third quarter of the sixteenth century. This is perhaps related to the claim that the development of the regional standard norm in Scotland first manifested itself chiefly in the well-established written genres. Recordings of trial proceedings are labelled 'speech-based' (Kytö 1996, Meurman-Solin 1993a: 79) in the HCOS, and the time-lag in the increase of markedly Scottish features in them (in recordings from St Andrews Kirk Sessions from 71% to 92%, in *Criminal Trials* from 62% to 87%) may be due to this relationship with spoken language.

Written texts classified as representatives of the same genre may be very different in terms of 'text type', the configuration of linguistic features. For instance Gilbert Skeyne's *Description of the Pest* (50%) reflects a lower percentage of distinctively Scottish features than his somewhat later tract *Description of the Well* (67%). The former is written in a learned fashion and in a more Latinate style than the latter, which discusses the beneficial effects of the water of a well near Aberdeen (see Meurman-Solin 1993a: 91–2). Elsewhere (Meurman-Solin forthcoming d), I discuss more fully the social function of written genres, their relationship to spoken language, and their evolution in terms of the dimension conservative versus innovative.

6   Concluding remarks

The criteria for defining a standard, namely that a standard is imposed from above, involves legislation and manifests an ideology of standardisation (Milroy 1994: 4), are not directly applicable to the rise of the Scottish Standard; this view is based on the idea that, in order to refer for instance to the imposition of a standard, at least some prescriptivist tendencies would have to be traceable. However, in Scotland, overtly prescriptive rules date from as late as the early eighteenth century. Instead, as summarised in Meurman-Solin (1997b: 3), 'the intensification of developments towards divergence in the fifteenth century is linked with the increase of Scotland's political and sociocultural independence. This process seems to have created a climate of consensus among those with access to wielders of political and economic power; such a climate supported the rise of a multi-purpose regional norm standard.' These developments are chiefly visible in written texts close to the 'common core', whereas a complete account of the variety will inevitably give evidence of continued variation.

In my concluding remarks I would like to suggest that the most central factors conditioning major diachronic developments in Scots are related to the social function of formal written texts and their audience; the degree of national or regional relevance is also important, whether attached to legal documents, political pamphlets, texts of the literary canon, or letters by high officials, including those addressed to royalty. The present study has repeatedly shown that the features of the national norm spread from the administrative, legal, political and cultural institutions to private domains. To what extent the regional and local norms are influenced by the national norm depends on the geographical, economic and social distance from the metropolitan area of

Edinburgh; elsewhere (Meurman-Solin forthcoming b, c) I show that, as compared with the southeast and the northeast, the time-lag is greater for the
diffusion of certain features to areas in the west. In addition, in areas on the
periphery there may be a strong feeling of solidarity towards the linguistic
practices of the local variety. In fact it is here assumed that resistance to outside
influence is stronger in communities where the norm is established by a
prestigious tradition of formal documents in the local vernacular. Further study
will be necessary to find out what the relative importance of the various urban
norms is as compared with the Edinburgh norm.

The HCOS was compiled to provide relatively representative data on the
Central Scots variety, although there are also a number of texts from the
Aberdeen region. In order to describe the hierarchical system of various norms
in the whole country, it has been necessary to widen the range of texts. Legal
documents currently being put into computer-readable form at the Institute for
Historical Dialectology in Edinburgh will certainly provide important evidence
for the reconstruction of such norms as regards the formal situations of language
use.

The launching of my new corpus project, the Corpus of Scottish Correspondence, was chiefly motivated by the need to make available texts that would
illustrate language use in more informal situations. More importantly, collec-
tions of letters were assumed to contain evidence of variation between idiolects
conditioned by language-external variables such as geographical and social
mobility. I have illustrated (Meurman-Solin forthcoming b) the relationship of
various coexisting norms with reference to sixteenth-century letters addressed
to Mary of Lorraine. The general assumption in that study is that an inherent
feature in such a hierarchy is 'the constant reordering of preferences as a result
of changes in social network patterns based on prestige and solidarity, or an
increase of weak ties with people representing a different norm'.

Finally, the present study has pointed out important developments that are
independent of the contact between the Scottish and the English varieties in the
history of the Scots language. It has been possible to show that less experienced
writers can function as informants of a unique kind as regards features of spoken
language, for instance in research tracing early adopters of certain phonological
variants. Despite a certain number of epistolary conventions, letters seem to be a
genre where degree of derivativeness is mostly sufficiently low to allow us to
discuss idiolectal practices. In order to identify *loci* of change within Scots, i.e.
changes independent of Southern English influence, it seems necessary to go on
searching for more texts by writers whose speech community is characterised by
strong ties, or by writers whose linguistic and stylistic competence only allows
them to use their own local variety.

Notes

1 Letters sent from school by Patrick Waus have a high frequency of phonetic spellings
as compared with his later letters (Meurman-Solin 1999).

2 There are important differences in the pace and pattern of change of individual linguistic features (for the different shapes of the curves depicting change, see Figures 1.2–1.4 in Meurman-Solin 1997b: 9–10).

3 In contrast with most other features discussed in Meurman-Solin (1993a), there is however very little evidence of the spread of variants with *l* and *n* mouillés (for example *assoilze*, 'assoil' and *fenze*, 'feign') to the western areas.

References

Aitken, A. J. 1977. 'How to pronounce Older Scots', in A. J. Aitken, Matthew P. McDiarmid and Derick S. Thomson (eds.) *Bards and Makars. Scottish Language and Literature, Mediaeval and Renaissance*, University of Glasgow Press, pp. 1–21.

1979. 'Scottish speech: a historical view with special reference to the Standard English of Scotland', in A. J. Aitken and Tom McArthur (eds.) *Languages of Scotland*, Association for Scottish Literary Studies, Occasional Papers no. 4, Edinburgh: Chambers, pp. 85–118.

1981. 'The Scottish Vowel Length Rule', in Michael Benskin and Michael L. Samuels *So meny people longages and tonges: philological essays in Scots and Mediaeval English presented to Angus McIntosh*, Edinburgh University Press, pp. 131–57.

Kytö, Merja 1996. *Manual to the Diachronic Part of the Helsinki Corpus of English Texts*, 3rd edn, Department of English, University of Helsinki.

Chambers, J. K. 1995. *Sociolinguistic Theory*, Cambridge, Mass. and Oxford: Blackwell.

Lass, Roger 1974. 'Linguistic orthogenesis? Scots vowel quantity and the English length conspiracy', in J. M. Anderson and C. Jones (eds.), *Historical Linguistics*, Amsterdam and Oxford: North-Holland vol. II, pp. 311–52.

Macafee, Caroline I. 1989. 'Middle Scots dialects – extrapolating backwards', in J. Derrick McClure and Michael R. G. Spiller (eds.), *Bryght Lanternis. Essays on the Language and Literature of Medieval and Renaissance Scotland*, Aberdeen University Press, 429–41.

Meurman-Solin, Anneli 1993a. *Variation and Change in Early Scottish Prose. Studies Based on the Helsinki Corpus of Older Scots*, Annales Academiae Scientiarum Fennicae, Diss. Humanarum Litterarum 65, Helsinki.

1993b. 'Introduction to the Helsinki Scots Corpus', in Matti Rissanen, Merja Kytö and Minna Palander-Collin (eds.), *Early English in the Computer Age. Explorations through the Helsinki Corpus*, Berlin and New York: Mouton de Gruyter, pp. 75–82.

1994. 'On the evolution of prose genres in Older Scots', *NOWELE* 23, 91–138.

1995a. 'A new tool: The Helsinki Corpus of Older Scots (1450–1700)', *ICAME Journal* 19, 49–62.

1995b. *The Helsinki Corpus of Older Scots*, WordCruncher version with 850,000 words of running text, distributors: Oxford Text Archive, Norwegian Computing Centre for the Humanities.

1997a. 'Text profiles in the study of language variation and change', in Raymond Hickey, Merja Kytö, Ian Lancashire and Matti Rissanen (eds.), *Tracing the Trail of Time, Proceedings from the Diachronic Corpora Workshop, Toronto, May 1995*, pp. 199–214.

1997b. 'On differentiation and standardization in Early Scots', in Jones, Charles (ed.), *The Edinburgh History of the Scots Language*, Edinburgh University Press, chapter 1 pp. 3–23.

1997c. 'A Corpus-based study on *t/d* deletion and insertion in Late Medieval and Renaissance Scottish English', in Terttu Nevalainen and Leena Kahlas-Tarkka (eds.), *To Explain the Present. Studies in the Changing English Language in Honour of Matti Rissanen*, Helsinki: Société Néophilologique, pp. 111–24.

1999. 'Letters as a source of data for reconstructing Early Spoken Scots', Irma Taavitsainen, Gunnel Melchers and Päivi Pahta (eds.), in *Dimensions of Writing in Non-Standard English*, Benjamins, pp. 305–22.

forthcoming a. 'Women's Scots: gender-based variation in Renaissance letters', in the proceedings of the International Conference on Medieval and Renaissance Scottish Literature and Language, Oxford, August 1996.

forthcoming b. 'The centre and the periphery. Competing norms on the dialect map of Renaissance Scotland', in Barisone, Ermanno (ed.), *The History of English and the Dynamics of Power*, Alessandria: Dell'Orso.

forthcoming c. 'On the conditioning of geographical and social distance in language variation and change in Renaissance Scots', in the proceedings of the International Conference on the History of English in a Social Context, Tulln 1997.

forthcoming d. 'Genre as a variable in sociohistorical linguistics', in *European Journal of English Studies*, vol. I, 2000.

Milroy, James 1992. *Linguistic Variation and Change*, Cambridge, Mass. and Oxford: Blackwell.

1994. 'The notion of "standard language" and its applicability to the study of Early Modern English pronunciation', in Dieter Stein and Ingrid Tieken-Boon van Ostade (eds.), *Towards a Standard English 1600–1800*, Berlin and New York: Mouton de Gruyter, pp. 19–29.

Murison, David 1977. *The Guid Scots Tongue*, Edinburgh: Blackwood.

1979. 'The historical background', in A. J. Aitken and Tom McArthur (eds.), *Languages of Scotland*, Association for Scottish Literary Studies, Occasional Papers no. 4, Edinburgh: Chambers, 2–13.

Nevalainen, Terttu 1996. 'Social stratification', in Nevalainen, Terttu and Helena Raumolin-Brunberg (eds.) 1996, pp. 57–76.

Nevalainen, Terttu and Helena Raumolin-Brunberg (eds.) 1996. *Sociolinguistics and Language History. Studies Based on the Corpus of Early English Correspondence*, Amsterdam and Atlanta, Ga: Rodopi.

Raumolin-Brunberg, Helena 1996. 'Historical sociolinguistics', in Nevalainen, Terttu and Helena Raumolin-Brunberg (eds.) 1996, pp. 11–37.

Romaine, Suzanne 1984. 'The sociolinguistic history of *t/d* deletion', *Folia Linguistica Historica*, 5.2, 221–55.

Trudgill, Peter 1996. 'Dialect typology: isolation, social network and phonological structure', in Gregory R. Guy, Crawford Feagin, Deborah Schiffrin and John Baugh (eds.), *Towards a Social Science of Language*, vol. I: *Variation and Change in Language and Society*, Amsterdam/Philadelphia: John Benjamins, pp. 3–22.

Wardhaugh, Ronald 1992. *An Introduction to Sociolinguistics*, 2nd edn, Cambridge, Mass. and Oxford: Blackwell.

Waus Correspondence. *Correspondence of Sir Patrick Waus of Barnbarroch, Knight, 1540–1597*, ed. Robert Vans Agnew, Edinburgh 1882.

10 Adjective comparison and standardisation processes in American and British English from 1620 to the present

MERJA KYTÖ AND SUZANNE ROMAINE

1 Introduction

In this paper we will address the standardisation processes in American and British English with reference to competing forms of adjective comparison. The primary competition is between the older inflectional comparative (e.g. *faster*) and the newer periphrastic construction (e.g. *more beautiful*), with the much less frequent double comparative (e.g. *more richer*) now considered non-standard.[1] In this study we will focus on the paradigm of the non-defective adjectives, a central category illustrated by the above uses. We thus omit from discussion the group of defective (or heterogeneous) adjectives (e.g. *good, better, best*).[2]

Our main sources of data here will be the pilot version of the Corpus of Early American English (1620–1720) and ARCHER (A Representative Corpus of Historical English Registers; see Biber et al. 1994a and 1994b). For the purposes of this study we have taken from ARCHER some 750,000 words representing five text types sampled from the subperiods containing texts from both British and American English, i.e. 1750–1800, 1850–1900, and 1950–1990. Together, this yields a corpus of nearly a million words which allows us to address similarities and differences in standardisation processes affecting these two varieties of English at the same time as it tests the potential of ARCHER for this type of comparative study. Both corpora comprise various text types, which allows us also to explore the question of the extent to which genre or text type influences standardisation. Previous diachronic research has revealed both word structure and text type as important factors. While word structure is a key linguistic factor (see 3.1), the influence of text type is not entirely straightforward, as we will show (see 3.2). Finally, we outline some issues and problems requiring further research and suggest some ways of investigating them. First, however, we will provide a brief overview of adjective comparison.

2   Adjective comparison in the history of English

Most grammars of contemporary English such as Quirk et al. (1985) treat adjective comparison in general terms. The topic is also covered in many handbooks on the history of English and in some specialist works (see e.g. Jespersen 1949, Knüpfer 1922 and Pound 1901). As far as we are aware, however, the issue of differences between British and American English (or for that matter between other varieties of English), has not been systematically addressed on a large scale, either diachronically or synchronically (see, however, Bauer 1994 and Loikkanen 1997 for a promising beginning). Some commentators have made rather casual and sometimes sweeping, though nonetheless intriguing, remarks which warrant further attention. For example, Nist (1963: 345) writes that American folk speech generally prefers -er for the comparative and -est for the superlative. Likewise, Mencken (1970: 464) observed even earlier the same tendency along with the use of double comparatives such as *more better*. In a comparison of what he called Vulgar (i.e. non-standard) with Standard English, Fries (1940: 200) also claimed that Vulgar English in the US was more conservative due to its more persistent use of inflected forms of comparison, while Standard English was more innovative because it made greater use of periphrasis.

From a historical point of view, the periphrastic constructions with more and most (e.g. *more effective*, *most effective*) are innovations. In Old English inflectional endings uniformly marked the comparative and superlative forms of adjectives, as in Modern English *bolder* and *boldest*, for instance. According to Mitchell (1985: 84–5), who lists the few attested possible examples in Old English, the periphrastic forms first appeared in the thirteenth century, possibly under the influence of Latin (and to a lesser extent French). Their use increased steadily after the fourteenth century until the beginning of the sixteenth century, by which time they had become as frequent as they are today (see Pound 1901: 19).

As with other syntactic innovations in the history of English, historians appealed to foreign influence as an explanatory factor. Some have also mentioned stylistic factors such as speakers' needs for emphasis and clarity. From a linguistic point of view, however, the loss of inflectional morphology accompanied the gradual shift in English towards a more analytical syntax, and the development of the periphrastic construction is consistent with this typological trend.

After the newer forms were introduced, however, change took another course. The new periphrastic type of comparison took hold in some environments, and eventually ousted the older ones completely. However, in other environments the newer forms declined at the expense of the older inflectional type. The use of the newer forms appears to have peaked during the Late Middle English period and the older inflectional type has been reasserting itself since the Early Modern period. Although a number of linguists writing in the

1950s and 60s such as Barber (1964: 131), Fries (1940: 96) and Potter (1975 [1969]: 146–7) seemed to think that periphrasis was in the process of replacing inflection, as Strang rightly observed (1970: 58) '[they] may be right, but we lack precise numerical information on the subject'. Contrary to what one might predict from the general trend in English towards a more analytical syntax, corpus-based studies have since revealed that the majority of both comparative and superlative adjectives in present-day English are inflectional (see Kytö 1996, and Kytö and Romaine 1997). In contemporary English some adjectives over-whelmingly show a preference for the newer periphrastic mode of comparison, some for the older inflectional form, while some fluctuate between the two. Bauer (1994: 60) concludes that what we have here is a case of 'regularisation of a confused situation', resulting in comparison becoming more predictable. Bauer's mention of the notion of regularisation suggests the need to take into account the effect of standardisation processes, as do the data presented earlier by Fries (1940: 200) with respect to standard and non-standard forms of American English.

In addition, the new periphrastic constructions introduced another option into the system, the so-called multiple or double comparatives, e.g. *more faster*, *most fastest*.[3] These hybrid forms in which *more* and *most* are combined with the inflectional adjective are also found in a limited number of words such as *lesser*, *worser*, *bestest*, *more better*. Thus, during the Middle English and Early Modern English periods, there were three alternative forms of comparison for an adjec-tive such as *fast*: inflectional (*faster/fastest*), periphrastic (*more fast/most fast*) and double (*more faster/most fastest*). For examples, see (1), (2) and (3).

(1)   I knew my Mother could not but be greatly affected with the Loss of her Son, who was always at hand to assist her, and in that *happier* than any of Us, And was not without Fears, How She would be able to get thorough so great a Trial, in her advanced Years. (Early AmEng/1670–1720/ Letter/Gurdon Saltonstall)

(2)   I hope, poor Mr. Fowler will be *more happy* than I could make him. (ARCHER/BrEng/1750–1800/Fiction/Samuel Richardson)

(3)   . . . and loke that your sherers, repers, or mowers geld not your beanes, that is to saye, to cutte the beanes so hye, that the nethermoste codde growe styll on the stalke; and whan they be bounden, they are the *more redyer* to lode and vnlode, to make a reke, and to take fro the mowe to thresshe. (HC/1500–1570/Handbook/Fitzherbert 36–7)

At all periods, however, the primary variants have been the inflectional and periphrastic types. The double forms have always been marginal. Although once used in the literary language, they gradually disappeared from the written language under the influence of standardisation. Both eighteenth-century and modern grammarians have condemned them.

An examination of the Corpus of Early American English texts considered in

Table 10.1. *The number of words in the subcorpus studied, drawn from the Early American Corpus (1620–1720) and the British and American English components of the ARCHER corpus (1750–1990).*

Early American English			Total
A 1620–1670			100,200
B 1670–1720			129,900
Subtotal			230,100

ARCHER	British English	American English	Total
A 1750–1800	122,700 (53%)	106,700 (47%)	229,400
B 1850–1900	137,000 (53%)	123,600 (47%)	260,600
C 1950–1990	137,100 (53%)	123,600 (47%)	260,700
Subtotal	396,800 (53%)	353,900 (47%)	750,700
Total			980,800

this study revealed no instances of the double forms. Nor could double forms be found in the ARCHER corpus from 1650 to 1990. The double forms occur today mainly in the most colloquial registers of spoken English (see Kytö and Romaine 1997).

3   Data

Table 10.1 provides an overview of our corpus consisting of nearly one million words taken from the Corpus of Early American English, divided into two subperiods, and the ARCHER data, for three main subperiods. As can be seen, the Corpus of Early American English contains 230,100 words distributed roughly equally over two periods: A = 1620–1670 (100,200 words) and B = 1670–1720 (129,900 words). This division reflects the generation gap between the early settlers and their descendants. The material comes primarily from the New England area (apart from one collection of depositions drawn from Virginia during the 1640s). It is divided into eight text types, some of which are common to the Helsinki Corpus and others characteristic of the settlement period: history, diaries/journals, correspondence (private and official), appeals and answers to the court, narratives (= prose of persuasion), sermons, trial records and witness depositions.

The ARCHER data comprise around 750,000 words roughly equally distributed across three subperiods and between the two varieties, with British English slightly better represented (53% of the total corpus) than American English (47%). Tables 10.2a and 10.2b give a more detailed breakdown of the five text

Table 10.2a. *The text types represented by the number of words in the Early American Corpus.*

Early AmEng	1620–1670	1670–1720	Total
History	10,200	26,000	36,200
Diary, journal	18,100	29,900	48,000
Letter	20,300	21,200	41,500
Sermon	10,600	13,800	24,400
Trial	17,200	3,400	20,600
Deposition	23,800	10,500	34,300
Appeal & answer	—	6,800	6,800
Narrative	—	18,300	18,300

Table 10.2b. *The text types represented by the number of words in ARCHER; A = 1750–1800, B = 1850–1900, C = 1950–1990.*

ARCHER		British English	American English	Total
Journal	A	22,000	21,800	43,800
	B	23,000	22,400	45,400
	C	22,500	22,400	44,900
Total		67,500	66,600	134,100
Letter	A	13,100	13,600	26,700
	B	12,000	12,000	24,000
	C	12,300	15,100	27,400
Total		37,400	40,700	78,100
Fiction	A	50,900	43,500	94,400
	B	49,400	44,800	94,200
	C	58,000	44,800	102,800
Total		158,300	133,100	291,400
Drama	A	25,500	16,600	42,100
	B	41,400	33,400	74,800
	C	31,800	30,700	62,500
Total		98,700	80,700	179,400
Sermon	A	11,200	11,200	22,400
	B	11,200	11,000	22,200
	C	12,500	10,600	23,100
Total		34,900	32,800	67,700

types (i.e. journals, letters, fiction, drama and sermons) represented across the three subperiods and two main varieties.

In the Corpus of Early American English each text type is represented by 10,000 to 30,000 words, with the exception of the category of appeals and answers to courts of law and later trial records. As for ARCHER, fiction is by far the best represented category, with nearly 300,000 words all in all; then follow drama (180,000 words) and journals (135,000 words). Sermons and letters are the smallest categories, represented by nearly 70,000 and 80,000 words, respectively.

Tables 10.3a and 10.3b show the distribution of inflectional and periphrastic forms in the Corpus of Early American English and the ARCHER subcorpus, respectively. As far as the Early American English data are concerned, there is a total of 393 non-defective adjectives, of which the majority (N = 218 or 55%) are comparative and 175 (45%), superlative. The majority of comparative forms for both periods A and B are inflectional, with period B showing a slight increase from period A, from 52% to 55%, while the occurrence of periphrastic forms declines from 48% to 45%. The superlatives on the other hand show the opposite tendency; there is a decrease in inflectional forms from 55% to 49% between the two subperiods.[4]

In ARCHER the majority of the comparative forms out of a total of 2,142 non-defective adjectives are also of the inflectional type for both British and American English with the exception of the earliest sample of American English in subperiod A from 1750 to 1800, where the periphrastic forms are more frequent (i.e. 57%) than the inflectional ones (43%). In British English for the same subperiod, the frequencies are reversed: 53% of the comparative forms are inflectional and 47% are periphrastic.

Interestingly, however, in each of the three ARCHER subperiods the two varieties show rather different ratios for inflectional versus periphrastic forms. For instance, in subperiod B from 1850–1900 the inflectional forms far outnumber (i.e. by 44%) the periphrastic ones in British English, while in American English they do so by only 20%. Similarly, in subperiod C from 1950 to 1990 the inflectional forms outnumber the periphrastic ones by 24% in British English, but by only 14% in American English. Thus, British English is slightly ahead of American English at each subperiod in terms of implementing the change towards the inflectional type.[5]

As far as the superlative forms of the adjectives in ARCHER are concerned, the inflectional forms are more frequent overall than the periphrastic forms, although there are fluctuations within subperiods. There is a clear trend within British English for the inflectional type to become more frequent over time, as can be seen in the increasing frequencies of inflectional forms from one subperiod to the next. For American English the tendency for the inflectional type to prevail is not quite as straightforward. Up until the 1950s, the two types are roughly equal in distribution and during the final subperiod the inflected forms catch up with the rate attested in British English. However, the rise of the

Table 10.3a. *Inflectional and periphrastic forms in the Corpus of Early American English. Inflect. = inflectional forms; Periphr. = Periphrastic forms. A = 1620–1670; B = 1670–1720.*

	COMPARATIVE			SUPERLATIVE		
	Inflect.	Periphr.	Total	Inflect.	Periphr.	Total
			(100%)			(100%)
A	59	55	114	43	35	78
	(52%)	(48%)		(55%)	(45%)	
B	57	47	104	48	49	97
	(55%)	(45%)		(49%)	(51%)	
Total	116	102	218	91	84	175
	(53%)	(47%)		(52%)	(48%)	

Table 10.3b. *Inflectional and periphrastic forms in the ARCHER subcorpus. Inflect. = inflectional forms; Periphr. = periphrastic forms. A = 1750–1800; B = 1850–1900; C = 1950–90.*

COMPARATIVE (N = 1106)						
	British English			American English		
	Inflect.	Periphr.	Total	Inflect.	Periphr.	Total
			(100%)			(100%)
A	93	83	176	67	88	155
	(53%)	(47%)		(43%)	(57%)	
B	151	59	210	109	73	182
	(72%)	(28%)		(60%)	(40%)	
C	128	80	208	100	75	175
	(62%)	(38%)		(57%)	(43%)	
Total	372	222	594	276	236	512
	(63%)	(37%)		(54%)	(46%)	
SUPERLATIVE (N = 1036)						
A	133	129	262	109	98	207
	(51%)	(49%)		(53%)	(47%)	
B	120	83	203	72	71	143
	(59%)	(41%)		(50%)	(50%)	
C	65	39	104	73	44	117
	(63%)	(37%)		(62%)	(38%)	
Total	318	251	569	254	213	467
	(56%)	(44%)		(54%)	(46%)	

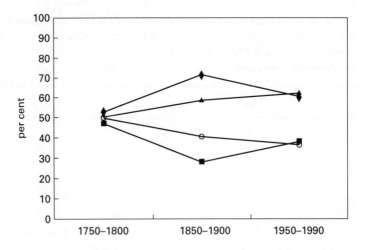

Figure 10.1a Percentage of inflectional and periphrastic forms in the ARCHER subcorpus: British English.

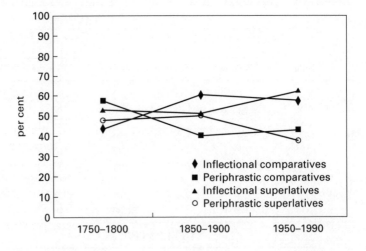

Figure 10.1b Percentage of inflectional and periphrastic forms in the ARCHER subcorpus: American English.

inflected forms was already anticipated in the first subperiod when these forms
were more frequent than the periphrastic forms by a margin of 6% (for a graphic
presentation of the results given in Table 10.3b, see Figures 10.1a and 10.1b).

The data thus suggest that the shift towards the inflectional type as the
predominant one did not proceed by steadily increasing frequencies from one

Table 10.4. *Inflectional and periphrastic forms in the British National Corpus (spoken component, South, dialogue), compared with Helsinki Corpus of English Texts (Late Middle and Early Modern English). Inflect. = inflectional forms; Periphr. = periphrastic forms.*

	COMPARATIVE			SUPERLATIVE		
	Inflect.	Periphr.	Total	Inflect.	Periphr.	Total
LME	211	172	383	152	189	341
	(55%)	(45%)		(45%)	(55%)	
EModE	382	267	649	370	366	736
	(59%)	(41%)		(50%)	(50%)	
BNC	1456	270	1726	433	159	592
	(84%)	(16%)		(73%)	(27%)	

subperiod to another. This may reflect inadequacies and gaps in our sample corpora, or that the pattern of change was somewhat irregular during certain subperiods. We will come back to this point in our discussion of text type in 3.2.

Overall, however, the long-term trend is clear. Over the centuries there has been a gradual increase in the inflectional forms for both comparatives and superlatives. This can be seen in Table 10.4, which shows data from the British National Corpus (1995), where most comparatives are of the inflectional type (84%), as are superlatives (73%).[6] The lower frequencies of inflectional forms in ARCHER compared to the British National Corpus can be accounted for by the fact that ARCHER like the Helsinki Corpus draws on written material compiled of various different text types, while our sample from BNC is taken from spoken dialogue (see Kytö and Romaine 1997: 335–6). By way of comparison, Leech and Culpeper (1997) recently calculated the figures for non-defective comparative forms found in the core written BNC (a million-word representative sample drawn from the 90 million words included in the written component of the corpus). In this material, too, inflectional forms dominate, albeit less conspicuously than in the spoken data: inflectional comparative forms prevail in 75% of the instances (N = 2494) as against 25% of instances with periphrastic forms (Leech and Culpeper 1997: 372–3, note 14).

Table 10.4 also includes for comparison Kytö's (1996) analysis of 930,000 words from Late Middle (1350–1500) and Early Modern English (1500–1710) in the Helsinki Corpus. We can detect here a gradual increase in the inflectional forms for both comparatives (from 55% to 59%) and superlatives (from 45% to 50%). There is a corresponding decline in periphrastic forms in comparatives (from 45% to 41%) and superlatives (from 55% to 50%). The data illustrate that the Late Modern English period, i.e. post-1710, is the critical period during which the present-day pattern of variation is established. The Early Modern English period overlaps with the Early American English Corpus and provides some comparative data for British English.

3.1   Word length as a conditioning factor on the choice between inflectional and periphrastic adjective comparison

Earlier scholars such as Pound (1901: 18) believed that the periphrastic and inflectional forms were in free variation and individual choice was the most important factor. Likewise, Jespersen (1949: 347) said with respect to the Modern English period that a 'good deal is left to the taste of the individual speaker or writer' and that the 'rules given in ordinary grammars are often too dogmatic'.

Despite these claims about free variation, Kytö (1996) found word length to be a powerful factor in accounting for much of the variation in the Helsinki Corpus material. The data from the ARCHER corpus confirm this general trend for monosyllabic words, where the range of variation in the periods 1650 to 1900 is ninety to ninety-five per cent. Disyllabic words, however, have always been subject to more variation. Trisyllabic adjectives and adjectives with more than three syllables favour the periphrastic forms overwhelmingly. Quirk et al. (1985: 462) in fact categorically rule out inflectional forms for trisyllabic adjectives in contemporary English, although a few can be found in colloquial English (see Kytö and Romaine 1997).

Tables 10.5a, 10.5b and 10.5c show the distribution of inflectional and periphrastic forms for the Early American English Corpus and the three subperiods of ARCHER, respectively. In Table 10.5a we can see that as far as the Early American English data are concerned, inflectional forms prevail in monosyllabic comparative adjectives, with an increase from 88% to 90% between the early and later subperiods, as well as in superlative adjectives, with an increase from 86% to 90%. In example (4) we have an exception to the rule and in (5) the prevailing form:

(4)   father condemn not thou me, but forgiue, and heal my backslidings . . . o do thou communicate thy sweet self who hast made me *more glad* than the wicked when their corn and oil increaseth. (AmEng/1620–1670/Diary/Michael Wigglesworth)

(5)   I desire the mayd that you provide me may be one that hath been vsed to all kind of work, and must refuse none if she haue skill in a dayrie I shall be the *gladder*. (AmEng/1620–1670/Letter/Margaret Dudley)

However, the greater the number of syllables, the greater the tendency towards the periphrastic type. In disyllabic adjectives, there is an increase in periphrastic forms for both comparatives (from 92% to 96%) and superlatives (83% to 86%) between the two periods. Information on adjectives containing three or more syllables is more scarce. Nevertheless, the trend is in the same direction. This set of adjectives nearly always favours the periphrastic, for both comparative and superlatives. In fact, it is only in the Early American English Corpus that we find any adjectives with three or more syllables forming the comparative or superlative inflectionally and there is only one instance of each (see examples 6 and 7).

(6)   Bable of one of the worst of men, among many others of which our Host made one, who, had he bin one degree *Impudenter*, would have outdone his Grandfather. And this I think is the most perplexed night I have yet had. (Early AmEng/1670–1720/Travel/Sarah Kemble Knight)

(7)   Whan Gods Servants qwarell and Contend for earthly honor ambition and proffit, it makes them the *unsavorest* men upon the Earth. (Early AmEng/1620–1670/Sermon/John Cotton)

By way of comparison, no more than two such instances of comparative forms and seventeen instances of superlative forms were found in the Early Modern English section of the Helsinki Corpus, which is more than twice the size of the Early American Corpus (Kytö 1996).

Table 10.5b shows the distribution of inflectional and periphrastic forms for comparative adjectives in the three subperiods of ARCHER. Monosyllabic comparative adjectives are nearly always inflectional, i.e. in over 90% of the instances, in both the British and American varieties, although there is a very slight tendency for the percentages to be higher in British English. Comparative adjective forms are categorically inflectional in both varieties even in the first subperiod. In the disyllabic comparative adjectives, however, the majority of uses are periphrastic to start with (in 83% of the instances in British English and in 89% in American English).[7] The number of inflectional uses reaches 41% in British English and 22% in American English by the 1900s. In subperiod C the incidence of inflectional forms sinks slightly for British English (38%), while it further increases for American English (50%). The rise in the use of the inflectional forms can be partly accounted for by the relatively great proportion of adjectives ending in *-y/-ly* in this category; this ending more readily takes the inflectional ending. In fact, though breakdown makes detailed counts less useful, we might point out that certain endings tend to promote the use of one variant form to a greater extent than that of the other. Among the more frequent endings promoting the use of the inflectional form, besides *-y* and *-ly*, is the ending *-le* (as in *simple*, *gentle*, and *noble*), and among those promoting the use of periphrastic endings are *-ful* and *-ous* (*watchful, joyful*, and *serious, specious*). This seems to hold for both British and American English. By way of illustration, see example (8) for the more regular use and example (9) for an exception.

(8)   How, then, can you explain faith? You are neither able to analyse it into parts, nor can you find anything *simpler* with which to compare it. (ARCHER/AmEng/1850–1900/ Sermon/John Broadus)

(9)   Did you ever think what he meant by that? In those days men were working their passage to heaven by keeping the ten commandments, and

Table 10.5a. *The Early American Corpus: adjective length in syllables.*
Inflect. = inflectional forms; Periphr. = periphrastic forms. A = 1620–70;
B = 1670–1720.

	COMPARATIVE			SUPERLATIVE		
	Inflect.	Periphr.	Total	Inflect.	Periphr.	Total
One syllable						
A	57 (88%)	8	65	38 (86%)	6	44
B	55 (90%)	6	61	44 (90%)	5	49
Total	112 (89%)	14	126	82 (88%)	11	93
Two syllables						
A	2	22 (92%)	24	4	20 (83%)	24
B	1	21 (96%)	22	4	24 (86%)	28
Total	3	43 (94%)	46	8	44 (85%)	52
Three or more syllables						
A	0	25 (100%)	25	1	9 (90%)	10
B	1	20 (95%)	21	0	20 (100%)	20
Total	1	45 (98%)	46	1	29 (97%)	30

the hundred and ten other commandments which they had manufactured out of them. Christ said, I will show you a *more simple* way. (ARCHER/BrEng/1850–1900/Sermon/Henry Drummond)

Table 10.5c shows the frequency of superlative adjective forms in the ARCHER corpus. Monosyllabic adjectives are nearly always inflectional, although there are very slight differences between American and British English. In the former the frequency of inflectional forms increases steadily from 96% to 100% across the three subperiods, while in the latter, it declines slightly from 98% to 95%. Superlative adjectives of three or more syllables are uniformly periphrastic in all subperiods for both varieties. Again, the disyllabic adjectives are the main locus of variation. British English shows a decrease from 68% to 52% in the frequency of periphrastic forms across the subperiods, while American English shows a rise in subperiod B from 60% to 68% before declining again to 39% in subperiod C. Thus, in the superlative forms British English shows a greater tendency towards the periphrastic type than does American English.

Table 10.5b. *Adjective length in syllables. Comparative forms.*
Inflect. = inflectional forms; Periphr. = periphrastic forms. A = 1750–1800;
B = 1850–1900; C = 1950–90.

| | COMPARATIVE | | | | | |
| | British English | | | American English | | |
	Inflect.	Periphr.	Total	Inflect.	Periphr.	Total
One syllable						
A	85	4	89	63	4	67
	(96%)			(94%)		
B	134	7	141	98	7	105
	(95%)			(93%)		
C	110	8	118	79	7	86
	(93%)			(92%)		
Total	329	19	348	240	18	258
	(95%)			(93%)		
Two syllables						
A	8	39	47	4	33	37
	(17%)	(83%)		(11%)	(89%)	
B	17	24	41	11	38	49
	(41%)	(59%)		(22%)	(78%)	
C	18	29	47	21	21	42
	(38%)	(62%)		(50%)	(50%)	
Total	43	92	135	36	92	128
	(32%)	(68%)		(28%)	(72%)	
Three or more syllables						
A	0	40	40	0	51	51
		(100%)			(100%)	
B	0	28	28	0	28	28
		(100%)			(100%)	
C	0	43	43	0	47	47
		(100%)			(100%)	
Total	0	111	111	0	126	126
		(100%)			(100%)	

Although the nature of the word-ending is also a prime determinant of the variation between inflectional and periphrastic adjective forms, we have not investigated that factor here due to the much smaller number of tokens for adjectives longer than one syllable, particularly in the Early American Corpus (see Kytö and Romaine 1997 for discussion of the ARCHER corpus). The majority of adjectives are monosyllabic. Other phonological as well as orthographic conditioning factors which we have not investigated may be at work here too for monosyllabic adjectives (see Jespersen 1949: 346, 349 for discussion).

Table 10.5c. *Adjective length in syllables. Superlative forms. Inflect. = inflectional forms; Periphr. = periphrastic forms. A = 1750–1800; B = 1850–1900; C = 1950–90.*

	SUPERLATIVE					
	British English			American English		
	Inflect.	Periphr.	Total	Inflect.	Periphr.	Total
One syllable						
A	106	2	108	84	4	88
	(98%)			(96%)		
B	102	1	103	60	2	62
	(99%)			(97%)		
C	54	3	57	59	0	59
	(95%)			(100%)		
Total	262	6	268	203	6	209
	(98%)			(97%)		
Two syllables						
A	27	58	85	25	37	62
	(32%)	(68%)		(40%)	(60%)	
B	18	24	42	12	25	37
	(43%)	(57%)		(32%)	(68%)	
C	11	12	23	14	9	23
	(48%)	(52%)		(61%)	(39%)	
Total	56	94	150	51	71	122
	(37%)	(63%)		(42%)	(58%)	
Three or more syllables						
A	0	69	69	0	57	57
		(100%)			(100%)	
B	0	58	58	0	44	44
		(100%)			(100%)	
C	0	24	24	0	35	35
		(100%)			(100%)	
Total	0	151	151	0	136	136
		(100%)			(100%)	

In the Corpus of Early American English we can find competing variants among the monosyllabic variants such as *aptest/most apt*, which are unlikely to be motivated by phonological or orthographic considerations. Compare, for instance, these two examples:

(10) In owr greatest inlargments whan owr hartes is most Comforted with the Consolations of God, than are we *most apt* to forget owr Selves . . . (Early AmEng/1620–1670/Sermon/John Cotton)

and

(11)   Our ploughes goe on with good successe, we are like to have 20 at worke
        next yeare: our lands are *aptest* for Rye and oats . . . (Early AmEng/1620–
        1670/Letter/John Winthrop)

Stylistic choice is presumably at work here and in other cases.

As far as polysyllabic adjectives ending in *-ous*, and other adjectives ending in
sibilants are concerned, one might be tempted to suppose that phonological
considerations explain the preference for the periphrastic type of comparative
with the superlative forms; namely, speakers avoid the co-occurrence of two
sibilants, e.g. **foolishest*, **famousest*. Nevertheless, Jespersen (1949: 355) found
more superlatives than comparatives of the inflectional type in such cases.

Although stylistic differences were claimed to be important by scholars such
as Pound and Jespersen, they have not been systematically investigated. Curme
(1931: 504) believed that there is a stylistic advantage to the periphrastic form
because the use of a separate word (*more*/*most*) instead of an inflectional ending
allows the speakers/writers to place additional stress on the comparative element, if they want to emphasise the idea of degree, or on the adjective to
emphasise the meaning. Jespersen (1949: 356) finds that the inflectional forms,
particularly in the superlative and in longer words, are generally perceived as
'more vigorous' and 'more emphatic' than the periphrastic forms, e.g. 'the
confoundedest, brazenest, ingeniousest piece of fraud' (Mark Twain). He noted
a tendency towards more frequent use of inflection in what he refers to as
'vulgar' speech. Although speakers can always rely on prosody to indicate which
parts of the utterance they wish to emphasise, writers must rely on other cues
such as word order, punctuation, word choice, etc. Periphrasis may possibly
have emerged as a stylistic option first in the written language to emphasise and
focus on the comparison itself rather than the quality referred to in the adjective.
In order to address that question, however, we need to look at the influence of
text type on the choice between inflection and periphrasis.

3.2   Text type as a conditioning factor in the choice between inflectional and periphrastic comparison

Overall, Kytö (1996) found that inflectional forms prevailed in matter-of-fact
text types in the Helsinki Corpus such as handbooks, and language written to
reflect spoken or colloquial registers. More rhetorical texts such as philosophical
and religious treatises, and correspondence, however, make greater use of
periphrastic forms. We argued in Kytö and Romaine (1997) that this may be
evidence for the origin of the periphrastic forms in written registers. We will
now explore that hypothesis using the data from the Corpus of Early American
English and ARCHER.

Table 10.2b which shows the distribution of the five text types in ARCHER,

Table 10.6. *Inflectional and periphrastic forms in the ARCHER subcorpus: text type distributions. Inflect. = inflectional forms; Periphr. = periphrastic forms.*

	British English			American English		
	Inflect.	Periphr.	Total	Inflect.	Periphr.	Total
COMPARATIVE						
Journal	85 (60%)	57	142	60 (59%)	41	101
Letter	31 (61%)	20	51	30 (50%)	30	60
Fiction	141 (62%)	86	227	103 (47%)	116	219
Drama	48 (68%)	23	71	42 (63%)	25	67
Sermon	67 (65%)	36	103	41 (63%)	24	65
SUPERLATIVE						
Journal	49 (44%)	62	111	38 (67%)	19	57
Letter	50 (56%)	40	90	44 (62%)	27	71
Fiction	110 (58%)	80	190	76 (46%)	90	166
Drama	67 (63%)	39	106	46 (54%)	39	85
Sermon	42 (58%)	30	72	50 (57%)	38	88

reveals considerable variation in sampling, with word counts ranging from 10,000 to 58,000 for different text types. Thus, fiction, journals and drama are better represented than letters and sermons. Such discrepancies arising from the unevenness of distribution of material across the text types make it difficult to say very much about how text type influenced the regularisation of this change. The bias against sermons and letters, however, may explain why we found no double comparatives; all things being equal, these are the text types one might expect to be closer to the spoken language.

We noted earlier that as far as comparative forms are concerned, British English appeared to be ahead of American English in implementing the shift to the inflectional type of adjective comparison. Table 10.6 shows that this is particularly the case for fiction, and to some extent for letters, but less so in journals, drama and sermons.[8] With respect to the superlatives, however, American English leads in the introduction of the inflectional type in journals

Table 10.7a. *Inflectional and periphrastic forms in the Early American Corpus: text type and subperiod distributions. Infl. = inflectional forms; Peri. = periphrastic forms. A = 1620–1670; B = 1670–1720.*

		Early American English					
		COMPARATIVE			SUPERLATIVE		
		Infl.	Peri.	Total	Infl.	Peri.	Total
History	A	21 (70%)	9	30	7	4	11
	B	8 (44%)	10	18	8	10	18
Diary/	A	11 (58%)	8	19	9 (56%)	7	16
Travel	B	15 (60%)	10	25	13 (57%)	10	23
Letter	A	12 (55%)	10	22	10 (34%)	19	29
	B	10 (59%)	7	17	8 (36%)	14	22
Appeal and	A	—	—	—	—	—	—
Answ.	B	1	2	3	1	1	2
Narrative	A	—	—	—	—	—	—
	B	12 (63%)	7	19	8	7	15
Sermon	A	1	4	5	17 (81%)	4	21
	B	4	10	14	8	5	13
Trial	A	13 (37%)	22	35	0	1	1
proceed.	B	5	1	6	2	1	3
Deposition	A	1	2	3	0	0	0
	B	2	0	2	0	1	1

and letters. In fiction and drama the trend is the same as for the comparative forms; namely, British English leads.[9]

Tables 10.7a, 10.7b and 10.7c show a more detailed distribution of inflectional and periphrastic forms of adjective comparison in the subperiods of the Corpus of Early American English (10.7a) and ARCHER (10.7b–c). The results here are highly variable, and some text types yield too few tokens to make reliable generalisations. For instance, in Table 10.7a the material available for the categories of appeals and depositions is particularly scanty, while diaries and journals are better represented. Similarly, in Table 10.7b some text types have fewer than 10 adjective forms per category within a subperiod.

Nevertheless, certain regularities can be observed. For example, Table 10.7b shows regularly increasing frequencies of inflectional forms in American English letters, fiction and drama from subperiod A to C. The shift towards the inflectional type of adjective comparison is, however, more uneven in journals and sermons. In British English, on the other hand, there is no monotonic progression in any of the text types from subperiod A to C. The frequencies fluctuate considerably.[10]

With respect to the superlative forms (see Table 10.7c), we can again pinpoint

Table 10.7b. *Inflectional and periphrastic comparative forms in the ARCHER corpus: text type and subperiod distributions. Infl. = inflectional forms; Peri. = periphrastic forms. A = 1750–1800; B = 1850–1900; C = 1950–90.*

		COMPARATIVE					
		British English			American English		
		Infl.	Peri.	Total	Infl.	Peri.	Total
Journal	A	19 (49%)	20	39	13 (68%)	6	19
	B	41 (72%)	16	57	20 (67%)	10	30
	C	25 (54%)	21	46	27 (52%)	25	52
Letter	A	10 (48%)	11	21	8 (42%)	11	19
	B	14 (82%)	3	17	8 (53%)	7	15
	C	7 (54%)	6	13	14 (54%)	12	26
Fiction	A	37 (50%)	37	74	22 (31%)	49	71
	B	48 (71%)	20	68	51 (54%)	43	94
	C	56 (66%)	29	85	30 (56%)	24	54
Drama	A	10 (77%)	3	13	12 (55%)	10	22
	B	19 (66%)	10	29	7 (58%)	5	12
	C	19 (66%)	10	29	23 (70%)	10	33
Sermon	A	17 (59%)	12	29	12 (50%)	12	24
	B	29 (74%)	10	39	23 (74%)	8	31
	C	21 (60%)	14	35	6 (60%)	4	10

a few regularities amidst a great deal of variation. For example, the text type of fiction is regular across both American English and British English; the frequency of the inflectional forms increases steadily from subperiod A to C. The same is true for letters in British English.[11]

It is probably no accident that the category of fiction reveals a great deal of regularity since it is so well represented in terms of number of texts. Another factor that might contribute to irregularities is the sometimes less homogeneous nature of the texts included in the corpus to represent a particular text type. The letter writers, for instance, represent a wide range of participant relationships (family members, close or more distant friends, business colleagues etc.) and writing styles (from informal to semi-formal and formal). Similarly, the category of journals includes travel journals, military journals, private diaries, and so forth, produced in various styles from telegraphic minute syntax to more elaborate phrasing. This variety reflects, of course, the intertextual variation characteristic of literary and non-literary production, but it may cause some unexpected irregularities in the more meagrely represented categories, in particular.

Table 10.7c. *Inflectional and periphrastic superlative forms in the ARCHER corpus: text type and subperiod distributions. Infl. = inflectional forms; Peri. = periphrastic forms. A = 1750–1800; B = 1850–1900; C = 1950–90.*

| | | SUPERLATIVE | | | | | |
| | | British English | | | American English | | |
		Infl.	Peri.	Total	Infl.	Peri.	Total
Journal	A	23 (41%)	33	56	11 (73%)	4	15
	B	13 (39%)	20	33	9 (47%)	10	19
	C	13 (59%)	9	22	18 (78%)	5	23
Letter	A	22 (47%)	25	47	17 (65%)	9	26
	B	17 (55%)	14	31	15 (71%)	6	21
	C	11 (92%)	1	12	12 (50%)	12	24
Fiction	A	46 (52%)	42	88	39 (42%)	55	94
	B	39 (63%)	23	62	21 (49%)	22	43
	C	25 (63%)	15	40	16 (55%)	13	29
Drama	A	28 (62%)	17	45	14 (50%)	14	28
	B	30 (67%)	15	45	15 (45%)	18	33
	C	9 (56%)	7	16	17 (71%)	7	24
Sermon	A	14 (54%)	12	26	28 (64%)	16	44
	B	21 (66%)	11	32	12 (44%)	15	27
	C	7 (50%)	7	14	10 (59%)	7	17

4   Discussion

We turn now to the issue of standardisation. Assuming one of the common definitions of standard as a written variety varying minimally in form and maximally in function, whose norms are codified in grammars and dictionaries (see e.g. Joseph 1987), we recognise that a standard does not arise via a 'natural' or inherent course of linguistic evolution, but by deliberate and conscious planning. Generally speaking, standard languages have been synonymous with élite varieties and they are imposed from above through institutions such as schools, printing houses, language academies, etc. Thus, standardisation is an ongoing process, spanning centuries in some cases, as the history of English clearly shows.

While the term 'King's English' was used by the end of the sixteenth century to label normative forms of English, not all royalty would have been considered good exemplars of it. The standards of the highest-class speakers were at first not necessarily those of the new self-constituted authorities on correctness of the seventeenth and eighteenth centuries. Even though, as Strang (1970: 107) points out, by 1770 English had a standard written form almost as invariable as today's, its norms were not universally embraced. Even Dr Johnson, who had a clearly thought-out opinion of how English was best to be spelled and is often given credit for fixing English spelling in its modern form, used two 'standards' of spelling, one in his dictionary and another in his private writings.

However, as pointed out by Romaine (1998: 13), 'a newly monied class of merchants in London would be eager to learn what H. C. Wyld (1920) called the "new-fangled English", i.e. the newly codified Standard English, as a sign of their upward mobility'. Sociolinguistic research of modern urban areas has, if anything, given us a revealing picture of the standard's uneven diffusion as it illustrates how social class boundaries act in similar ways to geographical ones in terms of their ability to impede or facilitate the spread of linguistic features.

During the period covered by the Corpus of Early American English we can probably still speak with some justification of there being only one national standard, i.e. British English, although subsequently a distinct American Standard was to emerge. London's norms, especially with regard to written English, were aspired to in the colonies, even after Noah Webster's (1789: 20) insistence on breaking ranks with an exogenous standard: 'As an independent nation our honour requires us to have a system of our own, in language as well as government. Great Britain, whose children we are, and whose language we speak, should no longer be our standard.' In any case, the American colonies lacked a single centre of linguistic prestige. Even though the major port cities of Boston, New York, Philadelphia and Charleston were important points of contact with Britain and centres of diffusion for their respective hinterlands, none was London's equal with respect to the development of Standard English.

We have already commented on some trends in our data which indicate that British English was slightly ahead of American English at each subperiod in terms of implementing the change towards the inflectional type of adjective comparison. This may be yet another instance of a phenomenon referred to as 'colonial lag' (see Marckwardt 1958: 59–80; Krapp 1960 [1925]: I,50ff.; Görlach 1987). Whether this particular aspect of the change in adjective comparison had anything to do with standardisation processes *per se* is doubtful, although we have already attributed the restricted occurrence of double forms to prescriptivism. In other words, the reassertion of the inflectional type as the primary one may simply reflect ordinary language change. A close examination of the prescriptive tradition in British and American English will be needed in order to clarify that question. Our analysis does, however, cast considerable doubt on the claims made by Barber, Fries and Potter about the tendency towards increasing use of periphrasis in the latter half of the twentieth century (see Tables 10.3a and 10.3b in particular).

To take an example of the prescriptivist viewpoint, in his landmark work *English Grammar* from 1795, Lindley Murray provides his readers with a list of 'rules' that are aimed at helping (as he puts it) 'to produce the agreement and right disposition of words in a sentence' (p. 87). In 'Rule VIII', Murray states that 'double comparatives and superlatives should be avoided':

Double comparatives and superlatives should be avoided, such as, 'A worser conduct;' 'on lesser hopes;' 'A more serener temper;' 'The most straitest sect': It should be 'worse conduct'; 'less hopes;' 'a more serene temper;' 'the straitest sect'. (Murray 1795: 103–4)

The absence of double forms in our data testifies to the success of this 'rule' advocated by the grammarians. Murray also proscribes the use of superlative forms of adjectives such as *chief*, *perfect*, *right* and *universal* that have in themselves 'a superlative signification':

> Adjectives that have in themselves a superlative signification do not properly admit of the superlative form superadded; such as, 'Chief, extreme, perfect, right; universal,' &c.; which are sometimes improperly written 'Chiefest, extremest, perfectest, rightest, most universal,' &c. The following expressions are therefore improper. 'He sometimes claims admission to the chiefest offices.' 'The quarrel was become so universal and national;' '*become universal.*' 'A method of attaining the rightest and greatest happiness.' (Murray 1795: 104)

To turn back to our data, our ARCHER subcorpus yielded three instances of 'most perfect' (example 12) and one instance of 'most universal', accompanied by an instance of 'chiefest' in the Early American Corpus.

(12)   SIR RICHARD: But so far as you can judge?
       INEZ: So far as I can judge, Sue is in a state of the *most perfect* indifference towards every man alive. (ARCHER/BrEng/1850–1900/Drama/Henry Arthur Jones)

Further evidence will be needed to address some of the issues we have raised here. We will need to apply techniques of sociohistorical reconstruction in order to obtain a fuller spectrum of text types and styles, particularly those most likely to reveal similarities to spoken language. We also need to examine, where possible, non-standard and regional varieties of English, which may have diverged from Standard English with respect to this development. A thorough investigation of the syntactic and semantic features that may block the occurrence of one or the other form in a given context is also in order. We hope to do this in further work on the topic.

Notes

We are indebted to Douglas Biber (Northern Arizona University) and Edward Finegan (University of Southern California) for access to the pilot version of the ARCHER corpus.
  1 Following the most common practice, we use the terms 'inflectional' and 'periphrastic' in this study (see Quirk et al. 1985), even though the term 'inflectional' is not

entirely accurate, since, strictly speaking, no inflection is involved (Pound 1901: 2). Our study is also confined to gradable adjectives, and thus excludes inflectional and periphrastic forms of adverb comparison. To expand the scope of discussion and situate our findings in the larger historical context, we compare our results with those obtained in Kytö and Romaine (1997), which focused on long-term developments in adjective comparison based on data from a number of corpora.

2 We have not included instances of negative adjective comparison with *less/least* in this discussion since there is no corresponding inflectional form. All in all, they are rare in the two corpora studied.

3 Various names such as double, multiple, pleonastic or hybrid have been given to forms such as *more nicer*. Strictly speaking, most of them are periphrastic in nature, except for a few common defective adjectives such as *worser*, *bestest*, etc., which are inflectional.

4 Owing to gaps in the representation of text types in the Corpus of Early American English, the use of the chi-square test (or other such tests of statistical significance) is not advisable.

5 The figures obtained for the comparative forms are significant (British English: chi-square $= 15.029$, df $= 2$, $p < 0.001$; American English: chi-square $= 10.476$, df $= 2$, $p < 0.01$). For the subsequent tables, the statistical significance of results is commented on only when the figures obtained are significant ($p < 0.05$, $p < 0.01$ or $p < 0.001$) and when the tables do not contain cells with expected values less than 5.

6 In Table 10.4 the figures obtained are significant (comparative: chi-square $= 246.410$, df $= 2$, $p < 0.001$; superlative: chi-square $= 98.100$, df $= 2$, $p < 0.001$).

7 In Table 10.5b the figures obtained for disyllabic comparative forms are significant (British English: chi-square $= 7.407$, df $= 2$, $p < 0.05$; American English: chi-square $= 16.210$, df $= 2$, $p < 0.001$).

8 The figures obtained for comparative forms in American English are significant (chi-square $= 10.042$, df $= 4$, $p < 0.05$).

9 The figures obtained for superlative forms in American English are significant (chi-square $= 10.277$, df $= 4$, $p < 0.05$).

10 In Table 10.7b the figures obtained for comparative forms in British journals and fiction are significant (chi-square $= 6.053$ and 7.203, respectively, with df $= 2$, and $p < 0.05$); the corresponding figures obtained for American fiction are significant as well (chi-square $= 10.882$, df $= 2$, $p < 0.01$).

11 In Table 10.7c the figures obtained for British letters are significant (chi-square $= 7.800$, df $= 2$, $p < 0.05$).

References

Barber, Charles L. 1964. *Linguistic Change in Present-Day English*, London: André Deutsch.

Bauer, Laurie 1994. *Watching English Change. An Introduction to the Study of Linguistic Change in Standard Englishes in the Twentieth Century*, London: Longman.

Biber, Douglas, Edward Finegan and Dwight Atkinson 1994a. 'ARCHER and its challenges: compiling and exploring a representative corpus of historical English registers', in *Creating and Using English Language Corpora. Papers from the Fourteenth International Conference on English Language Research on Computerized Cor-*

Adjective comparison in American and British English 193

pora, Zürich 1993, ed. Udo Fries, Gunnel Tottie and Peter Schneider, Amsterdam and Atlanta, Ga: Rodopi, pp. 1–13.

Biber, Douglas, Edward Finegan, Dwight Atkinson, Ann Beck, Dennis Burges and Jena Burges 1994b. 'The design and analysis of the ARCHER corpus: a progress report (a representative corpus of historical English registers)', *Corpora Across the Centuries. Proceedings of the First International Colloquium on English Diachronic Corpora, St Catharine's College Cambridge, 25–27 March 1993*, ed. Merja Kytö, Matti Rissanen and Susan Wright, Amsterdam and Atlanta, Ga: Rodopi, pp. 3–6.

BNC = The British National Corpus May 1995. Oxford University Computing Services.

Curme, George O. 1931. *A Grammar of the English Language.* Vol. II: *Syntax*, D. C. Heath and Company; repr. Essex: Verbatim Printing, 1977.

Fries, Charles C. 1940. *American English Grammar*, New York: Appleton-Century-Crofts.

Görlach, Manfred 1987. 'The colonial lag? The alleged conservative character of American English and other "colonial" varieties', *English World-Wide* 8.1, 41–60.

Helsinki Corpus = The Helsinki Corpus of English Texts, Department of English, University of Helsinki, 1991.

Jespersen, Otto 1949. *A Modern English Grammar on Historical Principles,* part VII: *Syntax*, Copenhagen and London: Ejnar Munksgaard, George Allen and Unwin.

Joseph, John E. 1987. *Eloquence and Power: The Rise of Language Standards and Standard Languages*, London: Pinter.

Knüpfer, Hans 1922. *Die Anfänge der periphrastischen Komparation im Englischen*, dissertation, Heidelberg; also in: *Englische Studien* 55 (1921), 321–89.

Krapp, G. P. 1960 [1925]. *The English Language in America*, 2 vols., New York: Frederick Ungar Publishing Co.

Kytö, Merja 1996. ' "The best and most excellentest way": the rivalling forms of adjective comparison in Late Middle and Early Modern English', *Words. Proceedings of an International Symposium, Lund, 25–26 August 1995*, ed. Jan Svartvik, Stockholm: Kungl. Vitterhets Historie och Antikvitets Akademien, pp. 123–44.

Kytö, Merja and Suzanne Romaine 1997. 'Competing forms of adjective comparison in Modern English: what could be *more quicker* and *easier* and *more effective?*', *To Explain the Present. Studies in the Changing English Language in Honour of Matti Rissanen*, ed. Terttu Nevalainen and Leena Kahlas-Tarkka, Helsinki: Société Néophilologique, pp. 329–52.

Leech, Geoffrey and Jonathan Culpeper 1997. 'The comparison of adjectives in recent British English', *To Explain the Present. Studies in the Changing English Language in Honour of Matti Rissanen*, ed. Terttu Nevalainen and Leena Kahlas-Tarkka, Helsinki: Société Néophilologique, pp. 353–73.

Loikkanen, Tuija 1997. 'Is it more common to say *more common* or *commoner*? Adjective comparison in BrE, AmE and AusE', Pro Gradu thesis, Department of English, University of Helsinki.

Marckwardt, Albert H. 1958. *American English*, New York: Oxford University Press.

Mencken, H. L. 1970. *The American Language. An Inquiry into the Development of English in the United States*, New York: Alfred A. Knopf (First edn 1919).

Mitchell, Bruce 1985. *Old English Syntax*, vol. I, Oxford: Clarendon Press.

Murray, Lindley 1795. *English Grammar, Adapted to the Different Classes of Learners. With an Appendix, Containing Rules and Observations for Promoting Perspicuity in Speaking and Writing*, York: Wilson, Spence and Mawman.

Nist, John 1963. 'Folk Speech', in *Aspects of American English*, ed. Elizabeth M. Kerr and Ralph M. Aderman, New York: Harcourt Brace Jovanovich, pp. 344–5.

Potter, Simeon 1975 [1969]. *Changing English*, London: Andre Deutsch (2nd revised edn).

Pound, Louise 1901. *The Comparison of Adjectives in English in the XV and the XVI Century*, Anglistische Forschungen 7, Heidelberg: Carl Winter.

Quirk, Randolph, Sidney Greenbaum, Geoffrey Leech and Jan Svartvik 1985. *A Comprehensive Grammar of the English Language*, London and New York: Longman.

Romaine, Suzanne 1998. 'Introduction', *The Cambridge History of the English Language*, vol. IV: *1776–1997*, ed. Suzanne Romaine, 1–56, Cambridge University Press.

Strang, Barbara M. H. 1970. *A History of English*, London: Methuen.

Webster, Noah 1789. *Dissertations on the English Language*, Boston: Thomas.

Wyld, H. C. 1920. *A History of Modern Colloquial English*, Oxford: Blackwell (3rd edn).

11   *The Spectator*, the politics of social networks, and language standardisation in eighteenth century England[1]

SUSAN FITZMAURICE

1   Introduction

It is accepted as a commonplace in the study of the history of modern Standard English that the grammar writers of the second half of the eighteenth century were instrumental in erecting the English grammar as a prescriptive device. Left unexamined, this commonplace obscures the social and political motivations of what amounts to a kind of prescriptivist movement in the period. In addition, it does not indicate the impact that this apparent movement has on speakers and writers. In this essay, I will consider the question of how the prescriptive grammarians came to identify a particular version or variety of English as a basic model for the construction of a Standard English. Did they discover its identifying features and exempla in the fabric of particular texts produced by specific writers? And if they did happen upon their model in this fashion, how did they choose these texts and these writers as appropriate sources of information for the variety that they would designate as prestigious, and prescribe and transmit as a standard? Put more succinctly, how did good linguistic practices become manifest to the eighteenth-century prescriptivists as sufficiently prestigious to be identified, selected and thereafter transmitted as a norm?

There is no simple answer to this set of questions. I will argue that the prescriptive grammarians took as one of the bases of their model of Standard English the periodical *The Spectator*. Importantly, it was not the paper's linguistic purity which most recommended it, for its pages furnished the prescriptivists with many examples of flawed, ungrammatical and incorrect English. Instead, the journal's extraordinary popularity both during and well after its lifetime, and its considerable cultural authority in matters of manners and politeness for many middle-class English men and women, made it one of the centrally important texts of the early eighteenth century. I argue that the prescriptivists use the cultural weight and literary reputation of *The Spectator* as an index of social prestige, and pay attention to the language of the periodical in consequence. To build a case in support of this claim, I will situate politically and socially the processes of linguistic standardisation in late eighteenth-century England (section 2), and then consider the stance of *The Spectator* regarding contemporary issues of polite language usage. In section 3 I consider the importance of the periodical for the status and social centrality of the men behind it, notably that of Joseph Addison and his circle. I draw upon social network theory to demonstrate how *The Spectator*'s social cohort works, and how the interests of the group shape the social and political stance of the periodical itself. In section 4 I examine a specific feature of the language of the network of men involved with the periodical to see how far their own usage matches or differs from the ideal prescribed by the prescriptivists. I hope to demonstrate how an approach informed by cultural and literary history may illuminate the politics of the construction of modern Standard English in the later eighteenth century.

2   Standardisation and codification

The role that individuals play, in selecting (unconsciously) particular forms and in attaching the necessary social prestige to those forms for them to become ideals of the standardisers is instrumental in the construction of the historical background to codification. The conscious activism of codification involved in standardisation occurs once features ripe for selection have already gained prestige, perhaps by virtue of being markers of identifiably powerful speakers. Social networks are mechanisms that link individual speakers as friends, literary collaborators or business associates. Occasionally, when conditions are optimal, they facilitate the spread of particular patterns or components of linguistic behaviour. This transmission of language patterns from speaker to speaker across a social network does not usually occur in an overt or organised fashion – it is a by-product rather than a goal of the social contact between speakers. By contrast, the business of implementing and stabilising a language standard typically takes the form of a process or set of processes undertaken by a group of speakers acting as authorities, whose task may include transmitting the result of standardisation (with its attendant values), by design, to as many speakers as possible. Unlike language spread as a consequence of social contact, the construction and implementation of a standard language is an intentional, ideologically motivated set of actions. Let us apply this view to the eighteenth century, and examine the resulting historical scenario.

The second half of the eighteenth century sees much change in the ways in which English speakers consider their language. From at least 1755, after the publication of Samuel Johnson's *Dictionary*, grammarians, school teachers and rhetoricians became increasingly interested in fixing and disseminating a model of written English that would be a standard and standard-bearer of the 'best' English language. This interest manifested itself in the proliferation of grammars, spelling books, rhetorics and letter-writing manuals which together constituted an arsenal of teach-yourself materials for the socially, economically and politically ambitious. The activism suggested by this production never resulted in the establishment of a formal academy for overseeing the progress of the English language. Crowley (1996: 56ff) discusses the celebration of English and the academy issue in the context of ideas of the nation's political uncertainty in the eighteenth century. Despite the lack of any formally or officially sanctioned body to ensure the preservation of the purity of the English language as envisaged by Johnson in his *Plan* of the Dictionary (1747: 32), there was a fairly explicit set of language-oriented practices and resources which teachers used in the English education of schoolboys belonging to or aspiring to the middling ranks, whether they were destined for trades or for the new professions (Earle, 1989).

Crowley (1996: 84) argues that language teaching in the eighteenth century was crucial in terms of 'the demarcation of bourgeois social space and the linguistic habitus required to in-habit it' and implies that this social space is a unified, undifferentiated thing. In fact, in social historical (rather than Bakh-tinian theoretical) terms, 'bourgeois social space' was by no means as unified an entity as the ideology of the inculcation of the 'habitus' suggests. Quite apart from the fact that London's middle state splintered into ranks differentiated by sources of income and type of occupation, the social and political rewards that mastery of the habitus brought varied. The social model of behaviour was based on a particularly late eighteenth-century notion of the 'polite' and the 'well-bred', and its aim was to secure everyone in his or her place. Politeness, one component of this bourgeois ideology that was signposted by clearly identifiable markers like correct language, was a means to divide further the middle states, to separate out the less from the more genteel merchant and trading classes. James Raven (1992: 140) points out that by contrast with the early part of the century, 'what was so different in the late eighteenth century was the fresh definition of social awkwardness and the particular consciousness of inferiority that went with it'. He also notes (1992: 141) the 'escalation of London-based pleas for standardised grammar and pronunciation' to meet the demand for education in politeness and taste, two entirely social concepts. In modern sociolinguistic terms, politeness becomes an attribute which the lower middle class must acquire if they are to join the group that they yearn to belong to – the solid middle middle class. Given a clearly-defined set of criteria (via do-it-yourself aids like handbooks of letter writing, manuals of etiquette and pronunciation guides), politeness – as embodied in a notion of correctness – was a commodity that could be bought. And one of its most transparent markers, language, was a product that could be marketed.

The proliferation of prescriptive grammars in the second half of the century is interesting in two respects. Firstly, it does the practical task of providing the concrete means of replacing a classical, liberal education with what Ash (1760) calls an *English* education suited to the needs of a modern, mighty trading nation. Secondly, the commercial and undoubted social value of the skills considered essential in this English education, such as penmanship, accounting and geography (Edwards, 1765) made the production of prescriptive grammars a profitable and competitive business for members of a profession which was not particularly well paid (Earle, 1989: 68; Holmes, 1982: 57). There were some highly respectable writers among the most successful producers of grammars, but many were very often 'little more than hack compilers or writer-booksellers with a quick appreciation of market potential' (Raven, 1992: 153).

Many grammars were practical digests of more authoritatively argued and philosophically based works, and were carefully targeted at a distinct market. Their writers were schoolteachers who designed their works for their own schools and academies, supplementing the basic grammars with readers: anthologies of moral writing for the general education and edification of their charges (Ward, 1777; 1789). These kinds of texts seemed to promise social advancement, whether they were supposed to help improve the prospects of a socially advantageous marriage for a woman of undistinguished family, or whether they were to help secure a permanent position for a beginning clerk. They also offered lower middle-class readers a way of distancing themselves from those they considered their immediate social inferiors by giving them the means of ascertaining the level of gentility attained. This discrimination was particularly salient where the 'price of admission to polite society' was economic success (Langford, 1989: 121).

In this context it is worth commenting briefly on the source and selection of those linguistic features designated 'polite' and thus 'correct' in the language. It was not enough for teachers to rely upon some abstract 'way of speaking'; they needed something material with which to drill their pupils. The writers of most English grammars in the early part of the century tended to describe the grammatical patterns commonly encountered and used in the language. The conception of such a project depends on an idealised notion of linguistic performance as largely uniform and homogeneous, reflecting in part the social inclinations and educational biases of the writers themselves.[2] As a result, the early eighteenth-century grammar writers were not interested principally in addressing or instructing a speech community divided by factors like class, gender, and education. (And if they were, it was with the object of smoothing away those differences.) But the purpose and nature of grammar-writing changed, precisely because of the needs and aspirations of a markedly heterogeneous community. In the second half of the century the grammar writer begins to assume the mantle of the judge and arbiter of correct and thus polite English.

What does this model of English consist of? The codification of language in the grammars of the second half of the century results in a clear sense of what low(-class) or *impolite* language is: archaic, colloquial and ungrammatical. Modern Standard English is up-to-date, formal and correct. Unlike traditional regional dialects, it is free from lexical and grammatical archaism. By contrast with the informal, intimate sociolects that are the communicative currency of local communities, it is free from colloquialism. And finally, in stark opposition to the casual sloppiness of uneducated writing, it is free from solecism. Sundby et al. (1991), and Leonard (1929) have produced anthologies of rules which they have identified as constitutive of correct English of the period, and there are ample details of the features which attained the status of norms.

One norm is the injunction to use the relative pronouns *who(m)* and *which* at the expense of the increasingly vilified *that* on the one hand, and the complete omission of relative marking, explicitly condemned, on the other. The question is how the prescriptivists (virtually by consensus) identify this rule as an important norm, and thereafter determine its selection as part of correct English.

The simple answer is that the prescriptivists pick up upon a choice already regularly practised in the writing of those speakers that many of them consider to be ideal models for standard written English. Of course the situation is more complicated than this; although the texts of writers like Addison, Pope and Swift are greatly admired, the writers themselves tend to be frequently condemned for incorrect usage.[3] One way of specifying what correct language is, is to demonstrate how the language perceived to be the politest of all is marred by colloquialism, archaic expression, and grammatical infelicity. And so writing hitherto considered to be critical to the polite canon begins to be scrutinised afresh in the new light shed by the notion of polite language as correct language. The critique of the best writers yields the best examples of both correct and improper usage. The grammarians are not so interested in removing these writers from the canon as in identifying for the practical education of their readers, the substance of correct and incorrect language (and consequently, style). By offering extensive illustrations and judicious corrections of bad grammar from the best authors, the grammarians arrive at a corpus of rules which can be seen in action. For example, the prescriptive grammarians regularly castigate Addison, Swift and Pope for their failure to observe the standard of modern, formal, correct English writing, and provide the reader with improved, grammatically correct versions of their offending constructions (Fitzmaurice, 1998). One text which turns up frequently in the grammarians' illustrative corpora of good and bad writing is *The Spectator*. This periodical furnishes extensive illustration of a range of prose styles on many topical issues in the period. The critics tend to admire and recommend the topics and their treatment, while criticising and correcting the style of the writing. This potent combination ensures the place of *The Spectator* as a central reference text for the remainder of the century.

3   *The Spectator* and the English Language

The Spectator of Joseph Addison, Richard Steele and their collaborators looms large in the cultural and intellectual life of England throughout the eighteenth century, despite its very short actual life.[4] The significance of *The Spectator* as an index of popular taste for the century is unchallenged, and its impact on many spheres of eighteenth century experience is undoubted. To understand its relation to the shape of the English language and the way in which it is studied in the century requires careful scrutiny of the basis of *The Spectator*'s influence. The stated aim of *The Spectator* to serve as a *vade mecum* of manners and mores for schoolboys, women and the emerging middle classes, in town and country, is well known. However, *The Spectator*'s own pronouncements on immodest and indelicate language, on the justness and purity of language, and on the 'genius' of the English language provide scant indication of the impact it comes to have on the language later in the century.

The linguistic influence of *The Spectator* is a (necessary) byproduct of its more general significance for the culture of eighteenth-century England. To understand this, we need to consider the nature of influence, and how this combines with the idea of the *spectator*. It is a commonplace that observation alters the state of the subject observed – we need look no further than Labov's 'observer's paradox'. This idea assumes that observation (spectatorship) is an act which has material consequences for the subject of scrutiny. The relationship between spectator and subject that we subsume in the expression 'observation' might be better characterised by the more socially resonant term 'influence'. As in the social sciences, influence cannot be discerned except in its results. The mere fact of *The Spectator*'s presence does not make it easy to theorise social influence, but its social position does help. If social influence can be traced to processes such as relations of authority, identification, expertise and competition, it is possible to build an account of *The Spectator*'s influence through citation.

A cursory examination of the contemporary press reveals constant reference to the periodical and the men behind it; and a beginning sense of *The Spectator*'s influence. Some pamphleteers attacked *The Spectator*,[5] while Gay, for one, praised the newcomer.[6] Swift's *Examiner* found little in it to attract his ire, and Defoe's *Review*, which had been hard at work since 1704, commented on the 'inimitable' *Spectator* 'not only for his learning and wit, but especially for his applying that learning and wit to the true ends for which they are given, viz., the establishing virtue in, and the shaming vice out of the world.' (Oct. 2, 1711; Evans, 1987). This sort of citation establishes relationships of identification and competition. Identification proceeds first by acknowledgement and thereafter by recognition, and however hostile the welcoming pamphlets, their attention to the periodical must count as influence. Competition too, signals the acknowledgement on the part of competitors that their target is important – after all what generates competition is the perception of influence.

The relationship of authority emerges and develops over time. *The Spectator*'s authority was acknowledged in the appearance of journals in England and on the Continent paying their respects by adopting its name. In 1721, the French playwright and novelist Marivaux launched *Le Spectateur Français*, a periodical in twenty-five issues which ran until 1724 (Haac 1973). In England twenty years later Eliza Haywood started her monthly periodical *Female Spectator* (1744–1746) ostensibly 'in imitation of my learned Brother, of ever precious memory' (Messenger 1986: 110).

If competition characterises contemporary citation of *The Spectator* and its authority is imprinted on those journals declaring themselves to be its offspring, at least in spirit, then the relationship of expertise must account for the enduring popularity of *The Spectator* as a key text in schoolboy composition exercises and the subject of translation into Latin and Greek (Bond (ed.) 1965, vol. I: cii). It is the dependably moral stance of the *Spectator* papers on matters of everyday life as well as on grave issues which probably qualifies it as a text worthy for the attention of schoolboys; even more so than the 'purity of taste, clothed in such exquisite language' that marked the *Spectator* essays as entirely suitable for use in grammar schools, according to Addison's editor, Richard Hurd (Hurd 1932: 76). Thomas Dilworth acknowledged this point, contrasting the virtuous *Spectator* with the Grubstreet Papers 'which only serve to corrupt and debauch the Principles of those, who are so unhappy as to spend their Time therein' (1751: viii–ix). The combination of authority and expertise results in the citation of *The Spectator* as representative of the best in English prose and thus as a candidate for the model *par excellence* of polite language of the period. By the second half of the eighteenth century, quotations from the periodical, with Addison invariably identified as the source of the quotation, come to be the staple fare offered by grammars characterising polite language. This kind of citation presents the linguistic aspect of good manners and behaviour. The grammarians cite and change *The Spectator*'s language to demonstrate how elegant language might be improved by grammatical correctness.

The compilers of the *Dictionary of English Normative Grammar* estimate that in the (187) prescriptive grammars published between 1700 and 1800, the frequency with which *The Spectator* is cited (149) is exceeded only by Swift (224), the New Testament (221), Hume (214), Addison himself (177) and Pope (155) (Sundby et al. 1991: 35). I discovered that in just one grammar, Ward (1765), *The Spectator* is quoted 59 times, exceeded only by the Old (88) and New (77) Testaments, more frequently than Addison (38) (Wright 1994: 244). These frequencies provide an idea of the status and visibility of *The Spectator* as an index of cultural (if not always linguistic) authority. For many grammar writers in the latter half of the century, *The Spectator* seems to encapsulate a representative, institutional sort of expression of the state of the English language, providing grist to the grammarians' prescriptive mill.

The Spectator also provides what is arguably the first 'authoritative' judgement before Bishop Lowth of the practice of omitting relative pronouns in expressions like (Addison's) 'in the temper of mind he was then' (*Spectator* 549). In *Spectator* 135, Addison discussed what he described as 'the suppressing of several Particles, which must be produced in other Tongues to make a Sentence intelligible', namely, the 'Relatives, *Who, which* or *that*'. Instead of issuing judgement himself, Addison adopts the convenient persona of Mr. Spectator, preferring to defer to 'something like an Academy, that by the best Authorities and Rules drawn from the Analogy of Languages shall settle all Controversies between Grammar and Idiom'.

The next significant occasion on which this feature receives critical scrutiny occurs as late as 1762, with Lowth's pronouncements in his *Introduction*. Lowth appears to be the first grammarian proper to take up the problem (Leonard 1929: 87–9; Sundby et al., 1991: 247–9). And when he does, he remarks simply that the 'Relative is often understood, or omitted', but his vigorous footnotes with illustrative examples indicate his view of omission as 'hazardous, and hardly justifiable' (Lowth 1762: 137). Lowth's disapproving line is picked up with relish by succeeding grammarians, like John Ash (1763), who designates omission of relative pronouns 'improper ellipsis'. The grammarians employ an array of expressions with which to label the offending ellipsis: from the comparatively harmless 'colloquial' (Elphinston 1765: 147; Crocker 1772: 38), through 'improper' (Bell 1769: 304; Blair 1783: 470), 'imprecise' (Ash 1763: 124; Story 1783: 36) and 'inaccurate' (Brittain 1788: 158), to downright 'bad' (Baker 1770: 101) and finally, the worst category 'solecism' (Lynch 1796: 89). These labels verge on the moralistic; to be sloppy or imprecise in speech implied a lapse in more than linguistic virtue. The result of this flurry of attention in the late eighteenth century is an enduring prescriptive rule which continues to carry weight in the matter of distinguishing between formal and familiar styles of writing on the one hand, and between writing and speaking on the other. The rule concerns the development of norms of polite language, and so it is not surprising that *The Spectator* should make the first observation of the eighteenth century to question the propriety of this feature.

Lowth evidently recognised and valued the weight of *The Spectator*'s general appeal. In this spirit, he uses *Spectators* 73 and 124 in his section on 'Punctuation' to exemplify the (correct) structure of simple and compound sentences (1762: 162–71). He, like many of his fellow-grammarians, finds himself in the awkward position of praising *The Spectator* on the one hand, and castigating it for its colloquialism and familiar style where a more lofty, formal one might be used, on the other. He metes out the same treatment to individual members of the network; Addison, Pope, Swift and Prior, some of the 'best' writers of the day, rarely escape vilification for improper, imprecise and colloquial usage.

The influence of *The Spectator* is not restricted to prescriptive grammars. Hugh Blair's lectures on Rhetoric and Belles Lettres, which focused on style rather than grammar, are similarly concerned with exemplification and critical instruction. In lectures 18 and 19, Blair presents a general overview of style, illustrating his definitions and discussion by reference to diverse authors, from Aristotle and Clarendon to Shaftesbury, Swift and Addison. In lectures 20–3, Blair proceeds with the critical examination of style, choosing Addison's *Spectator* essays on the Imagination for analysis.

4   Networks of power: the men behind *The Spectator*

4.1   Networks and history

The Spectator represents a collective view of politics, religion, morality and criticism – one developed and espoused by a powerful coterie of (principally Whig) gentlemen with a particularly clear social and political agenda. Joseph Addison might well have been the symbol of *The Spectator*'s values, and Addison and Richard Steele might well have been the articulators of this vision, but they were not solely responsible for it. *The Spectator*'s social plan for the English middle classes of the century can be traced to what might be called the hegemony of a network of powerful men. This hegemony is composed of a definable set of interests, political, financial, social, intellectual, which dominated the London scene (though not government) in the reign of Queen Anne. While the similarities and differences between the individuals representing these interests is not problematic, a precise and useful description of the social structure, dynamics and limits of the group is. It might be useful to sketch the historical context to illustrate this difficulty.

In the period following the so-called Glorious Revolution of 1688, London established itself as the centre of trade and the financial hub for the new provincially based industries. Merchants and shopkeepers were increasingly well-to-do and socially ambitious with their new wealth. The new professions of journalism, accountancy and stockbroking encouraged the liberalisation of the education system, providing a home for what Daniel Defoe called the 'middling sort'. In this social melting pot, diplomats and army officers rubbed shoulders with architects and playwrights, petty aristocrats with self-made men, churchmen with journalists. London was the centre of England's cultural, intellectual and political life, and so its people, especially those of the middling sort occupied an uncertain position – neither transparently upper-class nor evidently working-class. London grew dramatically in the course of the century, its population rising from 575,000 in 1700 to 900,000 in 1801 (Garside 1990: 476). By the end of the century, aristocratic values in city government had been replaced by a bourgeois and plutocratic ethos (481), as London's mercantile and financial bourgeoisie began to dominate an increasingly open and socially ambiguous polite society. Thus the social fabric of London changed in the course of the century, defying any straightforward analysis using sociological categories like class.

All of this suggests that social class, a historically specific, technical construct, is not necessarily an appropriate category to describe the historical and social conditioning of linguistic practice. To situate socially the practices and preferences among well-educated, political literary men in early eighteenth-century London, I will adopt a much adapted analysis using social networks. The notion of 'network' is also a technical one, developed in the fields of anthropology, social psychology, sociology, epidemiology, business studies, economics, and recently in sociolinguistics, to describe the relationship between individuals and the social structures which they construct and inhabit (Boissevain 1974; Wasserman and Galaskiewicz 1994; Milroy 1987; Milroy and Milroy 1985, 1992). By 'network', I mean a group of individuals with social ties of varying strengths, types and distances between one another. The network defining these individuals is not necessarily closed. This means that one might have ties with somebody that nobody else in the network is connected to. The degree of proximity between actors might be measured in terms of the nature of their ties. The criteria by which these ties are measured are: longevity of relationship, geographical proximity, formal social relationship in terms of comparative rank (social equal/superior/inferior) and type of relationship (intimates/equals/acquaintances; friendship/competition). The latter is inferred from the nature of evidence for the relationship (in the form of texts and other evidence connecting the actors, such as correspondence, memoirs, collaboration in pamphlets, editions, plays, etc.). These four represent a combination of subjective and objective parameters.[7] The calculation of these ties and the characterisation of the group in terms of the values attributed to the ties between actors provides the analyst with a structural basis for inferring and understanding social influence, both of one actor upon another and of the network as a whole on other networks in the community. The processes taken to underlie influence include 'relations of authority, identification, expertise and competition' (Marsden and Friedkin 1994: 3).

Studying this kind of coterie at such a historical remove cannot replicate the detail that social anthropological studies using the technique achieve. Subjects leave only partial personal historical records, leaving the linguist to do the work of historical detective, biographer and amateur psychologist. So the historical evidence for the nature, strength and number of ties between individuals is at best partial and at worst misleading. Because we cannot interrogate directly the perceptions of our historical informants we have to rely on a range of different textual material. Because the nature of the material itself is immutable and partial it does not readily supply the best raw data out of which to construct detailed ethnographic accounts of these peoples' lives and friendships. We might gain data that are comprehensive in quantity and range but they are rarely consistent, even, or representative. Notwithstanding these caveats, there are good reasons for trying out network analysis. The textual material accessible for this historical period favours a network analytic approach because the texts are the productions of individuals. My subjects have a repertoire of writings, but some have only the most personal kinds of textual testimony – letters to family, friends, associates. It is worth pointing out that these letters correspond to the kind of ethnographic detail usually collected to construct contemporary social networks. Although they are more impoverished than such data, they are the historical equivalent. These kinds of texts thus provide the source of both the raw linguistic data and valuable personal social information.

4.2   *Joseph Addison and his circle*

Joseph Addison and Richard Steele were the men behind *The Spectator* (1711–1714). They were the centre of a coterie of well-educated, politically ambitious men whose friendships were conducted publicly in Button's coffee-house, the political Kit-Cat Club and through collaborative literary enterprises, and privately in their correspondence. The coterie includes famous literary figures like Jonathan Swift and Matthew Prior as well as political men like Charles Montagu and Edward Wortley Montagu. We will situate Addison rather than Steele at the centre of the network under scrutiny because he, not Steele, is most closely associated with *The Spectator* both by his contemporaries and by later observers and critics (Wright 1997).

Addison's social circle varies its shape and density in accordance with the nature of the relationships that Addison contracts with different individuals. These relationships do not consist solely of friendships, though friendship is a historical factor, and one that is complicated by its very formal expression and construction in contemporary literary and political groups (such as Pope, Swift, Arbuthnot, Gay and the Scriblerians, and the Tory Brotherhood). The network is also dynamic, so that Addison's coterie changes over time with the changing political fortunes and allegiances, literary success or departures into obscurity and deaths of the members of his circle. After all, 'the formation, maintenance and dissolution of a friendship relation is a continuous combination of personality factors, relational factors and environmental factors' (Zeggelink 1994: 304). We need to describe Addison's changing network to reflect the perception that the connections he establishes with different members of his immediate social circle contrast with one another. The ties are not necessarily ones of friendship as we might understand this term today, though they are associations which are contracted strategically. Carley and Krackhardt (1996) offer a way of characterising the asymmetrical and occasionally non-reciprocal contacts that occur in the evolution of a relationship between individuals. They examine the evolution of friendship in terms of different points of view or perception of the relationship. Importantly, they assume that a friendship is *not* inherently symmetrical, and that it is best constructed using both sociometric and cognitive data: (a) two actors' (A, B) perceptions of the nature of the relationship that each 'sends to' the other; (b) the perception of a third person (X) of the nature of the relationship that Person A sends to Person B, and vice versa. This array allows the characterisation of nonsymmetrical ties at the level of the sociometric representation of the network, and might reflect non-reciprocity at the personal or cognitive level. It also licenses the necessary intervention by me (X) in trying to assess the ties between dead people who are unable to defend or challenge my conclusions, especially in the absence of reliable or robust self-report. The kinds of ties that Addison contracted with people over his lifetime and their very dynamic nature lead me to characterise his coterie as having some of the features of a coalition rather than a network of friendship.[8] A coalition is a particular kind

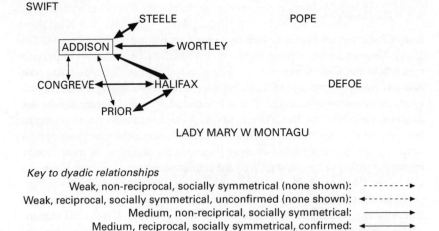

Figure 11.1 Addison's network in 1700 (The Kit-Cat Club).

of network, in which ties are contracted for particular purposes (social, political and literary patronage, for instance) for particular, variable periods of time (Boissevain 1974). For example, as we shall see, the connections forged between Steele and Wortley and Addison are of a different order from those built between Addison and Charles Montagu, or, for that matter, between Addison and Pope. We examine two points in the life of Addison's network in order to look at these dynamic and diverse characteristics of the group which emerged as instrumental in shaping the cultural icon, *The Spectator*.

4.2.1 Addison and the Kit-Cat Coalition in 1700. Let us drop in on Addison first in 1700, when he was a newcomer both to London's literary scene and to the political world. Figure 11.1 provides a graphic impression of part of Addison's network in 1700.

1700 sees Addison in London, a new member of the Kit-Cat Club, a dining club whose members were powerful political men (mainly Whig politicians), and writers who hoped to attract patronage for their literary projects by landing government jobs. Jacob Tonson, the publisher, was secretary and he introduced young hopefuls into the circle (Smithers 1968: 85). William Congreve, Charles Montagu and Matthew Prior were by this stage established members of the Club; Montagu and Prior had been fast friends since their university days in the 1680s. The equality and reciprocity of their relationship are marked in Prior's teasing, rather bawdy letters to Halifax, whom he affectionately calls 'old master'. Montagu's elevation to the title Earl of Halifax in 1704 as a reward for his work as Chancellor of the Exchequer (1694–1699) did not alter their relationship, but Halifax's failure to deliver a promise (in 1711) ruined his friendship with Prior.

Addison met Congreve perhaps through the agency of Jacob Tonson, with whom he had corresponded since 1694. Addison entered this circle an unknown poet and inexperienced man, who was looking for a job and access to the patronage of powerful men like Halifax. The point of the introduction to Halifax for Addison was to gain a protector and sponsor with political power and enough influence to aid his rise in London. As a younger man in years and a junior one in rank and social status at the outset of their connection, Addison remained Halifax's protégé and client for the duration of their relationship. There are other men in Addison's network whose ranks and consequent social status changed in the course of their lives, and this change means that relationships contracted with people at different stages in their careers may be different on account of the social distance or proximity between actors.[9]

By 1700, Addison had long been close friends with his long-time collaborator Richard Steele. Steele and Addison both attended Charterhouse school, and then Oxford. Despite going their separate ways in 1692, they renewed their friendship in 1704 in London, where they collaborated on literary projects like Steele's comedy, *The Tender Husband* (1705) and worked together in the office of the Secretaries of State. Apart from Addison's increasingly brief sojourns in Ireland, the two spent much time in close physical proximity until Addison's death in 1719. A possible indication of this geographical proximity is the fact that there is just one letter which survives between the two. Addison met Edward Wortley, a member of the powerful Montagu family (and later, husband of the much better-known Lady Mary Wortley Montagu), in 1699 in France (Smithers 1968: 52). They remained firm friends all Addison's life. As with many friendships, the closeness of their association relied on their shared experiences and intermittent rather than continuous physical proximity. After his Grand Tour of Europe, Addison's career as a civil servant based him first in London and then took him to Ireland, while Wortley spent the same period looking after his mining interests in the north of England, pursuing political office and favours in London, and working as a diplomat in Turkey. The place they renewed their connection was London, the geographical heart of the circle.

The Kit-Cat Club met regularly in London, and provided a central meeting point for its members. To understand the strategic and changing nature of the relationships which Addison contracted through his lifetime, let us pause and consider how the Kit-Cat Club might be considered as a likely context for a coalition. A club at this time was a body of men often not domiciled in any particular place, but meeting semi-informally with certain set purposes. Such was the Kit-Cat, but it was also aristocratic and highly distinguished; its two orders were reflected in the way that the members' portraits were hung in the room built by Tonson at Barn Elms. The great magnates were at eye-level, and the first flight of literary men were placed above (Smithers 1968: 243). So Whig grandees like Halifax, Somers and Sunderland welcomed the younger generation of talented politicos (Holmes 1993: 421) and accommodated the new professionals, among them journalists and architects (Holmes 1982). They also supported a gaggle of selected literary men and journalists, among them Maynwaring, Congreve, Rowe, Steele and, of course, Addison. This society was exclusive; it did not welcome the lesser fry of Whig pamphleteers and poets, who were the receivers of patronage, as the Kit-Cats were on the whole the givers. It is a useful reference point for trying to understand the nature of the ties contracted between its members. For while the ties between Prior and Montagu (Halifax) on the one hand, and between Addison and Steele, and Addison and Wortley on the other are evidently friendships in which there is social symmetry and reciprocity as well as affinity of age and experience, connections like that between Addison and Halifax and Congreve and Halifax are more strategic. Addison and Congreve stood to gain more out of the connection than their older, more powerful patron, Halifax. These are ties that might be best described as client–patron, dependency relationships. Addison and Steele both bring to their alliance the debts and responsibilities of the ties that each man contracted in the course of looking for commissions for literary work; the rewards for such work in the civil service professions which developed into a 'large career bureaucracy' increasingly departmentalised and specialised, a body that was 'largely non-political and in essentials, professional' (Holmes 1982: 242); and ultimately, the advancement of their civil and political careers. Addison's lifelong relationship with the Junto Whigs, Lord Halifax and Earl Somers, to whom volume I of the collected *Spectators* was dedicated, effectively exemplifies this type of connection.

The structure of Addison's network is multidimensional, encompassing connections characteristic of a patron–client relationship as well as more equal, reciprocal ones. The latter find expression and bear fruit in reciprocal acts of literary, political or even financial support (or hostility). The first kind results in payment or acknowledgement on the part of the client, often in the form of political support.

4.2.2 *The Spectator* and the great dictator in 1711. Between 1700 and 1710, with the launch of *The Spectator*, Addison's network changed. Figure 11.2 illustrates how we might represent part of Addison's network in 1711 graphically.

Increasingly, Addison contracted important close ties with men (and some women) who were his social equals, thus engendering reciprocal, occasionally conflict-ridden and often long-lived relationships. Addison introduced Swift to Steele, initiating one of the more stormy relationships in the network (Aitken 1889: 211). The nature of the relationship between Steele and Addison was qualitatively and temporally different from that between Steele and Swift, or indeed, Addison and Swift. However, it is possible to establish that they are all members of the same social circle that surrounds the life of the *Tatler* and the

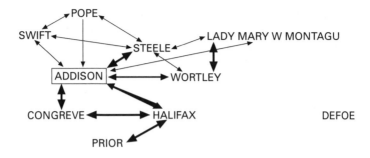

Figure 11.2 Addison's network in 1711 (*The Spectator*).

birth of *The Spectator*. They also had connections marked more by competitive-ness and rivalry than friendship, yet these were with equals rather than with superiors or inferiors. The formidable figure of Robert Harley, Earl of Oxford, the government manager who handled Whig and Tory parties alike from 1706 until Queen Anne's death, has ties, some hostile and some friendly, with most of the members of Addison's network (Downie 1979: 127). The reason for con-sidering these ties as part of the network, however peripheral, is that they provide a sense of the open-ended texture of the network, and the fact that it changes its structure over time.

1711 is the year which sees the success of the collaboration between Addison and Steele on the *Spectator* project. This enterprise made the literary (rather than political) reputations of the friends, and helped to fix their relationship as a sustained professional one, built on mutual reliance and trust. Swift's gossip in his *Journal to Stella*, and news in the letters of Wortley and his wife offer additional collaborative evidence for an intimate friendship. With the magnet of *The Spectator* behind them, the two men, especially Addison, began to attract potential clients and protégés. Addison was, for many years, Ambrose Philips' champion and Thomas Tickell's patron, and Steele helped the career of John Hughes. Addison might once have seen himself as Alexander Pope's patron. Alexander Pope went out of his way to woo Addison as a patron in 1711, and Addison, flattered, reciprocated by praising Pope's *Essay upon Criticism* (which appeared in May 1711) in *The Spectator*. But when Addison later recommended Ambrose Philips as a translator of Homer in preference to Pope, the latter viciously badmouthed him to his friends and anybody who would listen. However, in Pope's correspondence which he published himself in 1735, he includes several friendly letters to Addison, which are all fakes. The question is, what does this say about the perception of each about the other's friendship? In 1711 the young poet was apparently grateful for the praise despite the censure, because he contributed several pieces to *The Spectator*, and began to frequent Will's and then Button's Coffee House, where 'all the company sat at Addison's feet' (Smithers 1968: 243). In this period, although Swift was moving ever further from the Whig sentiments held so dearly by Steele in particular, in favour of the Tory pair of Bolingbroke and Harley, he stayed on the fringes of the *Spectator* coterie. By 1711, Lady Mary Pierrepont (who became Lady Mary Wortley Montagu in September 1712) was on the fringes of the coterie, and an occasional contributor to *The Spectator* too. Apart from Charlotte, Countess of Warwick, whom Addison had known since 1704, Lady Mary appears to be the only important woman with any significant and extensive contact with the coterie.

The coalition of men behind *The Spectator* is a group which develops identifiably political and literary ties to achieve particular goals. These goals include personal success and fame. Addison's own pursuit of the protection and sponsorship of powerful men like Halifax and Somers demonstrates quite clearly the usefulness of social networking, as does Pope's pursuit of Addison himself in 1710. The coalition is also allied with a particular political grouping, the Whig parliamentarians and government managers, who saw themselves as forward-looking and progressive by comparison with the Tories. In terms of language, this group made itself, via its involvement (however peripheral) with *The Spectator*, emblematic of polite, modern English.

4.3   *Shaping* The Spectator

The web of core and peripheral relationships in Addison's social network had a profound effect on the shape and function of *The Spectator*. Given the extent to which most members of this network knew most of the others (network density), and the social (geographical), and ideological proximity between them, we should be prepared to find that *The Spectator* expresses this network's ideology. What persuades us that the hegemony of *The Spectator* represents a network of interests is that its perspective encompasses the broad base of Whig concerns in the context of factionalism, which affected all areas of life. For example, *The Spectator* underlined the reasonableness of Locke's theories of government and education (Bond 1965, IV: 392–5; I: 263–4), popularised and made more comprehensible recent developments in science, and promoted the new business and entrepreneurial spirit, occasionally at the expense of the traditional professions of the clergy, the law and medicine (Bond 1965, I: 88–92). Its speculations both favoured the manners and fashions of the city and remarked on the provincialism of the country (Bond 1965, I: 486–8); it pursued a moderate line regarding the Anglican Church and Protestant dissenters, while maintaining an anti-Jacobite stance and (an enlightened?) virtual silence on papists (Bond 1965, II: 288). *The Spectator* also offered a line on eighteenth-century English culture that was accessible, digestible and, most importantly, apprehendable, to the increasingly middle-class readership. So the debate between the Ancients and Moderns finds expression in lessons on how to read modern literature as serious, as well as criticism of popular literature, remarks on proper and polite conversation (Bond

1965, II: 527–9), advice about appropriate dress for men and especially for women, and comments about polite manners and good behaviour.

5   The English language and the idea of standard modern English

In the light of the evident importance of *The Spectator* in shaping the cultural milieu of eighteenth-century London, and its role as exemplum of polite writing for a middle-class reading public, it is worth considering the extent to which the writing of some of its makers approaches the ideal set up by the prescriptivists. I have argued that the language of *The Spectator* (and thus its writers) provides the grammarians with a ready corpus of language which they might use as the basis of a model for modern Standard English. I claimed that they used this corpus to point out both good and bad writing, paying particular attention to demonstrating how the writers might have avoided infelicitous and ungrammatical English by following the rules. The question is how closely, if at all, the practice of *The Spectator* writers matches the prescriptions of the grammarians. After all, these are the writers whom the prescriptivists recommend as prestigious, but also caution as being frequently incorrect in their grammar.

Let us examine briefly the distribution of restrictive relative clause markers in some writing of Addison and his cohorts. The relative clause marker is a useful diagnostic feature with which to check the relation between prescription and practice because the relative rule is quite precisely stated by the prescriptivists. The writing I will consider consists of the personal letters of Addison, Steele, Pope, Swift, Congreve, Wortley, Prior, Lady Mary Wortley Montagu and Daniel Defoe (an outsider to the Addison circle, but connected loosely to others in the cohort). I have not included figures for Halifax because the data I have for him are too sparse. I have selected letters in preference to other texts because all of the members of the network share the familiar letter as part of their individual writing repertoires. Few by comparison share the essay, the pamphlet, prose drama or similar genres of poetry.

5.1   Results

The data consist of text samples of around 26,200 words each taken from the correspondence of Addison and his cohort, both published and manuscript. These data yield some interesting material for interpretation. Table 11.1 and Figure 11.3 illustrate relative marker choice across this group. The first question to consider is the extent to which relative clause marker choice for the group that makes up Addison's network reflects the preferences highlighted by the rule evolved by the prescriptivists. In other words, if it were the case that the prescriptive rule was based closely on practice, most of these (prestigious) users could be expected to prefer the *wh*-pronouns to the *that* complementiser, and disfavour ellipsis or zero-marking.

The answer to this question is that the practice of only one of the group,

Table 11.1. *Relative marker choice in the letters of Joseph Addison and his circle.*

	Joseph Addison	Richard Steele	Alexander Pope	Jonathan Swift	William Congreve	Edward Wortley	Matthew Prior	Lady Mary Wortley Montagu	Daniel Defoe
Date of letters	1710–15	1710–24	1713–16	1711–14	1692–1727	1710–42	1698–1720	1712–14	1711–13
text size	26,688 words	26,250 words	26,299 words	26,256 words	26,208 words	26,200 words	26,280 words	26,220 words	26,286 words
wh-	179*	179*	173	129	176*	71	129	27	176
that	51	29	49	42	59	113*	53	72*	31
Ø	60	69	139*	88	48	124	76	65*	101
N =	290	277	361	259	283	308	258	164	305

N = 2505, df = 16, chi-square test reveals statistical significance at p^2 0.001

* = standardized residual greater than absolute value of 2

Examples of relative clause choice:

wh: 'They are a sort of Gamesters *who* are eternally upon the Fret, though they play for nothing.' (*Spectator* 185, Tuesday, October 2, 1711)

that: 'His Pleasure arises from his Disappointments, and his Life is spent in Pursuit of a Secret *that* destroys his Happiness if he chance to find it.' *Spectator* 170, Friday, September 14, 1711)

Ø: 'This zealous and active Obedience however takes place in the great Point [Ø] we are recommending.' (*Spectator* 213, Saturday, November 3, 1711)

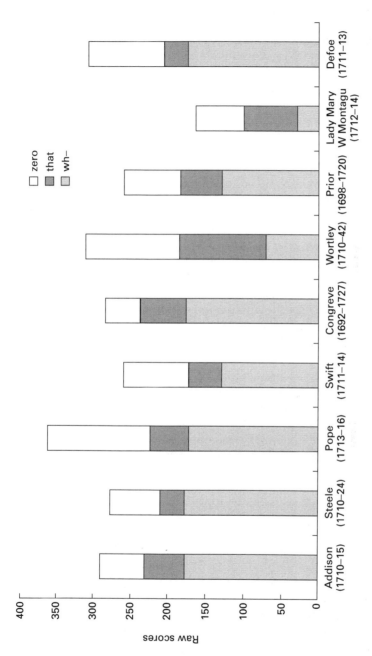

Figure 11.3 Addison and his circle: relative marker choice in letters.

namely William Congreve, anticipates the injunctions of the prescriptivists. He markedly prefers the *wh*-relative pronouns (*who(m)*, *which*) to *that*, indicating that he is three times more likely to choose a *wh*-pronoun than *that*. In addition, while he does not reject ellipsis altogether, he is more likely to avoid it in favour of *that* or a *wh*-pronoun. This usage is the closest that any of the group comes to matching the prescriptivist rule. Strikingly, while Addison is a prominent user of *wh*-pronouns for marking restrictive relative clauses, he seems to view *that* and zero-marking more or less equally. He appears to prefer zero to *that*, but this preference is not statistically significant. The remainder of the cohort demonstrates a much less ambiguous preference for zero-marking.

The second question concerns the comparison of the 'great dictator' Addison with his network – of his friends, colleagues, clients and patrons. This is relevant because it is arguable that while Addison's style is criticised by the grammarians, it is his hand which is generally considered to be at the heart of *The Spectator*'s prestige and importance as a model of style. In the register examined here, Addison and two of his immediate circle, Steele and Congreve, show similar patterns, with statistically significant choice of *wh*-relative markers. Wortley and his wife Lady Mary differ significantly from the rest of the circle with respect to their use of the *that* complementiser, and Lady Mary together with her admirer, Alexander Pope, demonstrate a statistically significant preference for ellipsis/ zero marking. Jonathan Swift, Matthew Prior and the outsider Daniel Defoe show no significant differences in their choice of relative markers. None of these men is very close to the central character, Addison, or to Steele or Congreve, by the time that *The Spectator* reaches its peak in 1712.

These results seem to indicate that the prescriptivist rule is not entirely an ideal construct unrelated to actual usage in the era of *The Spectator*. Indeed, by the time that William Congreve, the brilliantly successful author of the hit play *The Way of the World*, was twenty-five, he had anticipated the rule in his practice. Curiously, his writing appears to be all but invisible to the grammarians, perhaps because, unlike *The Spectator*, it is not a model of virtue and right thinking for successive generations of readers. After all, Congreve was a prime target of Jeremy Collier's blistering attack on the 'profaneness and immorality' of the English stage (1698).

5.2   Conclusion

In closing, let us return to some of the issues raised at the beginning of this essay. Select eighteenth-century texts had marked cultural value for most middle-class English men and women throughout the period, and their writers became emblematic of good conduct and polite language. For example, the eighteenth-century prescriptivists discovered in the prestigious language of Mr Spectator and his coterie, via *The Spectator*, the moral basis for sound linguistic practices. In identifying this variety as a basis for the construction of a Standard English, the prescriptive grammarians eschewed the more 'correct' language of more controversial, less establishment luminaries (like Congreve). Their task in constructing a modern Standard English was to demonstrate to their readers how the fabric of this language could be improved and further elevated by adhering to rules of grammatical correctness. Prescriptivist grammarians of the second half of the century went about the task of legislating their conception of written Standard English in a social and political climate in which the norms represented by *The Spectator* continued to be highly valued. Its agnostic political stance, its generality, and its ultimate conservatism made *The Spectator* a sure candidate for adoption as a model by the instructors and educators of the second half of the century.

Notes

1 Parts of the research reported here have been presented as conference papers: at ASECS, Tucson, Arizona, March 1995: 'Mr. Spectator, networks of power, and linguistic influence in 18th-century England'; at NWAVE, Las Vegas, Nevada, October 1996: 'Social network theory and stylistic variation in eighteenth century England'; and at the first International Conference on the Standardisation of English, Cambridge, UK, July 1997: 'Coalition for a cause: the politics of social networks and standardisation in eighteenth century England'. I am very grateful to Lesley Milroy and Laura Wright for their comments and suggestions.

2 See Charles Gildon's *A Grammar of the English Tongue* (1711).

3 It is important to make the subtle distinction between prescriptivist attitudes towards grammar and diction and the approbation in which the prescriptivists held the style of writers whose grammar appeared to be flawed, like Addison and Swift. Tieken (1997) fails to make this distinction, thus implying that prescriptivists like Lowth viewed writers like Addison as merely guilty of bad grammar.

4 The first number appeared on Thursday, 1 March 1711, and the paper appeared daily until December 1712 (first series: 555 numbers). It was continued for a further eighty issues in June 1714, managed principally by Eustace Budgell, and by then Thomas Tickell, Addison's private secretary, after Budgell's departure for Ireland to take up a government post procured for him by Addison.

5 The best-known examples are: *The Spectator Inspected* (London, 1711), published as an anonymous letter, dated 'Camp at Bouchain, Sept. 29, 1711', and *A Spy Upon the Spectator* (1711), a 24-page pamphlet of unknown authorship, published by the Tory John Morphew.

6 John Gay, *The Present State of Wit*, written as a letter to a friend in the country, dated from Westminster, May 3, 1711.

7 To introduce a degree of flexibility, I have judged each parameter for each relationship on a five-point scale. The overall calculation of 'proximity' is a mean of the aggregated scores: greatest proximity = 1, least proximity (greatest distance) = 5.

8 I am grateful to Lesley Milroy for suggesting that I look more closely at coalitions and their structure in trying to account for the complexity of Addison's connections with patrons.

9 A complementary factor is relative age. Although age may be adopted as an objective factor, there may be complex cultural values associated with advanced years which may

be historically sensitive. Also, because age interacts with social rank and occupation, it cannot be used in a categorical way.

References

A.   Primary

Ash, John 1760. *Grammatical institutes; or grammar, adapted to the genius of the English tongue*, Worcester.
   1763. *Grammatical Institutes; or, an easy introduction to Dr. Lowth's English grammar, designed for the use of school*, 4th edn, London.
Baker, Robert 1770. *Reflections on the English Language, in the Nature of Vaugelas's Reflections on the French; being a detection of many improper expressions used in conversation, and of many others to be found in authors*, London.
Bell, John 1769. *A Concise and Comprehensive System of English Grammar*, Glasgow.
Blair, Hugh 1783. *Lectures on Rhetoric and Belles Lettres*, Edinburgh.
Bond, Donald F. (ed.) 1965. *The Spectator*, 5 vols., Oxford: Clarendon Press.
Brittain, Lewis 1788. *Rudiments of English Grammar*, Louvain.
Collier, Jeremy 1698. *A Short View of the Immorality and Profaneness of the English Stage*, London.
Crocker, Abraham 1772. *A Practical Introduction to English Grammar and Rhetoric*, Sherborne.
Dilworth, Thomas 1751. *A New Guide to the English Tongue*, 13th edn; repr. in Robin C. Alston (ed.), *English Linguistics 1500–1800*, no. 4, Menston: Scolar Press, 1974.
Edwards, Samuel 1765. *An Abstract of English Grammar, Including Rhetoric and Pronunciation*, Dublin.
Elphinston, James 1765. *The Principles of the English Language Digested, or, English Grammar Reduced to Analogy*, London.
Gay, John 1711. *The Present State of Wit*, London.
Gildon, Charles (also attributed to Brightland, John) 1711. *A Grammar of the English Tongue*, London.
Haywood, Eliza 1744–46. *The Female Spectator*, London.
Hurd, Richard 1932. *Correspondence of Richard Hurd and William Mason*, ed. E. H. Pearce, Cambridge.
Johnson, Samuel 1747. *The Plan of a Dictionary of the English Language*, London; repr. in *English Linguistics 1500–1800*, no. 223, Menston: Scolar Press, 1974.
Lowth, Robert 1762. *A Short Introduction to English Grammar*, London.
Lynch, Patrick 1796. *The Pentaglot Preceptor; containing a complete grammar of the English tongue*, Carrick.
Story, Joshua 1783. *An Introduction to English Grammar*, 3rd edn, Newcastle upon Tyne.
Ward, H. 1777. *A Short, but Clear System of English Grammar, with Exercises of Bad English*, London.
   1789. *The Academic Reader*, London.
Ward, William 1765. *An Essay on Grammar*, London; repr. in *English Linguistics 1500–1800*, no. 15, Menston: Scolar Press, 1974.

B.   Secondary

Aitken, G. A. 1889. *Life of Richard Steele*, 2 vols.; repr. New York: Greenwood, 1968.

Boissevain, Jeremy 1974. *Friends of Friends: Networks, Manipulators and Coalitions*, New York: St. Martin's Press.

Carley, K. M. and Krackhardt, D. 1996. 'Cognitive inconsistencies and non-symmetrical friendship', *Social Networks* 18, 1–27.

Crowley, Tony 1996. *Language in History: Theories and Texts*, London and New York: Routledge.

Downie, J. A. 1979. *Robert Harley and the Press: Propaganda and Public Opinion in the Age of Swift and Defoe*, Cambridge University Press.

Earle, Peter 1989. *The Making of the English Middle Class: Business, Society and Family Life in London, 1660–1730*, Berkeley and Los Angeles: University of California Press.

Evans, J. E. 1987. 'Mr. Review on the "Glorious" Tatler and the "Inimitable" Spectator', *Journal of Newspaper and Periodical History* 3.1, 2–9.

Fitzmaurice, Susan 1998. 'The Commerce of Language and the changing face of politeness in eighteenth century England', *English Studies* 79.4, 309–28.

Garside, P. L. 1990. 'London and the Home Counties', in F. M. L. Thompson (ed.), *The Cambridge Social History of Britain 1750–1950*, vol. I: *Regions and Communities*, Cambridge University Press.

Haac, Oscar A. 1973. *Marivaux*, New York: Twayne Publishers.

Holmes, Geoffrey 1982. *Augustan England: Professions, State and Society 1680–1730*, London: George Allen and Unwin.

1993. *The Making of a Great Power: Late Stuart and Early Georgian Britain 1660–1722*, London: Longman.

Langford, Paul 1989. *A Polite and Commercial People: England 1727–1783*, Oxford: Clarendon Press.

Leonard, S. A. 1929. *The Doctrine of Correctness in English Usage 1700–1800*, repr. New York: University of Wisconsin Studies in Language and Literature, 1962.

Marsden, Peter V. and Friedkin, Noah E. 1994. 'Network Studies of Social Influence', in Wasserman and Galaskiewicz (eds.), *Advances in Social Network Analysis: Research in the Social and Behavioral Sciences*, London: Sage Publications.

Messenger, Ann 1986. 'Educational Spectators: Richard Steele, Joseph Addison, and Eliza Haywood', in *His and Hers: Essays in Restoration and Eighteenth Century Literature*, University Press of Kentucky.

Milroy, Lesley 1987. *Language and Social Networks*, 2nd edn, London: Blackwell.

Milroy, L. and Milroy, J. 1985. 'Linguistic change, social network and speaker innovation', *Journal of Linguistics* 21:2, 339–84.

1992. 'Social networks and social class: toward an integrated sociolinguistic model', *Language in Society* 21, 1–26.

Raven, James 1992. *Judging New Wealth: Popular Publishing and Responses to Commerce in England, 1750–1800*, Oxford University Press.

Smithers, Peter 1968. *The Life of Joseph Addison*, 2nd edn, Oxford: Clarendon.

Sundby, B., Bjørge, A. K. and Haugland, K. E. (eds.) 1991. *The Dictionary of English Normative Grammar 1700–1800*, Amsterdam: John Benjamins.

Tieken-Boon van Ostade, I. 1997. 'Lowth's Corpus of Prescriptivism', in T. Nevalainen and L. Kahlas-Tarkka (eds.), *To Explain the Present: Studies in the Changing English Language in Honour of Matti Rissanen*, Helsinki: Memoires de la Société Néophilologique de Helsinki.

Wasserman S. and Galaskiewicz, J. (eds.) 1994. *Advances in Social Network Analysis:*

Research in the Social and Behavioral Sciences, London: Sage Publications.

Wright [now Fitzmaurice], Susan 1994. 'Joseph Addison and the grammarians', in D. Stein and I. Tieken-Boon van Ostade (eds.), *Towards a Standard English, 1600–1800*, The Hague: Mouton de Gruyter.

1997. 'Speaker innovation, textual revision and the case of Joseph Addison', in T. Nevalainen and L. Kahlas-Tarkka (eds.), *To Explain the Present: Studies in the Changing English Language in Honour of Matti Rissanen*, Helsinki: Memoires de la Société Néophilologique de Helsinki.

Zeggelink, E. 1994. 'Dynamics of structure: an individual-oriented approach', *Social Networks 16*, 295–333.

12 A branching *path*: low vowel lengthening and its friends in the emerging standard

ROGER LASS

> Undoubtedly, the following account is hypothetical and oversimplified, but it has the virtue of organizing unruly observations. (Margulis 1993: 244)

1 Introduction: ME /a, o/ in modern RP

It is usually assumed that standardisation typically involves at least two major operations: elimination of variation, and codification (in dictionaries, grammars, orthoepic treatises, and other 'authorities') of the trimmed-down and 'authorised' version. In the case of English this is all true enough, globally and within limits. But English is unusual in the amount of time it took, and the lateness of the prescriptive or codifying grammatical (as opposed to phonological) tradition. And, somewhat paradoxically, the even greater lateness and variational latitude of the actual codification of parts of the phonology, even though pronunciation was from the earliest times taken as one of the hallmarks of the standard variety.

   The perception of a 'standard' or 'best' kind of English (as an ideal, if not an empirically localisable object) dates back at least to the sixteenth century. Leaving aside the now overfamiliar classic remarks of writers like Puttenham and Hart, here are two characterisations, one shortly before the period I'm concerned with here, and one from quite late. In the seventeenth century John Wallis (1653: 73) says he is describing 'puram et genuinam pronunciationem linguae Anglicanae'; specifically not 'singulas . . . variorum locorum dialectos, aut affectatas muliercularum ineptias, aliosve barbarismos'. And over three centuries on, A. J. Ellis (1874: 1089) says his 'object is to examine . . . the pronunciation at present used by educated English speakers'. Even though he adds the rider that he does not attempt 'to decide what is "correct"', he still defines his topic (p. 1090) as 'received English pronunciation'. This paper, then, to follow the style of traditional handbooks of earlier periods, deals with 'Proto-RP, Pre-RP, Early-RP', etc.

My topic is a micro-story from the middle of a macro-evolution: the development of the Early Modern English low vowels in the emerging southern Standard English of the seventeenth to nineteenth centuries. This evolution has a number of interesting features: (a) the enormous amount of time it took; (b) the occurrence of at least two 'reversals' or retrograde developments, one temporary and the other permanent; and (c) the question of evaluation. That is, the relevant phonetic changes are recognised by grammarians in the 1680s, but it is not until the 1790s that these well-noted observations develop a social value. Only in the very late eighteenth century do we find the first 'normative' remarks on lengthening and lowering or retraction of /æ/ < ME /a/ (*path*) and lengthening of /ɔ/ < ME /o/ (*cloth*): and curiously, in view of the steady spread of these novelties after the seventeenth century, and the later acceptance of at least one as a norm, the first comments are in the main negative. I return to this in section 4.

Middle English /a/ in modern Received Pronunciation and most other standard (non-Scots) modern British and later British-derived Englishes has at least five reflexes: [æ] (*cat*), [ɒ] (*want*), [æ:] (*man*), [a:] (*path*), [eɪ] (*name*). Middle English */o/ has at least three: [ɒ] (*pot*), [ɔ:] (*short*; *off* in archaic varieties: more on this below), [əu] (*foal*). I will be concerned here only with the *cat/path* and *pot/off* distinctions.

Lengthening of seventeenth-century /æ/ and its sequelae define one of the great English dialect divides. Lengthening alone separates the South and South Midlands from the North and North Midlands; quality-shift (lowering and retraction) of lengthened /æ/ (except before /r/) separates southeast England and the Southern Hemisphere Englishes from the North American ones. The intricacy and importance of these distinctions can be seen in a simplified chart of major regional types:

(1)

	N	US	WML	Aus	Mx	RP
cat	a	æ	a	æ/ɛ	æ	æ
path	a	æ:	a:	a:	*a:*	*a:*
far	a:	*a:*	a:	a:	*a:*	*a:*

N = SED Northern Counties: Orton and Halliday 1962
WML = SED Shropshire area 11.10: Orton and Barry 1969
Mx = rural Middlesex: Orton and Wakelin 1967
US = New York standard (my native dialect)
Aus = Australian, from my own observations.

These contemporary forms give a kind of historical snapshot, capturing the main lines of development:

(i) Lengthening before /r/ is universal (therefore by standard reconstructive imperatives earlier). Since ME /a/ never raised to [æ] in the North and

West Midlands, [aː] there shows simple lengthening, without quality-shift. So the phonetic type [aː] can be either conservative or innovative, depending on what it cohabits with: conservative if with short [a], innovative if with short [æ]. Thus WML [aː] is conservative, Australian [aː] innovative.

(ii) Of the regions with lengthening in *path,* the North and West Midlands are globally most conservative, showing no raising of [a] or quality-shift in lengthening environments. The US (except for some eastern coastal regions, which I will not discuss here) is innovative in showing raising to [æ] and lengthening; but it shows only the first stage of quality-shift, before /r/ (see below).

(iii) Australia, with raised EModE /a/ and [aː] in both lengthening environments, represents a further stage of development; actually very close to what the late eighteenth- to early nineteenth-century English standard would have been like. This makes good chronological sense, since the English settlement of Australia dates from the late eighteenth century.

(iv) Middlesex and RP, representing the newer standard type, are the most advanced, with raising to [æ] and retraction in both lengthening environments. Middlesex is however different with respect to ME /o/, which I turn to now.

ME /o/ underwent a number of changes as well, though much less radically than ME /a/, and less regionally defining. The dialect types above give this picture:

(2)

	N	US	WML	Mx	RP
pot	ɒ	ä	ɒ	ɒ	ɒ
off	ɒ	ɔː	ɒ	ɔː	ɒ
short	ɔː	ɔː	ɔː	ɔː	ɔː

(The unrounding of ME /o/ and raising of the long vowel are irrelevant to this story; Australian English by and large shows the same pattern as RP, and will not be treated separately.)

Note that the North, as before, shows lengthening only before /r/, as does the WML; the more southerly (rural or as we will see also urban conservative) varieties show a long vowel in *off,* but RP appears to have 'reverted' to the original state of lengthening only before /r/. This curious story (which is not a 'reversed merger') will be taken up later. But now we turn to earlier history.

2   The origin of [æ] (*cat*)

Typically English as [æ] seems to be, its 'native' distribution is limited. In Mainland vernaculars it is restricted roughly to an area south of a line from

North Norfolk to Staffordshire, and is commoner in the East than the West. All of the Midlands is north of this line; the North, Scotland, and Wales have nothing higher than [a] in *cat* except as importations from the South. (And [æ] is moving back to [a] again in many southern varieties, e.g. 'Sloane Ranger' and 'Estuary' English.) All the Extraterritorial Englishes have [æ] or something higher, presupposing input [æ]; the only exception is Hiberno-English, which retains [a] except in more anglicised varieties. So [æ] is a geographically restricted Early Modern development, with secondary spread due to London prestige.

Some writers (Zachrisson 1913, Kökeritz 1953) claim raising of ME /a/ to [æ] as early as the fifteenth century, on the basis of what they call 'approximative' spellings, i.e. with <e> for supposed ME /a/ (*understende*, etc.). These however are probably not 'attempts at [æ]' at all, but spellings of ME /e/; raising of /a/ to /e/ is widespread, and was commoner in the standard in earlier times. Nares (1784) for instance has /ɛ/ rather than /æ/ in *catch, gather, January, jasmine* (cf. the doublet *Jessamyn*), *many* (the latter now has /a/ only in Hiberno-English). This could account for both <e> spellings and apparent ME /a/:/e/ rhymes in the sixteenth century.

Both foreign and native sources generally indicate [a] in the sixteenth and early seventeenth centuries. The earliest description of a raised vowel is from the Scot Alexander Hume (c.1617: 8), who says that Southern English <a> 'is not far unlyke the sheepes bae, quhilk the greek symbolises be η not α, βη not βα'. He thinks the Scots 'pronounce it better'. It's unsurprising that a Scot with [a] would consider English [æ] somewhat [ɛ]-like (which is what this description amounts to). This is probably an advanced minority pronunciation; [æ] does not become the norm until mid-century.

For John Wallis (1653: 8), ME /a/ is a 'palatal' vowel, an '*a* exile'. Unlike the Germans, whose *a* is 'fat' (*pinguis*) and pronounced 'in the throat' (*in gutture*), the English raise the middle of the tongue so that 'aerem in Palato comprimant'. This can be taken as a safe indicator of [æ]. (Note that for John Hart 1569: 30a, this vowel is made 'with wyde opening the mouth, as when a man yauneth'.)

Wallis has the same quality long for ME /a:/ (*bate, pale*); so the two original low vowels are still qualitatively matched, but raised from earlier [a, a:]. This is perhaps supported by Wallis' observation that ME /a/ causes insertion of /j/ after a velar, just as the higher front vowels do: *can, get, begin* are pronounced *cyan, gyet, begyin* (p. 40). This is more likely before raised [æ] than open [a], though some modern Yorkshire dialects have this palatalisation before even centralised [ä]. (To be perhaps a bit in-group, anglicist cricket fans will find an excellent example in the speech of Geoffrey Boycott.)

Thirty years later Cooper (1687: 4f) calls this vowel '*a* lingual'; it is 'formed by the middle of the Tongue a little rais'd to the hollow of the Palate', and is distinct from '*e* lingual' (= ME /a:/ in *tale*), which has the tongue 'more rais'd . . . and extended'. The two are of different heights, and short *e* lingual is the value of ME /e/, i.e. [ɛ]. Wallis and Cooper must be describing something around [æ]: lower than [ɛ] and higher than [a]. We can date the stabilisation of [æ], then, to about the 1650s.

3   The origin of /ɒ/ (*pot*)

By the mid-seventeeth century ME /o/ had clearly lowered from its sixteenth-century value [ɔ] to [ɒ]. It is Wallis' (1653) lowest 'guttural' (= back) vowel. For Cooper (1687: 8) it is '*o* guttural', made 'by the root of the Tongue moved to the inner part of the Pallat, while the middle . . . is depressed, which causes the greatest space between the fore part of the Tongue and Pallat'. It 'hath the most open and full sound of all', which indicates [ɒ] rather than [ɔ]. We can assume that lowering began no later than the 1650s, and was firm by the end of the century.

Overall then, the story of the short vowel system can be summarised as follows, from c.1400–1650:

(3)

HIGH	i	u	i	u	i	u
HIGH–MID	e	o				
LOW–MID			ɛ	ɔ	ɛ	
LOW	a		a		æ	ɒ
	1400		1550		1650	

4   Lengthening I: New /æː/ (*far, path, plant*), /ɒː/ (*horn, off*)

The long nucleus system at c.1650 was:

(4)

iː	*meet*	uː	*boot*	iu	*due, dew*
eː	*meat*	oː	*boat*	ʌu	*out*
ɛː	*mate , date*			ʌi	*bite*
		ɒː	*bought*	ɒi	*boy*

For the first time since about the thirteenth century, English has an asymmetrical long vowel system, with an empty low unrounded slot; this is filled in during the next half-century or so.

The modern southern standard is poorer by one contrast than that in (4): *meat*, etc. have merged with *meet* or *mate*. It is also richer by at least five others: long monophthongs /ɑː/ (*far, pass*), /ɜː/ (*hurt, heard*), and centring diphthongs /ɪə/ (*fear*), /ɛə/ (*fair*), /ʊə/ (*poor*). The last four derive mainly from changes before /r/ and loss of /r/; /aː/, while partly of this origin, has other and more widespread sources.

Modern /a:/ largely represents lengthened and quality-shifted seventeenth-century /æ/; lowering to [a:] occurred during the course of the the eighteenth century, and there was gradual retraction during the later nineteenth. The lengthening occurred before /r/ (*far*), voiceless fricatives except /ʃ/ (*chaff, path*, *grass*), and to a certain extent before /ns, nt/ (*dance*, *plant*). Other minor sources of a long low vowel include sporadic lengthenings as in *father*, *rather*, and certain doublets of ME /au/ forms (*half*, *palm*). Despite the obvious allophonic conditioning, the change was never completed (except before /r/); there are still enough minimal or near-minimal pairs to ensure contrastiveness (/æ/ in *ass*, *ant*, *cam* vs. /a:/ in *arse*, *aunt*, *calm*; and see section 5 below).

This lengthening does not have a conventional name; the standard grammars list it 'atomistically' under the two vowels involved. But it is a single process and deserves christening: I call it Lengthening I, to distinguish it from the later lengthening of /æ/ before voiced stops and nasals (*bag*, *hand*), which is obviously Lengthening II (Lass 1990). This produces yet another ME /a/ reflex, [æ:]. Lengthening II has occurred in most Southern English dialects, and all extra-territorial ones except Hiberno-English (though it has never completely diffused, and there are still massive exceptions). Its output is distinct from that of Lengthening I except in most parts of the US, where it falls in with lengthened but unshifted [æ:] in *path*.

I will be concerned here only with the evolution of Lengthening I up to the earlier part of this century; the early history of Lengthening II is still obscure, and there seems so far to be little that can usefully be said about it. In any case, it is part of a different story, and its results are even more variable and confusing than those to be detailed below.

Lengthening I, because of its incomplete diffusion, creates a new phoneme /æ:/, later /a:/ < ME /a/. But it also affects ME /o/ in the same environments (before /r/ in *horn*, before voiceless fricatives in *off*, *cloth*, *loss*); these outputs however merge with ME /au/ (*all*, *law*) in /ɔ:/. Nowadays, as we will see, pre-fricative lengthening of ME /o/ has largely receded in favour of /ɒ/ in most standard British varieties, though some conservative standards and vernaculars still have the old /ɔ:/, as do eastern US and some South African dialects. Both long and short versions of *off*, *cloth*, etc. have coexisted since the late seventeenth century; the 'restoration of /ɒ/', as I noted above, is not a reversed merger, but a shift of prestige in a set of coexisting variants, as with *meet*/*meat*. (The restriction of Lengthening I to ME /a, o/ is not irrational: at the relevant time they are /æ, ɒ/, the natural class consisting of the only two low short vowels.)

The first solid witness is Cooper (1687), who shows a somewhat irregular pattern, typical of the early stages of diffusion:

(5)
ME /a/:   [æ] path, pass, bar, car
          [æ:] passed, cast, gasp, barge, dart
ME /o/:   [ɒ] loss, off
          [ɔ:] lost, frost, horn

He also notes general trends: *a* is long before /sC, rC/, and *o* 'commonly long' before /rn, st/. Lengthening I at this early stage is favoured by a following consonant cluster (*pass*, *bar* vs. *passed*, *barge*, *loss* vs. *lost*); the environment however simplifies over the next few decades. There is as yet no sign of quality-shift.

The history during the next century is complicated. By the 1740s there is already some shift of lengthened /æ/, notably lowering before /r/, which seems to precede lowering elsewhere, as the contemporary evidence in the last section also shows. The Geordie Mather Flint (1740) has [æ] in *chaff*, [æ:] or [a:] in *bath*, *castle*, *calf*, *half*, and [a:] only in *art*, *dart*, *part*. His testimony is particularly important because of his northern origins: coming from an area where /a/ had never shifted to [æ], he was specially sensitive, as a teacher of (southern) Standard English to foreigners, to the [æ]/[a] distinction (recall that the earliest reliable report of raised ME /a/ in the South is also from a northerner, the Scot Hume: cf. section 2).

It is hard to find two eighteenth-century sources in full agreement about which words have the new vowel, though there is consensus about its quality. By the 1760s it is commonly equated with long Italian <a> or the French vowel in *-age*, suggesting [a:]. By the 1780s its distribution for one type of speaker (but see below) is very close to modern, though there are still some lexical differences. Nares (1784) has 'open *A*' (/a:/) in *after*, *ask*, *ass* (now short), *bask*, *mask*, *glass*, *pass* ('and its compounds and derivatives': p. 5), and in *plant*, *grant*, *advance*, *alms*, *calm*, *palm* (on the last group see below). Data on ME /o/ is more sporadic, but Nares has 'broad *A*' (/ɒ:/) in *off*, *doff*, *offer*, *cross*, *toss*, *cloth*, as opposed to 'short *o*' (/ɒ/) in *moss*, *dross* (pp. 30f).

5 The late eighteenth-century reversal

Nares' rather modern-looking pattern is not the only one. There is a curious see-saw development: from the 1680s to the 1780s the use of the lengthened vowels expands; in the 1780s–90s a reaction sets in. So Walker (1791), perhaps the most influential of the late eighteenth-century normative lexicographers, has the 'long sound of the middle or Italian a' always before /r/ in monosyllables (*car*), and before <l> + labial (*balm*, *calf*). It was, he says, formerly commoner in *dance*, *glass*, etc. 'but this pronunciation . . . seems to have been for some years advancing [not being a historian he did not, as he ought to have done, say "retreating"] to the short sound'. To pronounce the <a> in *after*, *plant* 'as long as in *half*, *calf*, &c. borders on vulgarity' (pp. 10f).

This finger in the dyke is most likely a function of a more extreme quality-shift in London and neighbouring provincial vernaculars (especially before /r/: see the next section). In reaction, anything but [æ] (or perhaps [æ:]) was tarred with the non-standard or 'vulgar' brush. There seems then to have been a counter-fashion in the late eighteenth century (persisting in some lects into the nineteenth), which reserved lengthened and shifted /æ/ to two positions: before /r/, and where it was an alternative to ME /au/ (*dance*, *calm*, *half*). But both styles persisted, and the more general lengthening was finally adopted.

Lengthened ME /o/ was stigmatised at the same time; Walker says that just as it 'would be gross to a degree' to have the same vowel in *castle*, *plant* as in *palm*, so 'it would be equally exceptionable' to pronounce *moss*, *frost* as if they were spelled *mawse*, *frawst*. What Cooper a century earlier had simply noted as a fact about vowel length, and Flint half a century later as a fact about length and quality, had developed a social significance. Presumably the change became salient enough to attract a social value only in the later eighteenth century, when the quality had changed, and when this change was identified by at least some writers with more advanced (hence 'vulgar') dialects.

A good number of words (mainly French loans) that now have /ɑː/ once had doublets with ME /au/: especially before nasal clusters (*dance*, *grant*) and before /l/ + labial (*half*, *palm*). We would expect such words to have modern /ɔː/ < 18th-c. /ɒː/ (as some do, e.g. *haunt*, *flaunt*); but most have /ɑː/. Now if /aː/ presupposes earlier [æː], the modern forms must reflect a lineage that does not have ME /au/ here. We have good evidence for this competing type as early as the 1590s. In *Love's Labours' Lost* V.i.24f the pedant Holofernes condemns affected fashionable pronunciations by saying of Don Adriano de Armado: 'He clepeth a calf, caufe: halfe, haufe.' So in these words both ME /a/ ('calf') and ME /au/ ('caufe') were available, and more conservative speakers preferred ME /a/. The /au/ forms were apparently rather 'refayned'; though as late as 1701 Dr John Jones teaches /ɒː/ in *dance*. As with the *meet*/*meat* merger, and the later 'reversal' of lengthening in *off*, etc., one lineage has been substituted for another coexisting one.

6   The nineteenth-century developments (or not)

So far we have seen a progression like this: what for Cooper in 1687 was simply a (descriptive) fact about vowel length, and for Flint in 1740 the same kind of fact about length and quality, has become for Walker half a century later the basis for a prescriptive judgement, i.e. a sociolinguistic variable. This is clear from such evaluative terms as 'vulgar', 'gross', etc. Something of this persists well into the nineteenth century, probably for the same reasons, though the picture is complex and fuzzy, and there is a great deal of variation, both phonological and lexical.

In the earliest really good discussion, A. J. Ellis (1874: 1148) cites among other things a dictionary of the 1840s, which gives prescriptions for ME /a/ exactly like Walker's: [aː] only before < r, rm, lm, lf, lve >: *bar*, *harm*, *car*, *calm*, *half*, *halve*, but [æ] in the other canonical Lengthening I environments, e.g. before < ff, ft, ss, st, sp, st, nce >: *chaff*, *pass*, *past*, *dance*, etc. Ellis' own pronunciation (he was born in 1814), however, seems much more modern, as does that of many other 'educated speakers'. The norm appears at first to be [aː] in all lengthening I words; but there are variants, including unlengthened [æ], even before /r/, and sometimes lengthened but unshifted [æː].

That avoidance of lengthened and lowered [æ] is tied up with the earlier lengthening and quality-shift before /r/ is borne out by Ellis' remark (p. 1148) that some speakers (especially female) avoid [aː] through 'fear . . . that if they said (aask), (laaf), they would be accused of the vulgarity of inserting an *r*'. But in summary (or acknowledgement of the mess), Ellis finally says (ibid.):

> the words vary so much from mouth to mouth that *any* pronunciation would do; and short (a) would probably hit a mean to which no one would object. In a performance of *King John*, I heard Mrs. Charles Kean speak of '(kææf) skin,' with great emphasis, and Mr. Alfred Wigan immediately repeated it as '(kaaf) skin,' with equal distinctness.

He adds to these general comments observations of individual speakers, whose social position indicates the sort of accents one might expect them to have: an Oxbridge Professor has [aː] in *class*, [æː] or [aː] in *classes*, and [æ] or [aː] in *dance*; an Army Officer has [æ] or [aː] in *staff*, and the whole range [æ], or [a] or [aː] in *class*.

But aside from these particular remarks, Ellis explicitly acknowledges that his 'received' variety is in fact highly variable: his ultimate goal is description (p. 1089) of a 'generic' pronunciation; since 'from individual to individual there are great specific varieties, by comparing which alone can the generic character be properly evolved', we have to be 'content with a rather indefinite degree of approximation'. He sees no conflict in principle between a certain, even considerable amount of variability and 'standardness'.

Ellis has little to say about lengthened ME /oː/; most forms that 'ought' to have it do, and there seems to be none of the variability associated with /a/. But at roughly the same time, Henry Sweet (1877: 191) has a short vowel in *not*, *cloth*, *cross*, *soft*, though it may lengthen before *th*, *s*, *f* to the vowel of *broad*, *more*: a perfect illustration of Ellis' general point. He also allows (ibid.) for shortening in *glass*, *aunt*. Thus for Sweet's corner of RP-shire, lengthening of /oː/ appears to be, from a historical point of view, somewhat recessive, though apparently there are no judgements attached to the two values. Just after the turn of the century, on the other hand, still presumably describing the same cluster of lect types, a foreign observer, Moritz Trautmann (1903: 120) finds long [ɔː] only before /r/ and in ME /au/ words (*short*, *call*); otherwise the lengthening environments have short [ɒ] (*off*, *lost*, *soft*, *office*; though he does remark that in some cases this vowel is 'lang oder halblang gesprochen', but not in the best speech: 'Diese schleppende [drawling] Aussprache gilt jedoch für verwerflich'). Within the next two decades, we find at least two accounts that are more like Sweet's: in an adaptation of Viëtor's *Kleine Phonetik*, Walter Ripman (1918: 40) notes that a long vowel 'is frequently substituted for the short sound' before voiceless fricatives; while H. C. Wyld (1921: §245) describes [ɔː] in *cloth* etc., 'but not among all speakers'. (For further discussion of the nineteenth-century developments see Holmberg 1964: 36ff.)

It is only around the 1920s that we begin to approach the modern situation: Ida Ward (1929: §143) describes more or less the modern distribution of ME /a/

reflexes. But long ME /o/ (except before historical /r/) shows a more complex picture. In *cross, lost, off, soft, often*, a short vowel 'probably . . . is used by the majority', though 'many educated speakers' have a long vowel (§153). Ward thinks that the long vowel 'is dying out gradually' (§154); 'educated speakers who use [ɔ:] at the present day are mainly middle-aged, or conservative'. She also observes an element of lexical specificity associated with sociolinguistic judgements: *moss, boss, scoff* rarely have a long vowel, and in *toff* it is 'considered Cockney'; some speakers, she notes, have a long vowel in *cross* but a short one in *toss*.

The two lengthenings have clearly parted company by the 1920s, with the short variants largely re-generalised from some other lineage; the long ones remain in older speakers and as lexical fossils.

At the present time, the RP situation is more or less as follows. Both ME /a/ and /o/ are uniformly long before historical /r/. For ME /a/ the length and quality-shift is the norm, but there is still an undiffused remnant: fluctuation between [æ] and [a:] in *chaff, graph, hasp, Basque, masque* (but not *mask!*), *plastic, drastic, pasty* (Cornish), *Glasgow, stance, masturbate, transit, transport* and some others. As for ME /o/, Wells (1982: §3.2.6) notes that as of 1980, lengthened pre-fricative ME /o/ is 'a laughable archaism of 'affected' or aristocratic U-RP. The period of fluctuation or sociolinguistic variation in *cloth* words in England is thus now drawing to an end, with /ɒ/ re-established.'

This is really a very complicated and unsatisfactory history (at least if one is trying to operate in Neogrammarian mode). The lengthening and quality shift of ME /a/ spreads and recedes and then spreads again; that of ME /o/ spreads and recedes, and shows no signs of spreading again. What starts out as a unitary process eventually splits into two independent lineages, with one eventually 'received' and the other stigmatised to the point of disappearance.

References

Adamson, S., Law, V., Vincent, N., Wright, S. (eds.) 1990. *Papers from the 5th International Conference on English Historical Linguistics*, Amsterdam: John Benjamins.
Cooper, C. 1687. *The English teacher*, London: the Author.
Flint, M. 1740. *Prononciation de la langue Angloise*, Paris; repr. in H. Kökeritz (1944), *Mather Flint on Early Eighteenth-Century English Pronunciation*. Skrifta Utgivna af Kungl. Humanistiska Vetenskapsamfundet i Uppsala 37, Uppsala, 1944.
Hart, J. 1569. *An Orthographie, conteyning the due order and reason, howe to write or paint thimage of mannes voice, most like to the life or nature*, London.
Holmberg, B. 1964. *On the Concept of Standard English and the History of Modern English Pronunciation*, Lund: Gleerup.
Hume, A. c.1617. *Of the Orthographie and Conguitie of the Britan Tong*, ed. H. B. Wheatley, EETS OS 5, 1865.
Jones, J. 1701. *Dr John Jones' Practical Phonography*, London: Richard Smith.
Kökeritz, H. 1953. *Shakespeare's Pronunciation*, New Haven: Yale University Press.
Lass, R. 1990. 'Where do Extraterritorial Englishes come from? Dialect input and

recodification in transported Englishes', in Adamson et al., 1990, pp. 245–80.

Margulis, L. 1993. *Symbiosis in Cell Evolution. Microbial Communities in the Archean and Proterozoic Eons*, 2nd edn, New York: Freeman.

Nares, R. 1784. *Elements of Orthoepy: containing a distinct view of the whole analogy of the English language: so far as it relates to Pronunciation, Accent, and Quantity*, London: T. Payne and Son.

Orton, H. and Barry, M. V. 1969. *Survey of English Dialects. B, Basic Material: the West Midland Counties*, Leeds: Arnold.

Orton, H. and Halliday, W. 1962. *Survey of English Dialects. B, Basic Material: the Northern Counties and the Isle of Man*, Leeds: Arnold.

Orton, H. and Wakelin, M. 1967. *Survey of English Dialects. B, Basic Material: the Southern Counties*, Leeds: Arnold.

Ripman, W. 1918. *Elements of Phonetics. English, French and German. Translated and Adapted from Prof. Viëtor's "Kleine Phonetik"*, 7th edn, New York: E.P. Dutton.

Sweet, H. 1877. *A Handbook of Phonetics*, Oxford: Clarendon Press.

Trautmann, M. 1903. *Kleine Lautlehre des Deutschen Französischen und Englischen*, Bonn: Verlag von Carl Georgi's Universitäts-Buchdruckerei.

Walker, J. 1791. *A Critical Pronouncing Dictionary and Expositor of the English Language*, London: G.G.J. and J. Robinson.

Wallis, J. 1653. *Joannis Wallisii Grammatica Linguae Anglicanae*, 6th edn, London: William Bowyer.

Ward, I. 1929. *The Phonetics of English*, Cambridge: Heffer.

Wells, J. 1982. *Accents of English*, 3 vols., Cambridge University Press.

Wyld, H. C. 1936. *A Short History of English*, 2nd edn, London: John Murray.

Zachrisson, R. E. 1929. *The Pronunciation of English Vowels 1400–1700*, Göteborg: Wald, Zachrisson's Boktrykeri A-B.

Index

Printed in Great Britain
by Amazon.co.uk, Ltd.,
Marston Gate.